Magema M. Fuze, the author, was born in Zululand around 1840. His early conversion to Christianity and his lifelong association with Bishop Colenso's home and family did not separate him from his own people; he wrote as a Zulu, drawing on the rich store of oral tradition he assembled from his extraordinarily wide circle of contacts. In 1859 he accompanied Colenso on his famous visit to the king, Mpande, and at the Bishop's request he visited Cetshwayo shortly before the war of 1879. When Dinuzulu was exiled to St. Helena, Fuze was employed as his tutor.

Harry Lugg, the translator, served as court interpreter, magistrate and finally as Chief Commissioner for Native Affairs in Natal. He was famous for his sound and wonderful knowledge of the isiZulu language and the customs and beliefs of the people. He first met Magema in 1902.

Trevor Cope, the editor, was Professor and Head of the Department of Zulu Language and Literature at the University of Natal from 1970 to 1984.

Magema M. Fuze

THE BLACK PEOPLE

AND WHENCE THEY CAME

Translated by H.C. LUGG

Edited by A.T. COPE

UNIVERSITY OF KWAZULU-NATAL PRESS

Published in 2022 by University of KwaZulu-Natal Press
Private Bag X01
Scottsville, 3209
Pietermaritzburg
South Africa
Email:books@ukzn.ac.za
Website: www.ukznpress.co.za

© 2022 University of KwaZulu-Natal
The original English translation was first published in 1979 in hardback by the University of Natal

All rights reserved. No part of this publication may be reproduced or transmitted in any form or by electrical or mechanical means, including information storage and retrieval systems, without prior permission in writing from the publishers.

ISBNS: 978-1-86914-482-1
Ebook: 978-1-86914-484-5

Managing Editor: Elana Bregin
Typesetter: Patrica Comrie
Cover design: MDesign. Adapted from the original design by David Moon, based on 'The Border' by John Muafangejo, with acknowledgements to E.L.C. Art Centre, Rorke's Drift, and C. Struik (Pty) Ltd, Cape Town.

Special thanks to the National Institute for the Humanities and Social Sciences (NIHSS) for the funding that made this new edition possible.
And to Killie Campbell Africana Library for making the isiZulu material available.

Typeset in Baskerville 11 pt

Print administration by DJE Flexible Print Solutions, Cape Town

CONTENTS

Note on new edition	viii
Foreword by Hlonipha Mokoena	ix
Editor's Preface	xvii
Translator's Preface	xxiv

THE BLACK PEOPLE AND WHENCE THEY CAME

Abantu Abamnyama Original Cover	1
Photo of Magema Fuze	2
Author's prologue (*Isisusa*)	3
Introduction (*Inkondlo*)	7
Exhortations (*Amangebeza*)	9

PART I   HISTORICAL

1 The origin of the black people	11
2 Bushmen	12
3 Hottentots	14
4 Griquas	15
5 Where was the earliest origin? [The slave trade]	16
6 The white man and the black man [The slave trade]	17
7 Suggestions and comparisons [The problem of race]	19
8 They who remained behind [Christian Evangelists]	21
9 The dispersal of the people	22
10 More about the dispersed ones	24
11 More powerful clans	30

PART II   ETHNOGRAPHICAL

12 Life throughout the land	34
13 The head-ring and the top-knot	36
14 Circumcision and puberty	37
15 Engagement and marriage	41
16 Today is the day of dancing	44

17 Rectal bloodletting of a child	47
18 The departure of the army	49

PART III   ZULU HISTORY

19 The Ntungwa tribes	50
20 A kingdom foretold	50
21 Shaka's birth [and childhood]	52
22 Senzangakhona's visit to the Mthethwa	53
23 The arming of Shaka [against Zwide]	55
24 The Ndwandwe defeat	56
25 The Ngwane campaign	58
26 The attack on Macingwane	59
27 The dispersal of the Qwabe	61
28 The flight of Mzilikazi	63
29 The destruction of Nomagaga	64
30 The strengthening of Zulu power	65
31 The marriage and death of Nandi	67
32 The daughters of Jama	69
33 The death [and burial] of Nandi	71
34 Zulu royal residences	72
35 Shaka's attack on the Nyuswa	74
36 Matters already recorded [by J.W. Colenso]	76
37 Shaka [as told by the white people]	76
38 Dingane [as told by the white people]	79
39 Boers and British against Dingane	83
40 The dispute between Mpande and Dingane	89
41 The establishment of British rule	93
42 Wicked ruffians [British rule in Natal]	94
43 The Zulu kings	96
44 The first fruits ceremony	98
45 Mpande's good character	101
46 The reign of Mpande	103
47 The reigns of the Zulu kings	105
48 The reign of Cetshwayo	109
49 Cetshwayo's first fruits ceremonies	113
50 Magema's visit to Zululand	116
51 The European invasion	118
52 Zulu defeat and destruction	122
53 Restoration and expulsion	124

54 The death of Cetshwayo	127
55 The birth and childhood of Dinuzulu	129
56 The defeat of Zibhebhu	131
57 The Zibhebhu disturbances	133
58 The arrest of the princes	135
59 The trial of the princes	137
60 After the trial	138
61 The princes at St. Helena	141
62 Magema's mishap	142
63 The return of the royal family	144
64 False reports and rumours	146
65 Bambada's dispute	147
66 The Bambada rebellion	148
67 The arrest of Dinuzulu	151
68 The death of Dinuzulu	153
Epilogue	153
Notes	156

NOTE ON NEW EDITION

This English translation of *Abantu Abamnyama* is not an exact reproduction of the isiZulu original. In some sections Cope has exercised his editorial license, reassigning the sequence of passages for better flow or relevance, omitting repetitious fragments or 'confused and disjointed' remainders. These instances are indicated by Cope through the use of square brackets and explanatory inserts.

FOREWORD

As a writer, Magema Magwaza Fuze (c.1840–1922) did not intend to publish only one book. He had written to his contemporaries about writing an encyclopaedia on the origins of black people. His intention was that there should be volumes of books dedicated to the narrative of origins and migration. At the time, books were not published by publishers on the strength of peer reviews. Publication was based on subscriptions by potential readers. For many years, Fuze worked tirelessly to raise money to publish his book. The book that you are holding in your hand is therefore a mini version of what the author had originally intended. In my initial encounter with Fuze's writing, I described his 1922 book as an 'anti-climax'. Over the years, I have shifted my thinking and now I think of it as Magema Fuze's afterlife. Fuze knew that he was nearing the end of his life and he could not wait any longer for patrons and sponsors of his book, so he wrote the only kind of book that he could write – a self-scripted letter to posterity. It was a brave and reckless act for a writer of the isiZulu language to launch himself into the future of a literature that was uncertain. But, launch himself he did. That is why, one hundred years later, you are now holding his words in your hand, ready to read his work the way it should have been read a century ago. It is both exhilarating and daunting to write the foreword to a book that was published by a visionary writer. The daunting task is to give the readers a preview of what they can expect in the book while at the same time describing the cultural milieu which produced Magema Fuze – the author, the columnist, the printer, and the prolific letter writer. He achieved all these accolades at a time when the *amakholwa* were under immense pressure from the changing policies of the colonial and post-Union states. As a younger man, Fuze had enjoyed the tutelage and protection of John William Colenso (1814–1883) – the first and only missionary bishop of Natal, and Fuze's mentor – and his daughter Harriette Colenso (1847–1932). By the time Fuze published his book in 1922, Colenso Snr was already just a memory of a bygone era of missions and missionaries, and his daughters were struggling to keep his legacy alive in the face of the South African Anglican Church's vindictive excommunication of their father. It was therefore an inauspicious time to be a writer, especially to aspire to publish a book as astounding and intellectually dexterous as the one that Fuze ended up printing.

The story of a book does not begin when a writer sits down with pen and paper and decides to articulate his thoughts. Magema Fuze's book is no exception; the book began long before Fuze made the decision to be an author. When Colenso arrived in Natal in 1855, the young Magema (who had acquired the nickname 'Skelemu', implying that even at that age he was a 'trickster') had already prepared himself, and told his parents about a white man who would be coming for him. This prescient story opens the book *Abantu Abamnyama*, with Fuze placing it even before the description of his baptism and Colenso's wish that his converts be given isiZulu names rather than Hebrew ones from the Bible. This youthful eagerness to learn under a 'master' can be attributed to many historical causes; it reflects the widespread presence of mission schools in the Cape Colony as well as in Natal. Thus, the young Magema grew up already knowing that attending a mission school entailed leaving one's parents and surrendering oneself to the care of a missionary mentor. This is perhaps the most difficult narrative in Fuze's biography, because it suggests the loss of home, departure from his biological father and mother, and adoption by a 'white' father. Despite these complications, Fuze wrote about his move to Ekukhanyeni and Bishopstowe as an incidental episode. His life as a writer could be said to have begun soon after his baptism and renaming. In 1859, Colenso travelled to the Zulu kingdom to visit the reigning king, Mpande. He instructed his young converts to keep travel diaries and to write about their experiences. His *Three Native Accounts of the Visit of the Bishop of Natal in September and October, 1859, to Umpande* became an isiZulu language classic and was read for many decades after its publication. Fuze's debut appearance in print was not, however, the first example of his skills as a printer. In 1859 Colenso had also sent Sir George Grey a copy of Magema Fuze's printing exercise and composition titled 'Amazwi Abantu'. This latter text reveals a young man whose ear was already attuned to the scholarly demands of Colenso's growing interest in isiZulu linguistics and lexicography. The young Fuze composed a transcription of mundane and serious conversations he overheard around him and, in so doing, he preserved a record of the lives of the *amakholwa* who lived at Bishopstowe. Thus, both Three Native Accounts and 'Amazwi Abantu' could be said to have been the fountainhead and inspiration behind Fuze's youthful enthusiasm for the written word.

If the educational experiments at Ekukhanyeni had continued uninterrupted, then Fuze could have become an integral member of the *kholwa* elite – literate, opinionated, perceptive and, middle class. Events, however, soon made such an education impossible. Not only was the school closed in 1861 due to rumours of a Zulu invasion but in 1862 John William Colenso published his biblical criticism and exegesis, and this catapulted him and his converts into a world of literary and canonical notoriety and controversy. The *Pentateuch and Book of Joshua Critically Examined* (1862) was the outcome of Colenso's translation labours as well as his conversations with his young acolytes. Although he had not intended to radicalise biblical and missionary studies in Africa, Colenso's book caused his converts to become the centre of a global hysteria about how the 'Bishop of Natal had been converted' by the people he was supposed to be converting. This inversion of roles perhaps explains the vitriol and acerbic commentary that was levelled at Colenso's publication. Since Colenso owned his own printing press, it was Magema Fuze's skill as a printer that produced not just *The Pentateuch* but also Colenso's responses to his critics. This could be said to have been the beginning of both Colenso and Fuze's political careers and their baptism by fire.

Wherever Colenso's mind ranged, his converts were not far behind. The biblical and canonical controversies began a long battle between what became known as the 'Bishopstowe faction', the settler society of Natal, and the imperial government. Before long, Colenso found himself entangled in an even deeper political commitment as he befriended and supported the young Zulu king, Cetshwayo. Beginning with his visit in 1859, Colenso became acquainted with the affairs of the Zulu kingdom and its relationship with the colony of Natal and the Queen's government. As the guardian of the exiled prince, Mkhungo, who had arrived at Bishopstowe as a fugitive from the 1856 battle of Ndondakusuka where his brothers Mbuyazi and Cetshwayo fought a bitter and destructive war of succession, Colenso had already done more than most to ally himself with the Zulu royal family. The ascension to power by Cetshwayo in 1873 brought the Zulu kingdom into an even closer relationship with the colony of Natal, since Theophilus Shepstone officiated in the coronation. At the time no one could have predicted that Shepstone and Colenso would soon stand on opposing sides. This unraveling of a friendship that had begun with Colenso's arrival in 1855 was once again recorded by Ekukhanyeni's literati.

FOREWORD

While the coronation was happening, another political storm was brewing in the background. At issue was the fate of the amaHlubi chief Langalibalele who was accused of reneging on a promise to compel his young men to surrender their firearms to the Resident Magistrate John Macfarlane for registration. When the magistrate accused Langalibalele of insolence, Shepstone sent a summons to the chief to appear before him. When this was not obeyed, a messenger was sent to Langalibalele to demand that he appear in front of the Secretary for Native Affairs: Shepstone. This gave rise to a second accusation: Langalibalele's men had apparently stripped and searched Shepstone's messenger. When it became clear to the Hlubi chief that Shepstone could not be placated with the promise of paying a fine for his infractions, Langalibalele tried to flee over the Drakensberg to take refuge among the BaSotho. The incidents that led to Langalibalele's flight are still contested but what is important to know is that Colenso immediately took up his cause and attempted to intervene on behalf of a chief who was denied counsel. In his understanding of British justice, Colenso saw that Langalibalele had been unjustly treated by being court-martialled, and sent his converts to find mitigating evidence in favour of Langalibalele's cause. The report produced by Colenso is another moment of collective labour by the Ekukhanyeni faction. Not only did he write a rebuttal to the colonial accusation that Langalibalele's actions were treasonous, but Colenso also offered to his peers in the House of Lords ample reasons to distrust Shepstone's claims that he understood Africans and their culture. By offering alternative interpretations of Langalibalele's decision to flee, Colenso once again chose to involve himself in African affairs and thereby also draw his converts into the controversies.

As with other chiefs who fell out with the Natal government, Langalibalele was, despite Colenso's intervention, deposed and sent into exile. But this did not stop Colenso's work on his behalf. The important ingredient to note was the contribution of Magema Fuze to the testimonies included with the report. Fuze was therefore not just a scribe but a witness, who contradicted Shepstone's, and his indunas', vicious assassination of Langalibalele's conduct and character. The relationship between Colenso and Shepstone was finally broken and this fissure impacted on the lives of the Ekukhanyeni converts. Across the uThukela River, Cetshwayo's kingdom was also under pressure from the Boers who wanted, and claimed, more land; while the colony of Natal was also eyeing the kingdom's land, as well as its reservoir of youthful labour. In 1878 rumours started circulating that Cetshwayo was killing Christian converts and Magema Fuze was sent by Colenso to investigate the accusations. Fuze's travels to the Zulu country revealed several types of anxieties about the future of Zulu power and autonomy. These conversations with chiefs and commoners were faithfully recorded and published in England as 'A Visit to King Ketshwayo' (1878). Colenso reprised his role as the observer who was attempting to counteract frenzied rumour-mongering while giving an objective account of the situation in the Zulu kingdom. Needless to say, it was one more instance in which his convert, Magema Fuze, played a pivotal part. Fuze's words, as well as his audience with the Zulu king, left a mark on Colenso's understanding of the future of Zulu kingship. Although Fuze's text served its purpose of giving a faithful account of Cetshwayo's relationship with Christian converts, it did not undo the impact of what Colenso had called 'exaggerated accounts'. In fact, the report could be said to be prescient in its conclusions that these canards were merely pretexts to invade the Zulu country. Cetshwayo was about to face the same trials and tribulations that had destroyed Langalibalele.

From the beginning, Cetshwayo's reign as the Zulu king was beset by obstacles – his father, Mpande's long reign of thirty-two years cast a long shadow, while his own princely ambitions led to the elimination of potential rivals. By the time he was crowned king, the Zulu kingdom was already in a state of heightened anxiety and tension. Even without the internal dissension, the Zulu kingdom was uncomfortably sandwiched between the expanding Transvaal republic to the north and the restive colony of Natal to the south. This unenviable squeeze is the reason why Cetshwayo tried to play off the English against the Boers. Perhaps this would have worked were it not for the unexpected repercussions of the Sihayo incident in which Sihayo's wives tried to cross the border into Natal but were intercepted and murdered by one of Sihayo's sons. This was the pretext that the British had needed to act against Cetshwayo and soon enough there was talk of war. Again, Colenso's voice was the lone opposition; he preached against the settlers' excitability and their demand for an invasion. If there was any warmth left in the relationship between Colenso and Shepstone, it quickly dissipated. It is not necessary to re-enact the events of the Anglo-Zulu War save to say that the Ekukhanyeni faction moved into full gear and several books and pamphlets were published declaiming the war.

FOREWORD

The dismemberment of the Zulu kingdom from 1879–1887 was recorded in minute detail by Cetshwayo's sympathisers. For his part, Colenso made sure that even in his exile in Cape Town, Cetshwayo was kept abreast of what was happening in his country. When Colenso's advocacy won Cetshwayo an audience with the Queen of England, a whole world of political celebrity awaited Cetshwayo when he arrived in the United Kingdom. Here, too, the Colensos were in the picture, representing the Zulu cause as best as they could. The main point, however, is that when Cetshwayo returned to the Zulu country after his exile and his overseas visit, he found himself denuded of his actual kingdom. Although it may be speculative to infer this, it was, in all likelihood, the heartbreak caused by the civil war in the Zulu country that ultimately led to the deaths of Colenso in June 1883 and Cetshwayo in February 1884. These deaths marked the end of the autonomous Zulu kingdom but also the end of the influence and power of the peerage bestowed on the bishop of Natal. Ironically, this could be said to have been the beginning of Magema Fuze's independent voice and commentary. Once Colenso was gone, Fuze was free to reflect on the events of the previous three decades and reach his own conclusions.

It was necessary to give the historical context of Magema Fuze's emergence as a writer because without it, many of his published articles and columns wouldn't make sense. To say that Fuze was a monarchist would be to oversimplify the issue. Yet there is, in his writing, an evident attachment not just to the uSuthu nobility but to the idea of Queen Victoria as a magnanimous empress. These dual images of power, empire and kingship dominated many of Fuze's political views. The two newspapers that he began writing for were *Ipepa Lo Hlanga* (1894–1904) and *Inkanyiso Yase Natal* (1889–1896). Not surprisingly, these papers were mission-based and were printed at the mission stations using mission-trained printers. In these years, Fuze was a committed and prolific letter writer, stirring up various controversies and debates about what it meant to be a Christianised African. In 1901, for example, Fuze and another former Ekukhanyeni student, Mubi Nondenisa, revived the memory of their mentor by collaborating on a series of articles about John William Colenso (uSobantu) and the Ekukhanyeni institution. This series appeared on the pages of *Ipepa Lo Hlanga*. The establishment of *Ilanga lase Natal* (1903 to the present) by John Langalibalele Dube gave Fuze a new avenue for the expression of his views. By this time, it could be said that Fuze was already addressing a different generation to the one he had written for in *Ipepa* and *Inkanyiso*. To this readership, he was more historian than social commentator, and he used this position to full effect. Thus, for example, Fuze wrote extensively on his experiences on the island of St. Helena, where he was sent in 1896, as tutor and scribe for the exiled Zulu king Dinuzulu. His vested interest in Zuluness is evident in the fact that from 1915 onwards, Fuze wrote serialised articles for the newspaper *Ilanga lase Natal*, including 'Abantu Nemikuba Yabo Bengaka Biko Abelungu' (The Black People and their Customs before the Coming of the Whites), and 'Sapumapi Tina? Ukuhlazulula Uhlanga' (Where Do We Come From? A Clarification of Origins). His understanding of the unravelling of the Zulu kingdom and Zulu kingship was expressed in *Ilanga* articles such as 'Isipeto sikaZulu' (The End of the Zulu People, 1916); 'Ukuhlasela KwaBelungu KwaZulu' (The Attack of Zululand by the White People, 1919); and 'Umuntu Kafi Apele' (When a Person Dies, That Is Not the End of Him, 1916–1922). Fuze's articles and letters to the editor in these decades thus touched on Zulu history and customs, church history and *kholwa* identity, and sometimes the details of his personal life (such as when his daughter was murdered by her husband), and are notable for the robust and contrary views that they elicited from his readers. The liveliness of this exchange of ideas and queries suggests that the readers of *Ilanga* regarded the newspaper as a public forum apportioning space to each of them to express their views, however unpopular or idiosyncratic. These *kholwa* commentators constituted the audience to which Magema Fuze addressed his pleas for support of a book on the origins of the black people. The experience that Fuze had gained through his consistent publishing of columns meant that many readers knew what to expect from Fuze the book author – yet, they seem to have disappointed him by not suitably expressing their enthusiasm through funding of the book. Fuze's irritation with his readers' apathy is expressed in several letters and it may be worthwhile to quote one of these statements, if only to show how serious Fuze was about the idea that the origins of black people deserved a book-length and scholarly treatment. He chastised his readers by stating,

> Inningi leli litule liqintile, libheke ukuba inncwadi lena izicindezele yona ngokwayo, ukuze liti libona ibe sei yisideku esipeleleyo, esizenzileyo.

FOREWORD

> Kanti, bakiti, awuko nowodwa umsebenzi ozenzayo. Konke kwenziwa ng'abantu ngezandhla nangekanda. Seloku kwakunjalo nasendulo njengoba kuse njalo nanamuhla, abantu bayasebenza ngezandhla nangamatupana abo, basebenza imisebenzi eyakugcina ngokubukwa ng'abanye; bati bonke labo abayibukayo balinganise osongati ayenziwanga ngezandhla.
>
> (The majority of you are silent and idly standing by, expecting that the book will print itself, so that you will suddenly find that it is a substantial and complete thing that has made itself.
> On the contrary, folks, there is no work that completes itself. Everything is done by people with hands and mind. It's been like that since time immemorial and it's still like that today, people work with their hands and fingers, they do work that others will marvel at; and those who see the work will pass judgement [compare] as if it wasn't done by hands. (Fuze, M.M., 'Ngebhuku laBantu', *Ilanga lase Natal*, 25 February 1921.))

These words solidified what writing and authorship meant to Fuze. In 1921 when the above words were written, Fuze could not have known that his book, *Abantu Abamnyama, Lapa Bavela Ngakona* would not only be the realisation of his dream of a substantial volume on blackness and its origins, but that it would become a sourcebook for those who were interested in Zulu history. One hundred years later, his words of exasperation and resignation are prophetic rather than foreboding. He would be proud that his words are being reprinted as an affirmation of just how avant-garde his thinking was.

WISER, University of the Witwatersrand,   Hlonipha Mokoena
Johannesburg, 2021

EDITOR'S PREFACE

Abantu Abamnyama was the first major work ever written in isiZulu by a native speaker of the language. It was written shortly after the turn of the century, and privately published in 1922. Previously there had been transcriptions and translations by foreigners, some of them, particularly Bryant and Stuart, Callaway and Colenso, and less so the Samuelsons, dedicated to Zulu studies, and a few writings by Zulus, most notably the *Three Native Accounts of a Visit to King Mpande in 1860*, published by Colenso. On the Bishop's return from this visit, he had requested his three Zulu converts and companions to write these accounts as a sort of exercise. It appears that Magema Fuze was one of them, although he does not mention either the visit or the publication in this book.

The full title of the book is *Abantu Abamnyama* (The Black People) and, less prominently, *Lapa Bavela Ngakona* (Whence They Came). I have deliberately played down 'whence they came' in the title, for the interest here is not how much the author knows, but how little he knows (except in the matter of clan relationships and genealogies), and how limited his historical and geographical horizons. One's admiration for Bryant increases when one realises that it was from such shreds and scraps that he compiled his remarkably coherent picture entitled *Olden Times in Zululand and Natal* drawing the migrational routes and describing the settlements and subsequent histories of the various groups.[1] The date of the settlement of the people most conveniently labelled 'Nguni' is likely to be several centuries earlier than Bryant's 1600, so it is not surprising that Fuze is unable to describe these events.[2] It is rather to be noted that he has no doubts that the people were not here from time immemorial, but that they came down from the North. It is also to be noted that he stresses the common origin of these people, the common past history and the common genetic inheritance. Thus, although the bulk of the book expresses the achievements of the Zulu people under their royal leaders, Fuze also expresses the stirrings of a sense of nationalism wider than Zulu nationalism.

The book falls naturally into three sections, with a little editorial interference here and there, which is always clearly indicated by the use of square brackets. (Round brackets enclose Fuze's own comments.) Fuze does not state these sections himself, but as editor I have divided the book into three parts: historical, ethnographical, and Zulu history. Some readers may feel that the editor should have interfered far more freely. On the contrary, I have tried as far as possible to retain the original arrangement and order of chapters, for it would bring about distortion to impose foreign concepts of 'logical arrangement' and 'chronological order'. For instance, Chapter 44: 'The First Fruits Ceremony', although it may seem more appropriate to ethnography than to history, follows naturally and logically from the chapter on the Zulu kings with whom it was so closely associated, for it was primarily a ceremony to strengthen the king and thus the nation. As Fuze implies, it belongs to history rather than ethnography, for it ceased when the kingship ceased. It would seem very strange to find it among the domestic customs treated under ethnography. As to chronological order, the relevance of an historical event is seen more clearly if it is regarded from different points of view and from different points in time, as the Zulu praiser does in his chronicles of the kings, rather than as a constant point on an historical scale.

Similarly the general reader may wish that the editor had undertaken drastic deletions. He may regard the contents of Chapters 9, 10 and 11, as tedious detail, but it is useful material for specialists, and, as the footnote suggests, he may simply pass on to Part II. Here he will find the customs relating to birth and death, puberty and marriage, described in considerable detail. Again he may pass on to Part III, Zulu History, which comprises the bulk of the book. For the general reader, the main interest in the earlier parts lies in the expression of mind and the sociological reflections to be found in the first eight chapters and in the author's introductions. Here the reader should bear in mind the historical context in which the book was written. As a convert to Christianity in the nineteenth century colonial situation, even under a teacher so sympathetic as Bishop Colenso, the author stood at the forefront of the clash of cultures, values and interests. In fact the teacher's tolerance and sympathy towards local customs and attitudes laid an even greater responsibility and difficulty upon the convert. That he did not violently resist, that he did not completely capitulate, that he thought about the problems and came to his own conclusions, as these early chapters most clearly reflect, is a tribute to the man and to the many Zulu people like him.

A major interest of the book is the way in which Fuze lives in several worlds at once. He came to Bishop Colenso's mission station,

Ekukhanyeni (the place of enlightenment), from a country background, the influence of which remained with him throughout his life. The care and accuracy with which he describes the details of Zulu rural life suggest not only that he was still in sympathy with it, but that he was still in constant touch with it, even at the mission. At the same time, there is no doubt about the sincerity of his conversion and devotion to the world of education and enlightenment, and to the Christian God.

It is clear that it was the wider world of the mission that fostered a wider sense of identity and nationality, beyond the local community and even beyond the Zulu nation. He absorbed with great interest the information he heard of people to the North, beyond the Drakensberg, beyond the Limpopo, beyond the Zambezi, from the visitors who stayed at and passed through the Colenso household in the course of their evangelical travels. And on his own travels through Natal and Zululand on mission business, he gained a wider view than he could have gained from his original circumscribed background. It is also clear that the mission gave him a stronger sense of Zulu nationalism, for it was through the mission that he became acquainted with the Zulu royal family and with the issues borne by emissaries backwards and forwards across the Tugela River. Through Colenso he was in constant touch with the authorities, both black and white, on different sides of the river, for Colenso was a turbulent and political priest (in the eyes of his enemies), who did not see his mission as a retreat from the events of the time. One wonders to what extent Fuze influenced Colenso, not only in theological matters such as the capacity of Noah's Ark, but in political matters too, for Fuze had great respect and high praise for Cetshwayo, who was in his view so good and considerate and compassionate towards his people. One wishes that he had recorded his conversations with his mentor on these matters.

All these strands are woven together in Fuze's life and work: the traditional and the Christian, the local and the national, Zulu nationalism and African identity; he sees the value of both local custom and national unity, he has faith in both the past and the future. The historical and sociological value of Fuze's book lies largely in the way it 'straddles the several worlds he inhabits' and shows 'the linkages he forges between them'.[3]

The notes are entirely the responsibility of the editor. They are as brief as possible, for if they were to debate each question, point out every peculiarity, and supply all the details which Fuze omits, they would fill the greater part of the book. Rather than annotate Fuze out of his book, I have given the most useful and reliable references for the contents of the three parts, so that the reader may make his own investigations.[4] It is important that the book should remain Fuze's creation, and my main concern as editor has been to retain the quality of the book as closely as possible to the way he wrote it, with all its peculiarities, inconsistencies, errors and omissions.

The quality of the book depends largely upon its literary style, and we have done our best to retain it in translation. Mr Lugg in his preface mentions 'faults of style and errors of fact'. There are 'errors of fact', some of which have been corrected by the editor (in square brackets), but others I have been unable to detect or to correct, either through my own or general ignorance. As to the 'faults of style', they arise from the fact that the author's background was not a literate society, and he has no standard of literary style. He writes as he speaks, and natural speech, to quote Chomsky (*Aspects of the Theory of Syntax*) has 'numerous false starts, deviations from rules, changes of plan in mid-course (the course of the sentence), and so on'. He continues, 'We do not take these mistakes into account when we are listening . . . we sort it out according to a system of rules which resides in our minds, which is the grammar of our language'. Some of Fuze's 'faults of style' are, in fact, faults of syntax or sentence structure. Others are faults of literary style, for there was no such style in those days. When the style of natural speech is used in literature, it is sometimes difficult to comprehend the meaning, for we are not in a position to hear and see the vocal and facial expressions which are not only an accompaniment but a component of natural speech. Mr Lugg has made an excellent translation of a work stylistically difficult, peculiarly idiomatic, and sometimes slightly archaic, for Fuze's language is at least a hundred years old. My editorial responsibility, as far as the translation is concerned, has been to check for errors and omissions, and to see that both style and meaning have been preserved. Furthermore, I have been concerned that the translation should be as literal as possible. I hope Mr Lugg will forgive the alterations I have made in these interests.

Consistency in the spelling of Zulu names and in the translation of isiZulu words has also been an editorial responsibility. I have followed the convention of omitting the initial vowels of Zulu names: Mpande (not Umpande), Mzinyathi (not Umzinyathi), Mngeni (not Umngeni or Umgeni), Thukela or Tugela (not Uthukela), Sihlalo (not Isihlalo),

Sandlwana (not Isandlwana, although it is so well known as such); and also with locatives: Thekwini (not Ethekwini or eThekwini), except for a few: Eshowe, Ondini and Osuthu (royal residences). There may be a few further exceptions; for instance, *Embo*, because *Mba* is unpronounceable. The name of the Zulu royalist-loyalist faction is deliberately spelt *uSuthu* (the war cry which struck terror into the British troops and particularly the 'loyal' native troops), to distinguish it from the Suthu (*Sotho*) people of Basutoland (Lesotho); and for consistency its rival is spelt *iziGqoza*. The letters, *c*, *q*, *x*, represent the isiZulu clicks, which may also be voiced (*gc*, *gq*, *gx*) or aspirated (*ch*, *qh*, *xh*). Similarly, *kh*, *th* and *ph*, indicate aspiration, not 'th' as in English or 'ph' as in Greek. The isiZulu *k* sounds like *g* to English ears, but isiZulu *k* and *g* are different in the same way as *b* and *bh*: the former is 'light' and the latter is 'heavy'. The lateral fricatives (Welsh 'll')may be either voiceless (*hl*) or voiced (*dl*, once *dhl*), and so may the aspirate, although the distinction between *h* and *hh* is no longer reflected in the written language.

The concern for consistency in the translation of isiZulu words has seen, for instance, that *izikhulu* is always translated as dignitaries or important or prominent people, and that *inkosi* is always translated as chief, or, in the case of the Zulu paramount chief, as king. When Fuze uses it to refer to white people, he uses it in the sense of a high official such as a magistrate. The translation of *umnumzane* is the head of the household, important man or elder, that of *inceku* is an official, servant or attendant, that of *induna* is headman, councillor, leader, commander or general, but not 'induna' (which Mr Lugg had used quite often, as it is an item of our vocabulary), because of its later 'boss-boy' associations.

For similar reasons I have avoided the use of the words, 'hut' and 'kraal' (except in the sense of cattle kraal), throughout. A Zulu 'hut' (*indlu*) is either a room or a house. The household or homestead or residence (*umuzi*) comprises a collection of separate rooms or houses (*izindlu*), a vast collection in the case of the old royal residences. Also for similar reasons I have tried to avoid the use of the word 'tribe', but it has been unavoidable sometimes, to refer to the group between the clan and the nation, and sometimes appropriate, to refer to a large group of ultimately related people in a historical context. The word *impi* has been rendered as force or troop, regiment or army, battle or war, but not as 'impi' because of its large range of meanings referring to any sort of military activity. The *thakatha* concept is translated as witchcraft, although the Zulu belief has elements of sorcery as well as witchcraft.

EDITOR'S PREFACE

The only words that need no translation because they are so entrenched in our vocabulary are maas (curdled milk) and donga (eroded ravine; and lobolo (the noun) and lobola (the verb) are untranslatable (they refer to the transfer of cattle with marriage.

Mr Lugg has summed up the value of Magema Fuze's book very well in his preface. The illumination from 'the sidelights of Zulu history' is sometimes very revealing. Fuze's account of the circumstances of Shaka's birth is different in some important respects from Bryant's version. His views of Hamu and Zibhebhu are very different from the views of the white authorities of the time, and the Natal 'old timers' such as Dr Malcolm, Dr Edgar Brookes, William and Killie Campbell, and Mr Lugg himself, had a high regard for Zibhebhu as a man, general and diplomat, which was certainly not shared by Fuze. (Nor was it shared by Bishop Colenso and his family, nor is it shared by Dr J.J. Guy in his recent study of the civil war in Zululand.)[5] And there are other questions. Why indeed should the Zulus have revealed to a white man the real cause of Nandi's death? Why indeed should Cetshwayo have believed that the reason for the Zulu War was not simply to destroy his power? And Fuze's hints as to the cause of Cetshwayo's death could cause a scandal still!

The present publication is notable not only for its octogenarian author but also for its nonagenarian translator. Born and brought up in close contact with the Zulu people, he was well qualified by his sound and wonderful knowledge of the isiZulu language and of the beliefs and customs of the people, to serve as court interpreter, as magistrate, and finally as Chief Commissioner for Native Affairs in Natal; and, after his retirement, as social welfare officer at the large government hospital which serves the black people in Durban (King Edward VIII Hospital). At the age of over ninety, Harry Lugg was as mentally alert as Magema Fuze surely was at the age of over eighty. In spite of his great authority, he was humble enough and honest enough to admit that there were things he did not know about the Zulus. He recognised that he had never lived with the Zulus in the usual sense of 'to live'. Never did I hear him make such statements (which are fairly common) as, 'I was born and brought up amongst the Zulus' and 'I have lived with the Zulus all my life'. After all, it is against the laws of nature for a white man to be literally 'born and brought up amongst the Zulus'. However close the relationship, it can never be the closeness of family life with its complex of relationships, rituals and religious beliefs, and it can certainly never be the closeness of a mother's breast. And yet I would accord him the distinction of being the world's greatest authority, black or white, on the past traditional life of the Zulu people. A grand old man and a dear friend, he missed the publication of this book by only a few months.

Department of Bantu Languages A.T. Cope
University of Natal, Durban, 1977

NOTES
1. The modern reader must try not to allow Bryant's achievement to be overshadowed by his stylistic affectations, sense of superiority and attitude of condescension. Bryant's *Olden Times* is an important work which merits serious consideration. Originally published in 1929, it was reprinted by Struik of Cape Town in 1965.
2. The earliest Iron Age settlements in Natal date back to the latter part of the first millennium, but whereas they would almost certainly be Bantu, it is doubtful that they would be Nguni in culture, which seems to have arrived, or perhaps developed, relatively late in the Iron Age.
3. Dr Shula Marks (private letter). I am grateful to her for these insights, and for the notes marked 'S.M.', which add depth and historical value to this publication. As regards Fuze's later life, she writes:
    'After the Bishop's death, Fuze remained close to the Colenso family at Bishopstowe and closely in touch with Harriette, the Bishop's daughter, particularly in her long struggle on behalf of Cetshwayo's son, Dinuzulu.
    'In 1896 Fuze was summoned by Dinuzulu in exile on St. Helena, to be his secretary and to act as tutor to his children. He returned to Natal with the royal family in 1898.
    'As late as the second decade of the twentieth century, Fuze was still in close contact with Harriette, and seems to have acted as her intermediary to the Rev. John Dube, one of Natal's early nationalist leaders and the first president of the South African Native National Congress (later the African National Congress). In Harriette's diaries there are frequent allusions to meetings with Fuze and Dube between 1910 and 1920. It is perhaps to these contacts between Fuze and Dube that one must attribute Fuze's introductory acknowledgement to *Ilanga LaseNatal*, the African newspaper founded by Dube in 1903, as well as his clearly articulated African nationalism'. (Dr Shula Marks: personal communication).
4. For a full bibliography of fairly easily obtainable publications, with comments on the books, see *Select Bibliography relating to the Zulu People* (A.T. Cope, Department of Bantu Languages, University of Natal, 1974).
5. Unpublished doctorate, University of London, 1976: *The Destruction of the Zulu Kingdom: The Civil War in Zululand, 1879–1884* [since published under the same title by UKZN Press in 2012].

TRANSLATOR'S PREFACE

Abantu Abamnyama is the work of a Natal Zulu written in his old age, with the benefit of an elementary education. It was, as far as I know, the first book ever written by an African of this Province. It is written in rich, idiomatic and classical isiZulu, but as it was the writer's first attempt, it contains many faults of style and errors of fact, as might be expected. Nevertheless it contains much valuable information on the sidelights of Zulu history, the early life of the people, their tribal system, their clan relationships, their laws and customs, and their beliefs and attitudes, hitherto not contained in our records.

Born about 1840 and brought up under the influence of Bishop Colenso, Magema was so situated that he was in constant contact with most of the notable people of those days, both white and black, and was able to obtain information from men and women who had lived with and knew the early Zulu chiefs such as Senzangakhona, Shaka, Dingane and Mpande. The book incorporates almost the whole of Colenso's *Izindaba Zas'eNatal* which Magema interlards with his own views on these 'Natal Affairs'. Converted to Christianity at an early age by Bishop Colenso, he became a very religious and pious man, but at the same time he was still firmly attached to his old beliefs. Based on this background, his views on various problems are at times very vivid, and these glimpses of the working of his mind, the mind of a mature old man and an African mind, are one of the main interests of the book.

Possessed of a colossal memory and being a man of high birth, he has been able to list the tribal clans and sub-clans, as well as the pedigrees, running back many generations, of many early chiefs and other important people. He qualified as a compositor on Colenso's printing press, and for a time he taught this skill to the children at St. Alban's College in Pietermaritzburg. Also during his career he was employed in teaching Dinuzulu and his two uncles to read and write isiZulu during their detention at St. Helena. Magema accompanied Bishop Colenso when the latter visited King Mpande in 1859, and again just before the war of 1879 he visited Cetshwayo at the request of the Bishop.

I first met Magema in 1902. He had then written or partially written his book, and was a frequent visitor to our Native Affairs Department seeking financial aid for its publication, but as the Government coffers were then at a very low ebb owing to the recent Anglo-Boer War, we could not help him. The book was eventually published in 1922, but I do not know who assisted him.[1] I acquired my copy from the Estate of the late Mr J.Y. Gibson, judge of the Native High Court and author of *The Story of the Zulus*.[2] It is inscribed in the author's own handwriting, 'J.Y. Gibson, Esq., 1st August, 1923', and was probably a presentation copy. My translation of this book is dedicated as a tribute to the late Killie Campbell, and submitted for lodgement in the Africana Library which commemorates her name.

Durban, 1972   H.C. Lugg

NOTES

1. From the evidence of her letters, I think it may well have been Harriette Colenso. S.M.
2. Originally published in 1903, the revised edition was published by Longmans of London in 1911. It is simply and unpretentiously *The Story of the Zulus*, upon which the European presence increasingly encroaches.

ABANTU ABAMNYAMA,

LAPA BAVELA NGAKONA.

EKA M. M. FUZE.

PRICE 5/6

Magema Fuze

AUTHOR'S PROLOGUE

ISISUSA[1]

In as much as we all know that 'the *isisusa* wedding dance is always appreciated by being repeated' [Zulu proverb], it is fitting that I should tell you from the outset something about the person who relates to you the matters recorded in this book, so that you may know him and understand him, all you readers of this book. For today we are fortunate in the mutual acquaintance we receive through the services of the newspaper [*Ilanga laseNatal*] produced by the son of a chief of the Ngcobo people, the Rev. J.L. Dube, son of James, also son of a chief, which makes observations for us throughout this country of ours in Africa.[2]

In the territory of the Fuze clan of the Ngcobo tribe there lived a man by the name of Magwaza, son of Matomela son of Thoko, who had a number of wives. He produced four sons in the chief house,[3] in the second house five sons, and amongst the remaining wives three sons, that is twelve in all. And this Magwaza lived as a subject under Chief Ngoza son of Ludaba of the Majozi clan, a former headman under Somtseu son of Sonzica (Mr Shepstone, afterwards Sir Theophilus Shepstone, K.C.M.G.),[4] who managed the affairs of the black people of Natal on behalf of England.

The third son in the senior house of Magwaza was named Manawami, who followed the two eldest sons. There was also a brother, Mlingane, who was the eldest son in the junior house. Possibly you may know the meaning of the names Manawami and Mlingane,[5] that they have reference to your having married my daughter or to your son having married my daughter – they both refer to one thing only, my son-in-law. These two sons were named in relationship to one another as if the father realised the bond between them. They were born in this sequence: Manawami was born on the day on which the mother of Mlingane was married.

When Manawami attained the age of six or seven (I am not certain about that), he began to talk in a manner unintelligible to his parents, but they paid no heed to it, regarding it merely as child's talk. He was in the habit of making toy carts, together with the other children, with stones and aloe leaves. In his conversation with the other children he used to say, 'I am not going to grow up here at home. A white man of high rank will be coming here from across the sea; he is the one for whom I will work, and who will call me by the name of Skelemu.'[6] As he was always speaking in this way to the other children, his parents eventually discarded the name of Manawami, and Skelemu became his permanent name.

And so it happened. After a time there arrived Sobantu in 1854, the Right Rev. J.W. Colenso, D.O., L.L.D., Lord Bishop of Natal, 1853–1883. He came from overseas on a visit to Natal, having been sent by Queen Victoria to investigate it and become its Bishop. He travelled over it and made a thorough inspection of the whole country. Thereupon Somtseu kaSonzica [Shepstone] sent messages to all chiefs throughout the country, announcing the arrival of a great teacher, sent by the Queen to take charge of the province. This great teacher said that all children that were beginning to lose their first teeth should be gathered together and educated at his school which was going to be built at his home at Ekukhanyeni (Enlightenment). This message was dispatched to all chiefs, but with one voice they refused, saying their children would be taken and sent overseas.

On finding that the people had refused to send their children to be educated in accordance with the request of Sobantu, Somtseu assembled his headmen and all the elders under them – including the chiefs Ngoza kaLudaba of the Majozi clan and Zashuke kaMbheswa of the Ngubane clan, along with the important dignitaries under them – to inform them that all important people were to send their elder children to school at Ekukhanyeni where they would be educated, the elder children who would take control of the households[7] when their fathers were no longer living.

On this message reaching the elders, Magwaza (who was one of them) said to Skelemu, 'Today your great master of whom you have often spoken has arrived. You are to go to him.' And so he took Skelemu who was Manawami, together with Mlingane, to Ekukhanyeni to be schooled. When they were taken there, Skelemu was a small boy of about twelve, according to Sobantu's estimate, and Mlingane about ten or a little more. And they proceeded to study along with the rest. Later Mlingane became ill with a chest complaint and returned home, but Skelemu remained.

By that time Sobantu had already taken Manawami who was Skelemu together with several other boys and placed them with a white man named Mr Purcell, one of his employees in charge of his printing press, so that he should teach them to become compositors. This European taught them well. At this stage, one day of the same year, Magwaza arrived at Ekukhanyeni on a visit to the Bishop, to see his son. It was about the year 1859. Thereupon Sobantu spoke these words to Magwaza, 'Magwaza, I wish Skelemu to be baptised'. 'Sir, what do you mean by being baptised?', this question being put by Magwaza to Sobantu. And Sobantu replied to Magwaza saying, 'I wish him to abandon bad habits and follow the path of the King above.' 'Wo, Sir', replied Magwaza, 'then you wish to convert him into a Christian?'. And Sobantu admitted that it was so. Thereupon Magwaza said, 'Sir, I am afraid of my child becoming a Christian. There is a son of So-and-So at the Edendale Mission School over yonder who went there to study, and when his mother went to see him she found he was no longer there, and it was said he had simply left and no longer lived there. I am afraid, Sir, and do not wish my child to become a Christian, because he will defy me and his mother.' To this Sobantu made no reply, but picked up the Bible and opened it and ordered Skelemu to read the Ten Commandments so that his father could hear them. And so Skelemu read them in full. When he had done so, Magwaza said, 'Hau, Sir, then you wish to make my child honour me and his mother, and desist from the evil practices of stealing and fornicating? Wo, Sir, I have nothing to say, and I give my consent for you to do to him what you want to do to him. Even when in need of a blanket go and beg for one from Somtseu, and he gives me one; and when in need of a wife, I take cattle from my cattle kraal and pay them as lobolo to her father.[8] I give my consent, Sir, do as you wish with my child.' And there the matter ended.

On the day of the resurrection of the Lord (Easter 1859), Sobantu sent William Ngidi (who lived with the Bishop as his personal servant) to Skelemu to ask him, seeing that the time had come for him to be baptised, what name he wanted to be known by – he should decide. And Skelemu was at a loss what to do, but Ngidi came to his aid by suggesting that he refer to the New Testament and select a name suitable to him. And Skelemu went through the names contained in the Book. He selected two, that of Petros and that of Johane. And when Ngidi arrived to ask what name he had selected, he said he had selected that of Petros. Ngidi conveyed this name to the Bishop. But Sobantu said he did not want it. Again Ngidi came to Skelemu and told him that the Bishop would not accept it, and that he was to select another. And he chose that of Johane. And again Ngidi conveyed this name to the Bishop, but he refused to accept even this one, saying that he [Skelemu] was to concern himself no further as he himself would find a name suitable to him. He objected to African people being called by foreign names which meant nothing to them. After the midday meal William Ngidi went to Skelemu again and told him that the Bishop had chosen the name of Magema for him, and that he was no longer to be called Skelemu. Ngidi showed him a book in which were recorded many names, including that of Magema.[9] The evening service followed, and Bishop Sobantu baptised Skelemu by the name of Magema. And so Skelemu became Magema as he is known even at present.

And so in this way did this person, Magema son of Magwaza Fuze of the Ngcobo people, come into being. To proceed with this book, he had long begun questioning his people asking them, 'Where did we come from?', but they did not tell him exactly where they came from. But at a certain stage there came forward Mncindo kaDangadu kaMnyani kaNgqamuza kaNtomela of the Ngcobo people, to state that 'All of us of Ngcobo stock sprang from the reed beds of the Umvoti river'. Such an account, of course, is like a fool with neither head nor foot. I feel strongly that our people should know that we did not originate here in Southern Africa. And my kinsman who is in control of the whole clan, does not discuss this nonsense, but limits attention to the dispersal of our own small section of the Ngcobo, by being expelled by the senior section, the Nyuswa.

It is I who record this for you, One of you who loves you,

Pietermaritzburg, 1921   Magema M. Fuze

INTRODUCTION

INKONDLO[1]

For a very long time I have been urging our people to come together and produce a book about the black people and whence they came, but my entreaties have been to no avail. Had they complied, the book would have been produced many years ago.

Towards the end there came forward the son of the late Mr Nicholas Masuku of the Edendale Mission Station, Mr N.J.N. Masuku, and declared that by might and main he would endeavor to advance this book until it was finished, despite the failure of others to do so. Personally I admire the courage and determination of this person. I say that great is his courage and determination in endeavouring to overcome a difficulty that was evaded by our people.

Even though I may now be alone in this project, I think that there will be many of us desirous of having the book *Abantu Abamnyama* in our schools, in order that our children may get to know where they originally came from, because at present they do not know. It would be well for you all to know that many of our tribes were left behind by us at the Horn of Africa (Suez Canal). There are very many tribes there. From the extent and large size of Africa, I can safely assert that those of our people still living there are more enlightened than we are here. They wear clothes that they manufacture themselves. They breed sheep and goats which they shear and use the fleece for making blankets and clothes. Also those of our people there cultivate cotton, which is reaped and used for making sleeping blankets. They have their chiefs who govern them, as we do here. They also have boats which they use for crossing their large rivers – the Zambezi and the Congo – where many of our children were captured by the Portuguese and other wicked white people who were in the habit of selling our children and making them into slaves. In this respect I praise and thank Queen Victoria for putting a stop to such cruel and abominable practices.

As an indication that we were there for several centuries, there are many of our old women and men who heard about it or who actually witnessed the committing of these acts. The large animal known as

INTRODUCTION

Siququmadevu [hairy monster] is not an imaginary fancy but a monster actually seen by our people of those times – a ship for taking away our children who were found bathing in the rivers. As these two rivers were too large to be forded on foot but only by ships, the Portuguese and other wicked white people profited by these filthy tricks. At present there are large numbers who were stolen in this evil manner, numbered in hundreds and thousands, in America; and it was due to them that there came into being the people known as the St. Helenas who now fill the island of St. Helena, for when our people arrived there they had intercourse with the whites on the island, leading to the birth of double-breeds (*onhlobombili*).[2] And when these double-breeds began to increase and to intermarry among themselves, they changed colour and became as white as the whites themselves.

To return to the previous subject, the black people scattered and dispersed over the whole of Africa, for there are very many tribes that speak languages that are very similar although not exactly alike. For this reason the language of the Sotho, Mpondo, Swazi, Tonga, Ndawo, Tshweki, and all the northern and western tribes of Africa, is almost mutually intelligible and does not differ greatly in structure and in its speech from the isiZulu language.[3] And even as to those who still live beyond and this side of that great river, the Zambezi, their language is little different from that spoken by us, some words being similar, thus showing that although these people are no longer living together, they sprang from a common source, and there is no doubt that we were one in ancient times.

And so today, due to the words and determination of Mr N.J.N. Masuku, who with large teardrops pleaded and implored me to proceed with him in this matter and produce a book[4] in order that our children might know where we came from, I have consented, even though I am now very weak, having exceeded by far seventy years, being now almost eighty. But by the grace of God I may be able to accomplish that which is desired by Masuku. For this reason I am praying to the Almighty in his merciful grace to allow me to complete this book by which I am so anxious to enlighten those to come, including all our own ignorant children, as desired by Masuku.

EXHORTATIONS
AMANGEBEZA[1]

Members of the tribal assembly of our chief, and all you readers of this book, *Abantu Abamnyama*. Do not be surprised or disappointed to find that you are reading a book without horns [without effect] in that it treats events without dates, for you will see no year nor month nor day for the events which it treats. It is a matter of great distress and grief that it should be only now that we are beginning to discuss these matters which concern us, hundreds and thousands of years after we came into existence in the country. It is a matter of great concern, my friends,[2] but I am hoping that everybody will discover for themselves the dates of these events when they study the writings of the white people, if by chance they come upon them.

As to myself at present, my friends, I am joyful at having begun to tackle the task hip and thigh [arm and shoulder] that I have long since yearned for, thinking it should be done. For now I have seen and realised and no longer experience anxiety.

You all know that bridesmaids do not sing wedding songs without having seen the refreshments set apart for them; they sing when they have seen. In the same way a person should desist from folding his hands, wondering what to do seeing that it is long since passed. No indeed! Let it be for each to strive according to his lights, and diligently search for the dates of these events, so that in subsequent editions of books published now, they who wish to revise them may by their experience attempt to accomplish much more than we have done today, and so rouse our children from the deep sleep which we have slept for so long, giving the impression that we have been destined for such a state by our grandfathers and great-grandfathers; and when we began to be roused by foreign peoples, we then thought that we had sprung from the same source as they, ceasing to observe our own ways and respectful customs, and grasping those of the foreigners and then finding that we had been abandoned by the One above from whom we originated.[3] I now warn you to abandon all this pretence because it is of no benefit whatever. Adhere strictly to your own. It does not mean to say that because you see civilised people and wish to become like them, that you should discard your own which is good. It may happen that in seeking to do so, you may suddenly find yourselves being cast into a bottomless pit. The creator did not create us foolishly, but wisely, and there can be no doubt that if we love and acknowledge Him, He will uplift us like all the nations; but if we treat Him with disdain, and do not acknowledge Him, He will forsake us for ever.

In as much as there are some of us who like to examine, chapter and verse, the books of other nations, thinking that they contain the truth about the creation of heaven and earth and all else, visible and invisible, begin today to devote yourselves to this book which belongs to you and absorb it thoroughly, chapter and verse, for the sake of your children. Leave the enthusiasm for foreign affairs, and remember the fable of the chameleon and the salamander.[4] Yes indeed, I am also in agreement with it. A single goat can lead a flock of sheep to the slaughter; and even if there be hundreds or thousands they can still be led to complete extermination by that single goat. At the creation the sheep was designed as a stupid creature, cowardly and highly nervous and when frightened by the slightest thing running and killing itself in forlorn desperation, whereas the goat with its cunning nature, on observing a leopard dusting itself, runs toward it at the same time inviting other goats [surely the sheep?] to go with it, leading to all being devoured however great their numbers.[5] Pay heed therefore to that about which I speak. Many of our people are led to the slaughter because of ignorance like that of the sheep, in many groups and companies. But now I wish you all to adhere to what is your own and not that of other people.

You will attain nothing by your present state of disorganisation. Unite in friendliness like the enlightened nations. Do not merely look on heedlessly when others are being exploited. So long as you desire evil to one another, you will never be a people of any consequence; but you will become the manure for fertilising the crops of the enlightened nations, disorderly, useless, and without responsibility.

Seeing that dawn is about to break, listen all of you and understand. There are the bridesmaids chanting and asking for refreshments from the bridegroom. What do they say? They say, '*Wolete amangebeza, wolete*' [bring forth the refreshments, bring them forth]. And if the bridegroom should fail to do so, they will certainly not remain silent but subject him to perpetual and persistent protest throughout the night.

PART I: HISTORICAL[1]

Chapter 1
THE ORIGIN OF THE BLACK PEOPLE[2]

Our forebears tell us that all we black people originally came from the north. When we make close enquiry as to where this north may be, they point in an upward direction; but because no written records were left by those who came before us, all they can do is to point in that northerly direction upward of the country [*enhla nezwe*] which we hear referred to as the Horn of Africa near where the sea almost meets (Suez Canal). It is said that when they left that curve [*insonge*] they dispersed throughout the country, skirting the sea and travelling westwards and southwards. Those who went westwards are known as the Ntungwa, and those who skirted the sea and headed southwards as the Nguni.[3, 4]

The Nguni and the Ntungwa do not understand one another readily; they understand one another only slightly, certainly not completely. The Nguni are those people whose speech is soft and low, whilst that of the Ntungwa is hard and high, like that of the white people. If they say *inkomo* cow, the Sotho say *khomo*; *umuntu*, man, *motho*; *abantu*, people, *batho*; *amanzi*, water, *metsi*; *indlela*, way, *tsela*. The Nguni speak low [smoothly] but the Ntungwa speak high [harshly] like the English in their speech.

Further there is a big difference between the Ntungwa and the Nguni in that the Nguni is not ashamed to go about naked even amongst his own children, and his little covering at the back [*ibheshu*] and his little one in front [*isinene*] are merely to prevent shame; and when they are sitting about at home, the front covering is all they wear. But the Ntungwa are greatly afraid of seeing a person walking about naked, and they are even ashamed to look at him. It was for this reason that when Mzilikazi, the son of Mashobaba of the Khumalo clan, was driven out of Zululand by Shaka, the Sotho referred to his followers as Matebele because Mzilikazi's people went about naked.[5] But we regard even the Khumalo people as Ntungwa.[6]

Chapter 2
BUSHMEN[1]

A race about which little is known as to its origin, is the Bushmen, a diminutive people the size of children whose old men and women you can only recognise by the grey hairs on their heads, and then you see that 'Woshi! [My goodness!]This person is old!' It was for this reason that in olden times when one met a Bushman close at hand and was immediately questioned by him, 'When did you first see me?', one would reply, 'I first saw you in the far distance'. The Bushman would be pleased to hear that he had been seen at a great distance, and would then say, 'Ncinci! So I too must be tall'. For if one replied, 'I only saw you just here', the Bushman would be greatly angered, and as he is always armed with poisoned bow and arrows, would kill one instantly.

It is these people who arrived first in the country before we did, because our forebears tell us that they were already in occupation when we arrived. They did not dwell in homesteads such as are built by the Bantu people, but used to construct rough temporary shelters, so very small in size as to accommodate only two or three persons. Their occupation was only to hunt wild animals, large and small, especially large birds such as the bustard and others, and whenever a large animal was killed, they would remain there eating it until it was consumed, and then leave for elsewhere. Ant-heaps they excavated and then slept in the holes.

Their disappearance in this part of the country was due to intermarriage with our people, leading them to become taller, although some remained short as with all peoples, but they ceased to be the aboriginal Bushmen. Even now there is amongst us a clan by the name of Mutwa. This surname refers to those people about whom I am speaking, the Bushmen. But their language is not understood by anyone because it consists of a series of clicks such as '*Qam*! *Qim*! *Qu*! *Qu*! *Qu*!', and no one can grasp its meaning. It is a matter of much surprise for us to be told that whilst they can speak our language as well as ourselves, we cannot understand their clicking.

These people have many clever customs, of cunning and stealing. They can climb cliffs like baboons, where ordinary people cannot go, and they can drive cattle and horses along stony ways and dreadfully dangerous places. They can also stupefy people with smoke, causing them to go to sleep so that they can steal their property while they are in deep slumber. In former times they lived under the escarpment [Drakensberg] towards the south of the range, where they formed a large tribe and where they were in the habit of painting pictures of cattle and horses on the rocks of the Khahlamba [Drakensberg]. It is said that they too had their chiefs. Their clan name was said to be Nhlapo.[2]

That they should be no longer on this side of the escarpment is because they were driven out by the Bantu regiments which worried them by constant attacks, killing them whenever they attempted to steal their stock. The town of Bergville before it was established was the situation of great trouble to the Government and to everybody living to the east of the escarpment, because of the presence of these people. I am of the opinion that this town was established for the purpose of keeping a watch over these people, and to show the Government the trouble caused by the presence of the Bushmen. And conditions remained as such, but in 1848 the Hlubi people of Mthimkhulu arrived under their chief, Langalibalele, who was fleeing from Zululand. When they arrived here in Natal, the Government gave them permission to reside under the escarpment on its eastern side in order to prevent the Bushmen from troubling the country. It was he in truth, Langalibalele, who drove away the Bushmen, and they departed from this part of the country and moved over the escarpment to its western side, from where we hear it said that they moved into German West Africa.[3]

The Bushmen have no fear of snow, for when it snows, that is the time that pleases them most, for it is then that they plunder the people's stock. They do not feel the cold at all, being like a beast or dog or antelope that is not affected by cold, for they are also veld sleepers who do not bask before a fire for warmth as we do.

During the times when the Zulu kings, Shaka, Dingane and Mpande, ruled in Zululand, it often happened that the army when it was at a distance would come upon the Bushmen – not many, but only one or two – and the army would be afraid to speak to them, but they would speak without fear, even if faced with large numbers. And should the army fail to show respect towards a Bushman, he would severely scold it. On one occasion a member of one of Mpande's regiments, on speaking to a Bushman, rudely remarked, 'And what sort of person is this, that is merely the size of a child!' And he became very angry and threateningly said, 'And when you reach home you will beget one of the same size as myself'. And true enough, when he returned home his wife became pregnant and gave birth to a person the size of a child, Magwaqa or Mlambo, who came into Natal with the iziGqoza faction, the followers of Mbulazi.[4]

Chapter 3
HOTTENTOTS[1]

We are not the same as these people either, being different in bodily build. The creation of the Hottentot has produced something greatly different from the Bantu person. Look closely at their heads, noses, cheekbones, and their narrow foreheads, and see the differences between them and the Bantu person. The head of a Hottentot is as strong as that of a sheep, whose hard head can kill a bull. When a Hottentot fights with a person, the person should watch out for that very same head, for should he fail to do so, he will receive such a butt that will instantaneously put an end to him.

In very early times it would appear as if these people lived northwards towards German West Africa, from where they were removed by the Boers to the Cape, the Boers enticing them there by means of their drink known as 'grog', enticing them and telling them that they were taking them to a beautiful country known as 'Mooi Plaas', where, they said, if a person was fond of sweet potatoes, he could take his wagon, and wherever its wheel touched the ground a tuber would emerge as large as the body of a man. Well, the Hottentots having drunk a large quantity of grog, became very friendly with the Boers and agreed to leave their own country because of the temptation of the Boers. On reaching the Cape they became the slaves of the Boers, having been led to excessive drinking. In the end they forgot their own language and took to the language of the Boers only. Those of their people who remained behind they can no longer understand when they speak, and only a small number can now speak their original language.[2]

If you offer a person of that race grog, he is prepared to part with everything he possesses. Grog and bitter coffee are the two things that disrupt peace and happiness. The land of the Hottentots, a very extensive country, is said to have been sold for grog, for owing to the addiction of the Hottentots, the white people were able by degrees to acquire the whole country. In the end the owners of the land became the subjects of the white people with nowhere to live, because of their addiction to grog. You people, beware of grog because it is a serpent that bites. Chiefs who drink, and elders as well who owned large herds, no longer possess cattle-kraals because of drinking.

These are the people, by the way, whose god was an insect with many knees, which they worshipped in the full belief that it would save them when sick or in trouble, just as we Zulus rely on our fathers and mothers and all our relatives who are no longer alive, in the belief that they possess the power to save, and who, upon death, turn into snakes.[3] And so these people thoroughly believed that the mantis was their saviour and called it *Tixo*. And that is how this word came to be used for God among our people. For when the first missionaries arrived among the Xhosa, they asked them whom they referred to as the Lord that created the heaven and the earth and the people and all else. Well, the Xhosa having seen and heard other people, said it was *Tixo* having heard about it from the Hottentots. All of you know that the Xhosa get interested in foreign words, and then adopt them as their own. But as a matter of fact it was not fitting that the Father of all, who was known by all our people as *Mvelinqangi* [the first appearer], who created everything, the earth and the heaven, should be named after an insect as small and as repulsive as the mantis. But seeing that it was the first to be used, it is clear that in the course of time it will be found to be unsuitable and drop out of use, and thereafter our Father who created us will be known by the name of *Nkulunkulu* or *Somandla* [Almighty], and the ignorance of the Xhosa be abandoned.[4]

Chapter 4

GRIQUAS

The ancestor of these people is said to be Adam Kok, a Boer.[1] They originated a long time ago, they too being similar to the Hottentots but differing from them in certain respects that indicate that they are a mixture of two races – the black man and the white man. They are not exactly like the Hottentots, for on closely looking at him, you will observe that his facial features are those of a white man, and that he is not a Hottentot but a mixture.

I do not know from where this Boer obtained the girl through whom he produced the Griquas, but I fancy it was a Hottentot girl, because some Griquas resemble Hottentots. Also, their chief, Adam Kok,[2] once came to Pietermaritzburg some years ago, and whenever he stopped speaking the Boer language, he spoke a clicking language similar to that of the Bushmen. I maintain that these races – the Bushmen, Hottentots and Griquas – are a related family, and although I am unable to explain the matter clearly, it seems as if the Griquas are related on the maternal side to the Hottentots. Their origin appears to be one, as is the case with the Nguni and the Ntungwa, even though we have since increased exceedingly. But all these people, the Bushmen and the Hottentots, are not greatly different from us, and there is a great resemblance between us: their hair is the same as ours, and it is this which differentiates a white man and a black man; and so the Griqua is in truth a white man.[3]

Chapter 5

WHERE WAS THE EARLIEST ORIGIN?

[THE SLAVE TRADE]

It is not known where the people had originally come from when they left the Horn of Africa (Suez Canal), but some suggest that it was Egypt.[1] None of our predecessors tell us; they did not tell us anything about where we originated. Only one thing do they narrate, and that is that there were great rivers in the country where they formerly lived, which could only be crossed by boats. There, when children went to bathe, there appeared a monster known as *Siququmadevu* [shaggy-haired monster]. They said that it was a terrible animal indeed, because on arriving at a river where children were bathing, it would collect them all together without them realising what was happening – not by force but by kindness – by enticing them with tasty food, and giving it to them and providing them with amusement. (Perhaps they gave them biscuits, cakes and sweets, so much liked by children, but I could not be positive as to that). It is said that if a child began to cry, wanting to go home, saying, 'Give me my blanket', *Siququmadevu* would reply saying, 'Come here and get it'. And as soon as the child got there it would swallow it. (From a person's understanding of the position, it was then that the boat went off).[2]

Such a serious matter was told to us by the old people who were before us – telling us after nightfall at sleeping time – telling us that it was a fairy story. It was not fiction but the real truth. It is emphatically stated that it must not be told during daytime, it must be left until nightfall, at sleeping time, otherwise the old person narrating it would grow horns like a beast if he told it during daylight. For this reason we hear it at night, told by the old women when we are going to sleep.[3]

Chapter 6

THE WHITE MAN AND THE BLACK MAN

[THE SLAVE TRADE]

All of you can see for yourselves that there are no large rivers that could be navigated by ships in this country, and frequented by this enormous monster that used to move about collecting black children, filling its capacious stomach and then making off with them. This has reference to the ships of the Portuguese and other evil white men, going about hunting for black children bathing in rivers, to collect them and sell them to other white people to be turned into slaves, in order to acquire money. This evil practice was eventually brought to an end by the gracious English princess, Queen Victoria, who sent out great warships (Men of War) to patrol the seas, which on finding ships containing black children, apprehended them and deprived them of these children, who were sent to certain places established by her [Queen Victoria], and they were not sold.

It is due to this that so many of our people now fill America, for the Queen only saw to this latterly, after large numbers of children had been taken into slavery, for when she came to the throne this evil practice was already long in operation. Seeing that the two large rivers of which we know are the Zambezi and the Congo, if you give the matter thought, you will realise clearly that it was from these rivers that our children were taken.

I must tell you about the people from the Congo whom I saw at St. Helena at the time the Zulu princes were imprisoned there.[1] I saw them in 1896–7, they who were the same as those who were captured on the Congo river in former times – Cummings, Williams, George, together with Mbilimbili (I have forgotten the name by which the Europeans called him). These four men were captured on the Congo river as they were bathing, when they were small children, innocent and ignorant, and after they were captured they were rescued from the white men who had seized them by the ships of the Queen, and taken to the island of St. Helena by her orders. They remained there until they grew up into men, for now they are old men with homes of their own, except Mbilimbili who has no home and who still has a slight knowledge of our language, but the other three no longer know it except for a few words. This Mbilimbili was in the habit of telling me stories about Nqaba kaMbekwane Khumalo, the chief of his people, who was a man of much wisdom like Chakijana Bogcololo.[2]

I will not weary myself by telling you about the many of our people now in America, amounting to hundreds and thousands today, who were transported by and bartered and sold and turned into slaves of the white people. They, through the labour and great effort of their grandfathers in early times, were eventually able to obtain their release from slavery, and by the time they had children of their own, they had been freed and were important men in their own right. They have multiplied exceedingly, they have also been educated, they have prospered greatly, being numbered by hundreds and thousands in that country to which their grandfathers were taken and sold.

It is not the first time, for it started a long time ago, that the white people liken us to wild animals because of the colour given to us by God. Some white people do not think that the black person is a person but an animal, a baboon or a dog given them by the Almighty to work for them, hunt for them, and earn money for them to enable them to become the real people created by God. Oh!, they are mistaken!

There is only one white person who settled in the country who did not wish to discriminate against a person by his colour, and who announced that all people, regardless of race, were created by God at the same time – Queen Victoria was aware of that.[3]

But now there are many in the country who are double-breeds [*onhlobombili*], a mixture of white and black. There is a great tendency among worthless white men to marry our girls, finding them beautiful, thereby breaking the established rule that each race should marry with itself only, in accordance with its creation; but some white men have disregarded this, in spite of the fact that they know the laws of the Creator. We ourselves wished to see this behaviour on the part of the first white men, for they were given girls by Shaka from his harem: Mbuyazwe (Fynn), Wohlo (Ogle), and others,[4] who lived with their wives and built homes for them and did not abandon them. But why were these women and their children at a later date subsequently abandoned?[5]

Chapter 7
SUGGESTIONS AND COMPARISONS
[THE PROBLEM OF RACE]

There are some of our people who are in the habit of reading the scriptures of the Hebrews and who have come to the conclusion that we black people came from the people of Israel. And there is that important event following the death of King Solomon and the succession of Rehoboam to the throne, when ten tribes deserted him leaving only two, those of Juda and Benjamin. They inform us that even though it is stated that these ten tribes eventually appointed their own kings, it is not clear that all did so, and it is possible for some to have gone ahead since their desertion without wanting to have kings to rule over them.

All this is mere conjecture, for it is not possible for anyone to say definitely where we came from. Yet the migrations of the black people from the curve of the sea (Suez Canal) indicate to us that they were constantly moving forward, and also that there was something pursuing them from behind wanting to overtake them. Why? Because from the time they left the curve (Suez Canal) they were constantly on the move. And how is that apparent? It is apparent because there is nowhere that we settled, but we were always on the move. Every one of our people, of every variety that I have mentioned, on being closely questioned as to where he came from, will tell you he came from the north, from the upper part of the country, and he will never point to anywhere else. I refer to the Sotho, Swazi, Mutwa, Mpondo, Zulu, Xhosa, Ndawo, and all other black nations, even though now speaking different languages.

But by the way, may we agree with those who maintain that we are a branch of the Israelites? And by the way, were these Israelites absolutely black just like ourselves? I do not think that they were all black, for some were yellow like the Arabs; but we are different by being all black, whereas with them there are some who are yellowish. Well, and is it a fact that the people of Israel had tightly curled hair just like us?

The difference between a white and a black person is very great. Just examine the hair of a black person and then look at that of a white. Look at the nose of a black person and that of a white, and the lips and the eyes, and see if they are alike. There is one point of evidence that is clear, and that is that the Bushman and the Hottentot sprang from the same source as ourselves, because of their hair being similar to ours in its twisted curliness, which makes it perfectly clear that all of us together on our creation resembled the sheep among the animals, whilst the whites resembled the goat.

But if a black man should marry a white girl, and a white man marry a black girl, would the progeny resemble the black man? No! It will take after the white man, the blood of the black man being absorbed by that of the white, and after a few generations that progeny becomes absolutely white and the blackness disappears completely. What appears clear to me is that in the end all black people will become white and resemble the whites in colour finally, for the white men show much eagerness in their desire to have intercourse with black girls [they are *khaliphile* (sharp, quick and bold) with the *isinene* (frontal cover, euphemism for penis) among the black girls].

In the ancient writings of the Hebrews it is stated that one man and one woman were created. If it is perfectly true that there was only the one man and the one woman, it is likely that both the man and the wife were black. If they were white, well then, where did the blacks come from? And the yellow people and the others who are not white? For the whites do not change colour and become black. In the book of Genesis it is said that Adam begat Cain and Abel by Eve, but that the elder killed the younger because he was jealous of him. Cain was driven out into the country of Nod. Where did he get the girl who married him, seeing that his mother and father were the first and only people? (Genesis iv: 1–8). A person could weary himself to exhaustion over the ancient writings of the Hebrews. If this is true, who were the first to be created – white or black – seeing that there are many different races? Some are quite white, some yellow, some reddish, and others absolutely black. How does the ant have so many species? There is the completely black ant [*amahlwasisi*] that is eaten, also the completely black ant [*izimpompolo*] that bites, and the red ant [*amatsheketshe*] and others; there is the red ant [*ubutumusha*] that bites, and the reddish nocturnal flying ant [*izinhlwabusuku*] that is delicious to eat; there is the small flying ant [*izinkulungwane*] and the ant of the ant-heap [*ingange*] whose queen is known as *Qumbu*. Well then, are all these not known collectively under one name? Why does the human being fancy himself to be something special, seeing that he has been formed in exactly the same way as all animals created by the Creator?

Pay heed to this: Why should the story not be true that the first person to be created was a baboon, and that in the course of time the baboons developed into humans such as us? Afterwards the people dispersed over the face of the earth. There is the account that states that the members of the Thusi clan are baboons, that becoming weary of cultivating crops, they went to live in the veld and inserted their hoe handles into their rumps, where they grew into tails. Is there not another account that asserts that in the high mountains of Switzerland there are animals similar to our baboons, but they are white with long hair? Would it be a miracle to suggest that the white people evolved from these animals? No one can be positive on the subject of the first man and the first woman, of whom it is said she was created out of the rib of the man. Such talk completely confounds us![1]

Chapter 8

THEY WHO REMAINED BEHIND

[CHRISTIAN EVANGELISTS]

Even if the people continued to move towards the west of the country, there were many who remained behind, tribe by tribe; and today there are many living beyond and on this side of the Zambezi, governed by their own chiefs. Some have submitted to British rule, some to French, some to German, and some are under the Portuguese. And in those places the Word of God is preached. There are missionaries who are spreading it. But the language of these people does not differ greatly from ours, some words being the same.

Not many years have passed since Archdeacon Mackenzie of Mlazi in Natal was sent to enlighten those at the Zambezi and to be Bishop there. But his mission there did not meet with success because the people of those parts were still like wild animals. He crossed that great river, the Zambezi, with difficulty, with fighting and shooting in the river itself, but he nevertheless succeeded in crossing. He did not live there very long because of the severe fever of that country, and soon died, which caused great sorrow to us all who knew him and his human qualities.[1]

After the lapse of a few years, there arrived a lady, Miss Alice Werner, from the Zambezi where she had been teaching, bringing books from those parts because she was able then to speak a little of their language. She related to us the details of those people, and the great work that had been undertaken to evangelise them, and how they were able to weave their own clothes; and she told us that they bred large flocks of sheep and herds of goats, and cultivated cotton.[2]

Chapter 9
THE DISPERSAL OF THE PEOPLE[1]

The dispersal of the people throughout the country indicates that they were in search of places in which to settle. But even those who found such places still moved on. The great tribe of Mnguni went in the direction of the setting sun, but as with the locusts, found itself barred by the sea.[2] It was this Mnguni that begot Mxhosa, who was apparently the first-born of Mnguni. This tribe has for many years lived apart from its brothers that it left behind.

A noted clan was that of Sibiya, of which it is said, 'The Sibiya people fence their cattle-kraals with cattle whilst others use branches'.[3] It is said that when this clan arrived here, appearing from the north, it settled between the two Mfolozi rivers, the White and the Black. It was the first clan to arrive in Zululand, and it is said to have possessed large herds. It would appear that the praise, 'The Sibiya people fence their cattle-kraals with cattle whilst others use branches', refers to their large herds.

Another tribe that moved off a long time ago is the Mpondo, leaving behind the people of Madango whose brothers are the people of Xulu, for if a person were to greet a Xulu by his formal salute [*isithakazelo*], he would say 'Mpondonde Madango', for they are not distantly related, even if those of Faku kaNgqungqushe [the Mpondo of Pondoland] appear to be so, which came about because Madango remained behind, but they were begot by one person, the senior being Mpondo. There are also the Xasibe of Nxele, closely related to the Mpondo in every respect, and not distantly related. It was only great disputes that led the family not to wear the same brass necklace.

The dispersal of the people throughout the country was due to dissensions and quarrelling. When a younger brother found that he was not living on good terms with his brother, he broke away to go and establish a home in his own place, where he could live in peace and happiness without being disturbed by anyone, for indeed the land was extensive and available to all.

A large tribe that remained behind was that of Makhasana kaTembe, where the chieftainship has stood for a long time. Furthermore they are not a warlike people and dislike quarrelling. It is an old-established tribe, which has been there for a very long time. I am referring to the people of Noziyingili.[4] They have always been a people who live peaceably. It is for this reason that when they find people looking at them enviously and threateningly, they resort to the use of medicines for retaliation against them who cause them trouble, thus giving rise to the saying that 'the Tonga are a race of sorcerers, and worthless people'.[5]

Not far from the Tembe are the Swazi, a large tribe that has developed from many small clans, now occupying a large tract of country.[6] From them emerged the Embo people of Mkhize,[7] who left because of a dispute. And this Mkhize tribe now has large numbers of clans today. Near to these people is now a collection of Tonga and Swazi and other remnants.

A great tribe was that of the Nxumalo, which comprised two large clans, that of Zwide kaLanga, the great chief of the Ndwandwe, and that of his kinsman, Soshangana kaManukuza, both being great chiefs with a great many people.[8]

Yonder is the Mthethwa clan whose chief was Jobe who had two sons, Tana and Godongwana; and when there was a dispute over castor oil plants which had grown on a deserted site,[9] Jobe got angry, realising that they were rivals for his position and that in the end they would kill him. He thereupon closed in upon them with a regiment one morning, killing the elder, Tana, but Godongwana escaped and went away towards the west. There he remained until he heard that his father Jobe was dead, and then he returned as Dingiswayo and assumed his father's position and became chief of the Mthethwa people.[10]

The large tribe of Malandela comprised the clans of Qwabe and his brother, Zulu kaNtombela, both of which covered large areas. It is said that on one occasion Nozidiya, the great chief of the Qwabe clan, wishing to set his household in order, slaughtered a large ox, and placed all the joints in a large heap. He then called all his sons so that each should take the joint he wanted. It was then that Mayiwe selected a large leg. Thereupon it was said of him, 'You are now a person of no consequence because of having behaved disrespectfully by taking such a large piece'. After him came Msomi who selected the ribs of beef. It was said of him, 'You are a chief by having taken this meat'. And he, Msomi, begot Mbhedu, his first-born son, and also Gasa of the junior house of his family, and then Singila, his heir. Singila begot Vumane who begot Kude and Moyeni. The Qwabe also produced the people of Mhlongo, by which I mean those of Zincuma.[11]

You should understand that I am enumerating only some of the tribes, so do not think that you will get them all here, for some produce other small ones. It depends on population increase. After four or five generations, people call themselves by a younger forefather and abandon the older one.

Chapter 10
MORE ABOUT THE DISPERSED ONES

Yonder is a man known by the name of Bhede of the Ngwenya clan, and he was constantly wandering about like all the others coming from Swaziland. He made his way westward where he established himself on the top of a mountain and below it, and there begot Mokhatshana who begot Moshweshwe [Moshesh]. The place where he thus settled is known as *esihlabeni* (Thaba Bosiu, which means Night Mountain), his main stronghold.[1]

And there is also Mchunu who on arrival established himself between the two Tala mountains, the large and the small. It was he who produced many descendants [the Chunu clan] at that spot. He begot Lubhoko who begot Macingwane. He begot Ndima who begot Lembede (whose name is said to be Bayeni). It was these people who once disputed with Macingwane. Lembede's bush, which marks the place where he was buried, is at Sikhaleni-sebomvu, between the two Tala mountains, the large and the small. The larger one is towards the north whilst the small one is towards the south, where the Church of South Africa school is now to be found. Towards the upper side of where the school is situated, is a large pile of stones, the grave of Lubhoko. It is said that after the fighting in which Lembede was defeated, Lubhoko assumed the Chunu chieftainship.

Over towards the Mhlathuze river and overlooking it, is a large bush, the burial place of Mbhoma. He was chief of the Sikakana clan. These people are noted for their medical skill, and in olden times they were mostly medicine men.

Over there are the Cube of Dlaba, chief of the Shezi clan at Nkandla, together with the Majozi. It was from here that the Camane originated to make their way across the Tugela.

Near Nkandla are the Ndlovu people, whose chief was Ngema who begot Lumula, and Lumula begot Zingelwayo who begot Mpongo, the father of Manzezulu. The Ndlovu contested hotly with Macingwane [the Chunu chief]. Mpongo had great powers and he sent two Bateleur eagles to attack Macingwane before he himself arrived on the scene. Macingwane also sought the aid of his own medicine man, who bewitched a leopard and sent it to kill Mpongo at night when he was asleep. It mounted the hut as Mpongo was sleeping, and descended and destroyed him as he was sleeping at his home in the large forest of Nomangce. And so his tribe was dispersed and Macingwane assumed the chieftainship.

There is also Tshisi, chief of the Nxamalala, who arrived from the north having separated from the rest of his Sotho people. He begot Matomela, the father of Lugaju. And the people multiplied.

Over yonder towards the north of the country are the Zibisi, who gained the praise, 'The Zimpisi [hyenas] are red mouthed from lapping people's blood', because they are all great warriors. Their chief was Nomashingili kaBango. It was these people who accompanied Dingiswayo, the Mthethwa chief, on his return to his Mthethwa domain. He went down riding a white horse given to him by white men.

There are the Ngcobo people also coming down, moving in large columns together with a number of small clans that had attached themselves to them. And it was during these movements that they gained the praise, 'Those who thatch and unthatch like a buck', because on their travels when the people were very weary, even if the chief had announced the previous day that they would be up and away again, they would agree and immediately thatch their temporary shelters, thinking that they would not be observed, for they were tired of travelling, having come from far away, and it was a long time since they first set out.

The following clans are branches of the great Ngcobo tribe which came down from the north. You know, of course, that Ngcobo was the son of Vumezitha who had separated from the Tembe people. They are as follows: the Nyuswa, the chiefhouse of them all; the Qadi section of the chief house; the Bhelesi; the Ngongoma of Ngcobo's original ancestral home [*isizinda*]; Nomazocwana kaNdlela; Mkhetshane kaNgcobo (Shangase); Mnguni kaKhuzwayo (Ngidi); Ndelu of the Bhulose; of the Wosiyana; the Mfene; the Cele of Ndosi; the Goba, along with many other clans whose names I cannot remember. It does not surprise these people to address one another as 'Ngcobo', even though they now have different surnames and normally intermarry with one another.[2] The Nyuswa marry into all these sections, with the exception of the Qadi section. The Ngwane, 'mighty milkers who milk with the suction of a yearling' [clan praise] – their principal chief was

Matiwane. It was the Ngwane that possessed a powerful chieftainship. It was Matiwane kaMasumpa who fought Shaka for a long time, but because of Shaka's persistence he fled and became a wanderer. On his return, defeated, he sent a message to Shaka: 'An exhausted clod seeks sanctuary of you, son of Senzangakhona, for I am now overcome by failure'. Shaka agreed to accept him, but due to the wickedness of the Zulu people, they spitefully accused him of seeking chiefly power, and Shaka put him to death.[3] And the cliff [of execution] came to be known as 'KwaMatiwane' even today. This happened in 1812 after Matiwane had submitted and given himself up to Shaka.[4]

Near the Ngwane are the Zizi of Sijadu under their great chief, Dweba, who settled on the land round about the Mtshezi river. This chief enjoyed wide dominion. On one occasion when the Dlamini of Nongcama kaMndlovu (who were their neighbours) went to lobola a girl of the Zizi clan, they began constantly to address one another as well as the people of the place where they had gone on a marriage visit (the Zizi), by the formal salute 'Dlamini', which was very pleasing to the Zizi. On their departure, Dweba offered them a heifer for permission to use the surname 'Dlamini', and so ever since then the salutation surname [*isithakazelo*] of the Zizi has been Dlamini.

Note that there are many branches of the Dlamini tribe: there is the senior branch of the right-hand side under Bhidla kaNgonyama; the Emakhuzeni under Khukhela; the Esiphahleni under Mbazwana; the Egugwini under Fodo; the Enhlangwini under Sidoyi, and there are other sub-branches.

The settlements were not far apart. The Hlubi under Bhungane kaNsele were where the present Boer town of Utrecht stands,[5] living adjacent to the Ngwane, the Zizi and the Enhlangwini (Dlamini).

At Umvoti there were the Dunge – the European town known as Mgungundlovana (Greytown) is on an old site of theirs – where they lived in large numbers, eventually extending across the Tugela to occupy the whole of the Mandlalati area, which some call 'Mangralatsi'.[6]

And the Ngcolosi are not far from them, living always with mutually respected spaces between them. At the present time the Ngcolosi consist of two clans, that of Ndlokolo kaNkungu and that of his brother Hlangabeza. This was caused by the dispute between them over the chieftainship of their father, Nkunguthe son of Mepho kaNgwane kaBhengu. It is this surname 'Bhengu' by which they are now addressed.

There are two Bhengu sections in the country, if I enumerate those known to me, the Ngcolosi and a small remnant of the Embo of Mkhize, they of Bhulu kaBhengu, [namely] the Mvubu of Shongwe and the Mahoyiza of Mlandu, whose chief was Mfacane kaMpalampala kaMatomela, and who were defeated in heavy fighting with the Embo of Khabazele kaMavovo, over an inheritance dispute. Thus were overthrown the descendants of the great-grandfather of Mfacane. Among the Ngcolosi there are several small clans – those of Jali and those of Peta.

I cannot omit to include the people of Nzama (the Wosiyana) even though they are a branch of the Ngcobo. In early times they were also a considerable clan. It is these people who in the latter years when Shaka appeared on the scene and everybody was deprived of their cattle, the chief of the Wosiyana, Ngcugcwa by name, obtained some magic medicine – whether from the Bushmen I am unable to say – and resorted to trickery for stealing people's cattle at night without being seen, but eventually he was caught. On being brought before Shaka in the morning, Shaka greeted him saying, 'sakubona Gcugcwa' [the Zulu greeting, 'we see you'], to which he replied, 'Yes Ndabezitha [your majesty], I also see you'. Again Shaka said 'sakubona Gcugcwa', and did so three times greeting him thus;[7] and then Ngcugcwa said, 'Yes Sir, you see me now, but others will see you later on'; whereupon Shaka said, 'seize him'. And so the expression arose when a person greeted another joyfully with 'sakubona So-and-So', he would reply cheerfully, 'Yes, you see me now, but others will see you later on', as Ngcugcwa said. It was done because in the end Shaka was put to death by his brothers as foretold by Ngcugcwa who said, 'And others will see you later on'. And so it became a saying even up to the present day.

Over there is the powerful clan of Mzilikazi kaMashobana,[8] the Khumalo; together with the small related clans of Mabaso and Mangwe. There is also close at hand the large clan of Khanyile adjacent to the Zulu – or perhaps the Phunga or the Mageba at that time.[9]

There are also the people of Mevana who used to rule themselves, by which I mean the Buthelezi. Mnyamana kaNgqengelele was chief councillor to Cetshwayo, the last of the Zulu kings, his father Ngqengelele having appeared amongst those people [the Zulu] during the time of Shaka. Ngqengelele arrived in the Zulu country without having pierced his ears.[10] On his arrival, Ngqengelele was appointed as attendant [*inceku*] to share the king's private apartment ['gentleman of the bed-chamber', to wait intimately upon the king], to receive the king's spittle and phlegm when the king found it necessary to expectorate.[11] But he had a brother, Khoboyela, the father of Klwana, commander of the army in the time of Dingane. Klwana was put to death by Mnyamana during the reign of Mpande. Klwana was a famous man as commander of the army. When Mpande succeeded to the kingship, Mnyamana was then in a high place, and he put Klwana to death on the grounds that he was appropriating the estate of his [Mnyamana's] father Ngqengelele, to which he [Klwana] had no right as he was the son of his [Ngqengelele's] brother Khoboyela. I think Ngqengelele's father was Shenge, a name used as an oath by Mnyamana, but I am not sure of it.[12]

Then there are the people of Manti, the great chief of the Thuli clan, of whom it is said that when he separated from the people of Luthuli who remained behind, he referred to them as 'Luthuli lwangodzi',[13] and that is how they came to be separated from the Thuli clan. Of the clans who spoke the *tekela* dialect by making the tongue lie down [*lala*] when they spoke,[14] there was the Cele of Ndosi, and also the Nganga of Lushozi, a large clan that ruled itself.

There were many clans that arrived here and settled wherever they pleased, because even those of Dube living along the Mhlathuze, and those of Sokhulu who lived below them towards the sea, ruled themselves independently under their own chiefs. And there were many independent clans, large and small, which I have not enumerated here.

There are the Zondi of Nondaba, formerly ruled by their chief, Dlaba, now comprising many clans: those of Mhlola, Dambada, Laduma, and Bhevu. In olden times they were all under one person and not as we see today.

There are the Ntambo of Khwela whose chief was Nokwena who made haste towards the Cape.[15] Nokwena was the father of Mgwada.

Here again are the Phephetha, the clan of Mnyeka, also well established like the rest.

The great tribe of Mkhuphukeli, the Thembu, comprises many clans today. Even over yonder in the Cape Colony are four small chiefs, but the senior chief of them all is Ngqamuzana kaMganu kaNodada kaNgoza kaMkhuphukeli kaMnyandeni kaMvelase. The chief of this clan does not eat maas, nor even beef, merely chewing it without swallowing it, extracting the juices and ejecting the rest. He eats the flesh of the hare and the antelope only, and that of the partridge.[16]

When Ngoza fled from Shaka he was in flight with Macingwane who perished at Ensikeni. And he (Ngoza) died in Pondoland, for he fought with the Mpondos. His clan then became scattered. His heir, Nodada, returned to Natal, to Cacane near Nambithi [Ladysmith], and settled there between Phakade [the Chunu chief] and Matshana kaMondisa [the Sithole chief].

The Embo parted a long time ago from the Langeni (the Swazi), the Embo also being Swazi.[17] They also parted from the Shange of Dumakude. On an occasion when the Embo chief wished to appoint his heir, he slaughtered a large ox and laid out the meat. It was about the time of Sibiside. It was then that Shange pounced upon the leg, and it was then that Mavovo took the brisket and the chieftainship.[18] The Embo chief was Gubhela who begot Kubone who begot Mngebelezana who begot Dlozela who begot Sibiside who begot Mavovo who begot Khabazele who begot Gcwabe who begot Zihlandlo who begot Siyingela who be got Ngunezi, the father of Tilongo and Sikukuku. Zihlandlo was the only one allowed by Shaka to have a harem [*isigodlo*], treating him as a younger brother and destroying all other chiefs.

LESS IMPORTANT CLANS

[Extract from Fuze's next chapter, Chapter 11, which is treated in this edition as Chapter 12 in Part II, because it is mainly ethnographical rather than historical.]

If I have omitted some people from here, it is not a matter of serious concern.[19] I have told you that some small clans sprang from large ones. To me it does not seem necessary to include an insignificant clan such as the Khabeleni of Dlomo, from which people coined the phrase because of their small size, 'You say it is but a single person? Then it is at Fabase's'.[20]

There is no need for me to include the Ngidi because they sprang from the Ngcobo and are still Ngcobo. And the Ndelu of Bhulose and the Cele of Ndosi, along with the Mfene and the Goba, they are all of Ngcobo stock.

But as for the Thusi, they are a race apart. People of olden times are most emphatic in declaring that they are one with the baboons, and that these baboons used to be human beings just as we are. For the Thusi, because they were too indolent to cultivate crops, abandoned their homes and went to live in the veld, consuming the seed that was to be used for sowing. Then with their hoe handles inserted into their

CLANS

hindquarters, they were afraid to return to human habitations to meet people, and continued to live in the veld. In consequence they grew fur like animals.

Then there are the Sithole, their chief being Mbhadu kaNtshiba, but his clan became depleted, and his headman Jobe rose to power and occupied the habitation sites vacated by Ntshiba who removed elsewhere. Jobe remained in the original sites, and the Sithole people eventually acknowledged him as the chief of the clan. When he came to beget Mondisa his position as chief was finally confirmed. And when Mondisa begot Matshana there was no longer the slightest doubt as to who was the chief of the Sithole clan. Yet in truth, the real hereditary chief is Mbhulungeni kaMbhadu kaNtshiba.

The following insignificant clans that sprang from others would not be of much use to me: Msweli, Nala, Hlophe, Mgwaba, Seme, Camu, Masondo, Sokhela, Mlilo, Ntanzi, Duma, Maphanga, Mweli, Madondo, Zimu, Nzimande, Geza, Cagwe, Mathe, Luvuno, Nkabini, Mseleku, Mahlanjeni, Nhlanzini, Nyembe, Zungu, Mthalane, Majola, Manyoni, Masuku, Zelemu, Nyawo, Thusini, Nyathela, Ximba (Mlaba), Sondezi, Mbhatha, Thole, Nkomo, Nyathi, Nyawose, Gcwabaza, Bafazini, Nhlamvu, Mbuyazi, Lamula, Mbheje, Maduna, Magwaza, Lumbo, Sengqela, Mthwazi, Ngiba, Mphungose, Gazu, Gcabashe, Senzela, Mbambo, Meyiwa, Mbomvu (Ngubane), Ngcoya, Mbonambi, Ncobeni, Cebekhulu, Nhlangoti, Mdluli, Njele, Manzi, Ncwabe, Nkala, Ndumo, Xaba, Msimanga, Mzolo, Madlala (which we well know to have come from Basutoland), and Zindela (also from Basutoland, as also the Malinga, who also came here seeking to settle just like all the rest).

Chapter 11[1]

MORE POWERFUL CLANS

There was the clan of Mokhatshana kaBhede, the chief of the Ngwenya, who arrived away up north and drove out the Sotho people. For Bhede himself was not a true Sotho but a member of the Ngwenya clan like the rest. He attained his nationality as a Sotho [his Sotho-ness] later, after the birth of his son Mokhatshana. When Mokhatshana begot Moshweshwe, he became a real Sotho. The clan name of Ngwenya was then changed to Kwena. Moshweshwe through growing wise and teaching his people and his own children, became the most powerful chief of all the people thereabouts.[2]

The clan of Ngqungqushe, the chief of the Mpondo people, was a powerful clan in that land beyond the Mtamvuna river. When he broke away from his own Madango people, he came to increase exceedingly in that part of the country, along with many other clans that were with him such as the Xasibe and the Nxele and others. When he produced Faku, he then became a powerful chief, with the Mpondomusa [Mpondomise] and other clans under him.[3]

There are three related clans which appear to be separate today, the Makhoba, the Zungu and the Gwamanda. Even though they may appear to be separate they are really not. Among the Zungu was born the mother of Cetshwayo, Ngqumbazi, the daughter of the Mbhonde kaTshana. Their chief was Mfanawendlela kaThanga kaManzini kaTshana. The clan of Makhoba was that of Joko, the father of Mangcengce, his eldest son, and his brother Magwaza. The clan of Gwamanda I do not know their chief, but I do know the important teacher Joseph Gwamanda who was stationed at New Hanover, later to proceed to Zululand to undertake teaching there, and also Manzini, the father of Nkofana, an important dignitary of the Gwamanda.

The clan of Ndungunya has always remained in the same place since its arrival from the north,[4] and he begot a son Sobhuza. And when troubled by other clans, he was able to use the caves which abound in his country, and thereby got the better of them. And the Swazi people continued to increase until they became very numerous. From them emerged the Embo of Mkhize and a number of other small clans of that place.[5, 6]

The clan of Makhasana kaTembe has for a very long time continued to live where it is at present. It is very large indeed and it has long been established there, for they are not a restless people.[7]

The clan of Mzilikazi son of Mashobana (the Khumalo people) was a very large, powerful and warlike clan. The chief of these people together with other people similar to them, does not eat maas, like the chief of the Hlubi, the Ngweni and the Mabaso.[8] The Khumalo were both numerous and powerful, and when Shaka became prominent, disrupting all the clans, they left with much fighting to go and settle far to the north, which is now known as Bulawayo, the name of Mzilikazi's capital. And here back in Zululand, Shaka built his great capital and called it by the name of Gibixhegu [Root out the Old Man], which was later known as Bulawayo.[9]

The Ngwane, the people of Luhlongwane, were a very powerful clan indeed. Even when Shaka appeared, Matiwane kaMasumpa fought fiercely against him. It was he who when driven from home, became a wanderer. Eventually he returned to Zululand without an army, and on arrival before the king said, 'The clod is weary with exhaustion, son of Senzangakhona, accept me for I now belong to you'. If Matiwane was subsequently put to death it was due to the bloodthirstiness of the Zulu people.[10]

Many clans emerge from others, such as the Bomvu of Ngubane which emerged from the Ngwane. Just take note here: Nomafu begot Ngwane; Ngwane begot Ngcukumane; Ngcukumane begot Myaluza who begot Ngogo; Ngogo begot Ngubane; and he begot Nomaphikela, the father of Mbomvu who begot Nyonemnyama who begot Ndlovu who begot Matomela, the father of Nzombane who begot Somahashi, the father of Mawele who begot Nyoniyezwe.[11] There are now many clans, the Ngwane, the Bomvu, the Sibhunge of Homoyi and the Njengabantu of Sobuza, all descended from Nzombane.

The Mthethwa clan was very large, their chief Dingiswayo ka Jobe having been a powerful man. But he was put to death by Zwide whilst on a peaceful visit to him.[12] This was the cause of the quarrel between Shaka and Zwide, for in fact Shaka had grown up under Dingiswayo, who nourished and supported him. His son, Somveli [Dingiswayo's son], fled at the time of the conflict between Shaka and Zwide, the Ndwandwe chief.

The Hlubi clan was very powerful during the reign of Mthimkhulu, and it was this clan that assisted Shaka in his great encounters with Zwide.

The Chunu clan was very powerful during the reign of Macingwane. It was he who fought a great battle against Shaka. Eventually he fled to the Cape Colony where he died at Ensikeni.

The great clan of Nozidiya kaQwabe kaMalandela, which is one in origin with that of Zulu kaNtombela kaMalandela, was powerful indeed. The chief, Phakathwayo kaKhondlo, was famous for his greatness. But when Shaka kaSenzangakhona kaJama kaNdaba kaPhunga kaMageba kaNkosinkulu kaZulu kaNtombela arrived on the scene, who was his [Phakathwayo's] kinsman by birth [by blood], Phakathwayo was fearful and lacked the strength to wage war against Shaka, for it is said that he was in the habit of speaking about him contemptuously saying, 'Eya! What is that troublesome stumpy little stick [*igamathandukwana*] which, whilst eating with a meat platter in the one hand and a mash of mealies in the other, is approached and buffeted by a dog with its head?'[13] Both these persons were descended from Malandela. The senior was Qwabe and Zulu was the junior. Senzangakhona [Shaka's father] lived amicably with Phakathwayo, without quarrelling.

These clans to which I have referred were the most powerful of all, although they did not rule the other clans of the country. But they were acknowledged by the whole country as the most powerful.

PART II: ETHNOGRAPHICAL[1]

Chapter 12[2]

LIFE THROUGHOUT THE LAND

All the people lived independently, without interference, and free from disturbance and quarrelling among themselves. [Here follows the passage that has been extracted and added to Chapter 10]. All these clans that I have enumerated and those I have not, lived in harmony and without enmity.[3] If a quarrel arose between two clans, the males would meet at a pre-arranged place, armed with shields and many spears. As soon as they met they would throw their spears at one another, each one shouting 'Heiye!' as he hurled his spear at the enemy. When one was wounded, those of his side would run away. And at the same time those who had inflicted the wound would stand still and refrain from pursuing those who were running away, and then depart for their homes. The following day messengers would be sent to express regret. There was no emnity between them.[4]

Furthermore fighting was not the normal thing among the people; it happened only occasionally, it was not a daily occurrence. Spears were carried in large numbers in a man's shield, unlike today when only two are carried. In those days the people were very friendly, and if someone was seriously injured he was not abandoned but cared for and helped to reach home.

Today if a person injures another in a fight, he finishes him off by killing him outright, and then proceeds to disembowel him by sticking his spear into his stomach, so that his innards fall out. They tell us that this is done to prevent the assailant's [not the victim's] stomach from swelling, but that is just nonsense.[5]

ON THE DEATH OF A PERSON

On the death of a person, his relatives and neighbours are informed. They go to his home and the men dig the grave. If it is the head of the household, the grave is dug within the cattle kraal. The grave is made round and not elongated, and it is dug deep. When it is of the desired depth, a niche is hollowed out to receive the body. The body is then removed from the room in which the head of the household has died, and brought to the cattle kraal on a mat, covered with his clothes. All his family stand around the grave, with the eldest son holding his father's weapons. The body is delivered into the grave by two persons, one below standing in the grave, and the other above to lower it to the one below. All the while the body is bound together into a sitting position as if the person were alive.

When the body is lowered down and placed in the niche, the attendant in the grave supports it with stones starting at the bottom until he reaches the head. The one above supplies the one below with stones with which to support the body. After this work is quite complete, the soil is replaced. And then when everything is finished, the death wail is raised with loud lamentations. Afterwards everybody proceeds to the river to wash with the cleansing medicines [*intelezi*] which have been provided for them. After they have washed, they go home. Then a medicine man is sought to provide them with medicine [*umlawu*] to take internally, and the next day a medicine man is sought to prepare medicinal roots and barks [*amakhubalo*, for purification and protection purposes]. A beast or yearling calf is slaughtered to take with this medicine. All the meat of this animal must be consumed on that day. Then there is abstention for a few days, and there is no singing for a month. After the lapse of about six months, a great feast with beer is held, with a beast and goats being slaughtered, to bring back [*buyisa*] the dead man; and his spirit [*idlozi*] is addressed with prayer and praise [*ukuthetha idlozi*]. Then all the members of his family rejoice. On that day his widows (those that still want to lead a married life) choose from among his brothers those who would marry them [by the custom of *ukungena*] and raise seed for the deceased.[6]

ON THE DEATH OF A CHIEF

On the death of a chief, all the members of his clan are assembled, armed with shields. They chant their clan songs, but do not dance. It is customary for the body of a chief to lie unburied for three or four days or even for a week, pending the full assemblage of the clan. While the body is waiting for such a time, oxen are slaughtered and the skins wrapped round the corpse so that there should be no smell of decomposition in the home.

DEATH

All the people having assembled, the body is interred with all its personal belongings; the head-ring is severed and buried with the corpse. During these proceedings all his sons are present, standing around the grave with the eldest son holding his father's weapons, and all the men standing with their shields and surrounding the grave. And so it is. But all deaths are the same, only that of a chief is different in that all the men shave their heads as the women do on the death of their husbands, for the chief is regarded as the husband of all the men who are bereaved.

And then after all this, a large hunting party goes out to hunt antelope. If there is an enemy hostile to the chief, the funeral hunt [*ihlambo*, the washing of spears] goes out as an army to attack the enemy and its chief. But if it is a minor chief or headman, there is only a hunt for antelope and no thought of war.

After the lapse of a number of months, the clan is assembled to partake in a large feast to bring back [*buyisa*] the chief. On that day the meat is so plentiful that even a number of dogs could not dispose of it, and the beer is contained even in cracked and chipped pots, with more than enough for everyone, and the drunkards caper around unconscious of what they are doing. The widows appear dressed to perfection and ready to select those [of the deceased's brothers] who would enter into *ukungena* marriages with them. On that day the spirit of the chief is brought back into the home.

Chapter 13

THE HEAD-RING AND THE TOP-KNOT

At one time the man's head-ring [*isicoco*] and the woman's top-knot [*inkehli*] were unknown.[1] A man went about without a ring on his head, and the women also were without these top-knots on their heads. But the women did used to rub red ochre into their heads as is done by the Bhaca people, without raising the hair, it being left to lie down in exactly the same manner as the Bhaca. The head-ring first appeared in Shaka's time,[2] the one who turned the people into soldiers. He decreed that no man or woman should marry before he had given the command.

I myself do not think that Shaka invented on his own account the idea that men should wear head-rings; I think he was directed to do so by God. Just study a man's head and see what it looks like. A boy grows up even as you are watching him, with beautiful black hair, but after he has attained fifty years of age, you will notice that his head shows signs of disarray. Long before the appearance of grey hairs, you will notice that there is a bare patch on the back of the head without a single hair on it – simply a smooth spot. When Shaka observed this, he was inspired by God and gave orders for the head-ring to be sewn on to that spot, on the first appearance of baldness, to improve the person's appearance and also to show that he was a fully mature man.

It was thus that this custom was introduced, which had been unknown formerly. You will realise how disparaging it is for a man to be without a head-ring; he is not like the wearer of a handsome and dignified head-ring, who has a sense of maturity and confidence. I do not think that a little bald-headed grey-haired old man is an object of beauty; in fact he is known by all as only a little old bald-head [*impandlana*]. These defects are to be found even among the white people, who do not wear head-rings, but they are saved by the hats they wear on their heads, for, if they did not do so, they would look even worse and more unbecoming.

Chapter 14
CIRCUMCISION AND PUBERTY[1]

At one time circumcision was practised. An uncircumcised person was not recognised as a man, he was addressed merely as 'boy' [*umfana*] however old he might be, and regarded as a worthless woman and a coward who was afraid to face the spear at the flat stone [where circumcisions were performed].

At certain suitable times it was customary for the boys of various localities to assemble in age groups for the purpose of circumcision, at their own particular places. Women did not visit the youths that had been circumcised, it was only the old women who went to them to take them food. Meat was never lacking for the circumcised youths, it being provided in the main by the slaughter of yearlings and not sucking calves.

This custom among the people was terminated by Shaka,[2] and circumcision was completely abolished. He established the custom that a whole age group should assemble in its various localities to serve as herd-boys [*kleza*][3] at the military barracks [*amakhanda*], and they who were gathered together in such a great establishment were to be known as the enrolment or regiment [*ibutho*] of such and such a place.

PUBERTY

And girls were also formed into regiments and they also lived under restraint, without being allowed to marry even to a chief, without the owner's consent.[4]

All those who misbehaved by breaking the rule were put to death. However, it was no crime for a young man and his sweetheart to have sexual intercourse without marriage,[5] and this was regarded as desirable.

[Extract from Fuze's Chapter 19]

In olden days a girl would have sexual intercourse [*soma*] once a month, and then wait to ascertain whether she had got into trouble; after that she would do it again, if so desired. But they would be examined by their mothers every month, a spoiled girl being detected at once. It was not as things are today with all girls being in effect married women [*abafazi*], for today girls often get pregnant while still living at home, doing that which was not done in olden days and ignoring ancient customs.

[Extract from Fuze's Chapter 46]

Although it was permissable for a girl to have sexual intercourse [*soma*] once a month, whenever she did so she would hold herself together and not expose herself.[6] If she did so [open herself], her lover would be wary for fear of trouble.

It was not permitted for a girl to get pregnant and give birth at her home; that was a serious disgrace. Furthermore it was not permitted for a girl who had given birth at her home to go to a festivity and dance with the other girls who were taking part; it was a disgrace.

It merits death to have intercourse with one's sister, one's father's wife,[7] one's father's sister, one's mother's sister, one's cousin, one's brother-in-law's or sister-in-law's children who stand in the same relation to oneself as one's brother's or sister's children . . . [and so Fuze goes on, at length and to complications which, in Mr Lugg's words, are 'incomprehensible'].

According to our ways, grandchildren should reach ten generations before the family begins to separate, and until then they are still under the restriction to recognise one another as brothers and sisters, until the separation is brought about by the chief, after which they may intermarry. Only the chief of the original patrilineal line could do this [confirm the separation]. [End of Extract]

PUBERTY AMONG BOYS

After Shaka had put an end to circumcision, the custom relating to the attainment of puberty by a boy was as follows. When the boy has an emission, the next day the cattle will be found to be missing from the kraal, the boy having secretly removed them all before dawn, leaving only the calves behind, tethered in the huts. Unobserved he removes all the cattle and drives them off to a distant grazing ground.

By the time the people begin to wake up at home, there is not a single animal in the cattle kraal, only the calves calling to their mothers from the huts. All the elders know by this that so and so has attained puberty, when they enquire among the small boys about who is absent.

The one who has attained puberty drives away the cattle, eventually returning with them late in the morning or in the early afternoon. On arrival at his home with the cattle, he remains absolutely silent, speaking to no one. Then those wishing to make him speak or laugh approach him, but no, he still remains silent, not speaking or laughing with a soul.

His father now summons a doctor to treat him and give him food mixed with medicines. He is not allowed to drink cold water, only warm. If he gets thirsty, a hoe is removed from its handle, heated in the fire until it is red hot, and dipped in to cold water to make it tepid for him to drink. He continues to be silent until his father has slaughtered a goat for him and his head is shaved. After this he will talk to people again as before, and his father presents him with a spear to show that he is now a man.

The silence on the part of a boy who has reached puberty is imposed to prevent him from going wrong and becoming an incessant talker. It is similar to the silence of a bereaved person. We speak of a person who is always talking as being 'spoilt', 'hysterical' or 'conceited'. The old people are positive that if a bereaved person speaks in a loud voice, he will never get out of the habit and will go on chattering incessantly, and never be quite like other people. And in regard to this abstention from drinking cold water, the old people are also certain that if a person drinks cold water on being bereaved or on attaining puberty, he will continue to drink large quantities of water.

These customs are no longer observed, and the people have become worthless in consequence.

PUBERTY AMONG GIRLS

With a young girl this event becomes known by hearing the girls continually singing puberty songs. These puberty songs are very bad and disgusting, and refer to matters not spoken about by a well-mannered person and spoken about only by an evil-minded person with no sense of respect. But such songs are composed as a warning to both those who have attained puberty and those who have not, that to do these filthy acts is evil, and that it is a worthless girl who does them.[8] Puberty rites are carried out to enable girls to get to know one other, so that a girl who has already had a child should not associate with those that have never been spoilt, and in this way become ashamed and dejected by being ostracised.

It is for this reason that if a person insults a girl by calling her a married woman [*umfazi*] and a girl of no worth, all the girls of that particular locality will be greatly angered, and proceed to slaughter an ox belonging to the offender's family and cleanse themselves with its stomach contents. Such an act is not an offence, and it is reported to the head of the family, who thereupon sets aside a room for his daughter's puberty attainment.[9] After this, he sends messengers to invite the girls of the neighbouring homesteads, reporting also to relatives both near and far that his daughter has attained puberty, and that it is fitting that the young girls [*amantombazana*, either pre-pubertal girls, or a polite term, rather than *izintombi*, for girls] should come and perform her puberty rites [*thombisa*, to help her to mature].

The girl is then taken into the room set apart for her by her father and mother. All the girls go to the river to collect the soft *incapha* grass [*Scirpus costatus*] and place it in that special room. Then they build a small enclosure at the top end of the room with blankets, where the puberty subject [*umamgonqo*] will remain in seclusion. A friction drum [*ingungu*] is constructed out of a skin,[10] and in the evening the girls play it, producing a rumbling boom [*ukuduma*] like the drum of the European soldiers. And then they sing and chant those same puberty songs.

Then the young men of another locality [another locality presumes another clan] invite others to join them, and proceed to the place of seclusion [*umgonqo*] to court the girls. They arrive in a body in the same manner as a bridegroom's party, at that homestead where the puberty rites are being performed. Their arrival will already be known and reported to the head of the family. They first present the token by which they can court at that homestead, a spear. Such proceedings are known as '*ugelo*'.

After all this, the young men perform a grunting chant [*ukuchwaya*] in the room, with the girls and members of the family looking on as spectators. After this the girls choose [*qoma*] from among the young men their lovers. In accordance with custom, one of the young men is left alone as a buffoon [*iyobo*] to be laughed at and made a fool of. Before the courting ceremony takes place, the girls who are about to choose send one of the young men back to his home to report that he left them choosing, but he is not treated in the same way as the one who is left alone when they choose, who is called '*iyobo*'.

The girl will remain in seclusion for a month with these ceremonies being observed. When she comes out of seclusion, all the girls assemble, for she is now going to 'come out' in preparation for marriage [*ukwemula*]. Her father slaughters a goat for her, which is known as the '*umhlonyane*' goat, and a beast which is known as the '*ukemula*' beast. The girls dance on that day, and the people gather together as at a wedding. They are provided with refreshments of beer and meat, after which they disperse and the proceedings come to an end.

Chapter 15
ENGAGEMENT AND MARRIAGE[1]

On a young man falling in love with the daughter of So-and-So and being afraid to tell his father, he speaks to someone who is on good terms with his father, and informs him that his son is in love with the daughter of So-and-So, who would like to marry him [*gana*]. Some men consent, but others do not. Nevertheless, that girl leaves her home and proceeds to that homestead to become engaged [*gana*]. She is dressed significantly in her leather skirt [*isidwaba*],[2] and accompanied by a young girl as her maid. She leaves home towards evening, arriving there at dusk. She passes through the gate so as to enter the homestead on the left-hand side, followed by her maid, and advances to go and take up a position at the top, next to a house at the upper end. When she gets there, she stands erect, and then squats down on her haunches with her hands on her knees. When those who are at home see her, they give vent to shouts of joy, saying, 'Hi-hi-hi! You are welcome, virgin girl!', to be followed by much noise and chatter.

On being questioned as to whom she has come to see, she names him. On being accepted by the head of the family, she is invited into a room which is set aside for her. She then occupies the room together with her companion maid. After a time, young boys and girls of the family come and keep her company. Food is brought but only the young girl companion eats. She who is about to become engaged does not touch it, and goes to sleep without having eaten. As soon as she rises in the morning, she goes to the river to bathe. If she has relatives there, they will bring her food there at the river. On returning to the home of her engagement, she enters in the same way as she did on her arrival in the evening – on the left-hand side [*ikhohlo*]. She goes and stands at the same spot where she stood the previous evening, and the womenfolk come forward and clothe her with a blanket (for indeed since yester day she has gone about uncovered, girded round the lower regions only by the leather skirt). When they provide her with the blanket, she veils herself and covers her head with it. After this, she returns to the room into which she was shown the previous evening. She is given food, but she only looks at it and does not touch it until she is given a goat. This goat is known as the '*indlakudla*' [to permit to eat], but it is not slaughtered until the arrival of the girls of her home, who are summoned to do the slaughtering, for indeed she is not permitted to eat the meat from the home of her people-in-law until after her marriage, when she is then a wife of the home.

The presentation of the blanket to cover the head imposes the observance of respect [*ukuhlonipha*] upon her. Thereafter she can no longer go about with her head uncovered, also she can no longer walk about in front of the houses like other people, but keeps at the back of them.

At dawn on the day after her arrival, the head of the family sends someone to report to her father with the message, 'seek hither now,[3] you of So-and-So' (mentioning his surname); and then he [the messenger] sits down and describes to her father a particular lobolo beast (black, red, or what sort).

On his acceptance of the beast, the father of the girl enumerates the cattle required by him in order to obtain his consent to the marriage. The messenger then goes home and reports these words to the father of the man to be married.

After a few days the girls [of the girl's family] come to partake of the goats, the *inklakudla* goat and others, in accordance with custom. After all these observances, the engaged girl is escorted back to her home, acccompanied by the bridegroom's people (males and females). When they arrive at the girl's home (with ample supplies of beer provided), as they stand outside they announce, 'Hail, friend, you of So-and-So (his surname), we come with certain cattle (they enumerate them as to their colours). We have come to request a desirable relative, and we wish you to give us your daughter in marriage'. They are provided with a room for their accommodation. A certain number of goats are slaughtered for them, including one for the engaged girl. Wo! The beer is so plentiful that no questions are asked about it; and the meat too is in abundance. And there is feasting to repletion.

Thereafter the bridegroom's people return home, with the answer of the girl's father. If he has consented,[4] preparations are then made for the wedding.

On the day of the arrival of the bride's party [on its return from the bridegroom's home], the marriage intermediary [*umhlaleli*, acting on behalf of the bridegroom's family] is sent to obtain the consent of the bride's father for her to marry. His consent means that the malt may now be soaked [to make the beer for the wedding feast]. When the day comes that the malt has sprouted, the intermediary goes and reports the fact. Thereupon the father [of the bride] calls for the spears of his sons and his own, for the purpose of severing his daughter from the home. By then his wives have come to shave the bride and trim her hair so that it may be built into a top-knot [*inkehli*] for which a fee [probably a goat] is required by the bride's father.

On a certain day the bridal procession [*udwendwe*] leaves the home, the father having first provided his daughter with a goat as food for the journey [*umncamo*] which is slaughtered and eaten by the bride on that particular day that she leaves.

So what do you know? The marriage intermediary[5] is again in attendance to lead out the procession, but on that day he is not treated with civility by anyone at the home, but as an evil person who is about to deprive them of their child, and they sometimes insult him and try to strike him. And so he heads out the procession. He is then handed his mat on which he sits until he is presented with a goat in the open space [*isigcawu*] in front of the homestead, a goat that will arrive with the bridal party [*umthimba*] on the wedding day. The bridal party does not leave when the moon is finished ['dead'], it leaves a few days after the new moon. The bridal party is provided with the meat of a beast known as the beast of the '*izibhoma*' [gifts of meat], which is to be distributed among the homesteads in the neighbourhood of the bridegroom's homestead, for indeed the bridal party is obstructed at all the homesteads it passes on its way. The bridal party arrives singing its chant [*ihubo*] the evening before bed-time. Well then! Everybody of the bridegroom's home stays awake that night together with all the families in the neighbourhood. When the bridal party arrives, it is stopped at the gate and then it distributes the *izibhoma* gifts of meat, as well as other requirements.

The bridal party now enters the homestead, to be greeted with a great din of welcome and jubilation. It is then ushered in to a room and presented with a goat known as the '*isiwukulu*', and another known as the '*umnyango*' [entrance or admission]. Then there is feasting on beer and meat, and there is no sleep until daylight because the girls are singing and demanding from the bridegroom the goat for the bridesmaids' refreshments [*amangebeza*].

Chapter 16
TODAY IS THE DAY OF DANCING

The next day the bridal party leaves the homestead at dawn and settles by a clump of bushes [*esihlahleni*].[1] There it eats and drinks and practises the wedding songs that will be danced[2] by the girls and the males. Later someone is sent to call them from the clump of bushes and they come up to the homestead. The girls dance, beginning with the grand wedding dance [*inkondlo*] after which the bride makes her appearance. As she begins to dance, her father stands up and salutes and addresses his father and grandfather [his forefathers in the male line] on behalf of his child, praising them and requesting them to bless his child with a fortunate situation. He also refers to the lobolo cattle which are still due, and to the fact that the son-in-law should bear them in mind and hand them over to him some time. At this stage the bridegroom's people get up and withdraw from the arena, going to dress and adorn themselves at home.[3] The bridegroom's party [*ikhetho*] then appears, advancing in a hush of silence, executing its movements, carrying its shields, and dressed to perfection. When they arrive at the arena where the bridal girls have been dancing, they also perform their wedding dance and everything is nice, gay and merry.[4]

MARRIAGE

The father of the bridegroom also makes a formal salutation. He stands up and salutes and thanks his counterpart [*umlingane*, here the father of the bride] for the good he has done in consenting to give him his child. He also praises his father and grandfather, and gives thanks for the presents brought to him by his daughter-in-law, and the beast known as the '*umbeka*' [to install the bride, and which is slaughtered at the wedding]. After this the celebrations terminate. The bride [*umlobokazi*] – up to now only the term *umakoti* has been used, but hereafter both words are used] now invites all those deserving to be presented with the gifts she has brought with her[5] – blankets, sleeping mats, eating mats, and brooms; and a blanket each for her husband's father and mother, and gifts for all other deserving cases such as the daughters and the husband's brothers, in accordance with the custom of the place. Then follows a general dispersal.

The following day the bridesmaids slaughter the *umbhubuzo* beast [*bhubuza* means to steal or capture] in honour of the bride.[6] They do the selecting themselves, and if one is in poor condition they leave it and choose one that is good and fat. It is then killed, but if the person who stabs it [who is always a man of the husband's family] does so without killing it outright, it is a serious fault, and the spear with which he stabbed becomes the bride's, to be redeemed with a forfeit, and it continues so, the spear having to be redeemed whether it is one, two, three, or ten times. The beast is slaughtered as the bridesmaids chant, 'May it rise! Yes, may it rise!', wishing on their part that it would not die until it has been stabbed several times, so that the bridegroom should pay out further forfeits on account of the stabbed beast not dying.

After dropping to the ground, the beast lies there for some time before being skinned. Only after the bridesmaids have entered the cattle kraal do the skinners enter to skin it. The skinner should take great care not to puncture the stomach and release the chyme, for if he does so, it will be regarded as a most serious fault by the bridesmaids, requiring a penalty or sometimes even the replacement of the slaughtered beast by another. It is correct for the bride to come out of her room and do the puncturing herself after the beast has been skinned. Thereafter the skinners dismember it and send the joints to her room. At this stage the bride and bridesmaids are formed up and dancing in the cattle kraal. The knife she uses for puncturing the paunch is not hers but her husband's. This is the day for the distribution of gifts.[7] It is then that the bridesmaids take a leg to the cattle kraal where the people are gathered, and roast it. This leg is known as '*umbhubuzo*'. After this the bride is sprinkled with the gall, and as she is sprinkled, the bridesmaids scramble for pieces of meat and strike the men who are eating meat in the cattle kraal.

The bride requests the married women of the family to examine her to ascertain whether she is still a virgin unspoilt by a man. There is the song requesting the women to examine her: 'I invite you, married women of my husband's home. Hoya! Ewu-yeye! Hoya!' And indeed the women examine her, and it is good if they find her to be still complete in virginity. This is the day for the consummation of the marriage.[8] But she does not consent to her husband without resisting strongly, until he overpowers her by force and with all his strength; for if the husband fails to overcome the bride, she being stronger than her husband, the matter will be deferred to some other time. If the bride is overcome, everybody at home knows it when she laments and sings this song: 'I have lost my virginity![9] Don't you see that I have lost my virginity? O mayi-hoya!' Then all the girls of her home who have remained behind for this event after the others have gone home, begin to sing.

On the previous day she was sprinkled with the gall of the *umbhubuzo* beast to testify that she was now a fully fledged wife of that household, for it would not be possible for a mere girl to be sprinkled with the gall without having married into that household, and it would be a serious offence punishable by the fine of a large goat or even a beast.

After these observances[10] the bride is now a married woman of that household like all the rest.[11] She will rise early in the morning to go and draw water at the river for the several houses of the homestead, and she also grinds food for them. She will rise very early when it is still dark and sweep the spaces between the houses,[12] and do everything that ought to be done by a married woman in her own house. Even if there is a spare room [*ilawu*] in which she sleeps with her husband, when she gets up in the morning she does not return to it to live, but to the house of her husband's mother where she cooks and eats, until after the lapse of a year. She does not enter the cattle kraal, but sends a child to get cow dung for her if she wants to smear the floor of a room. She does not go to the side of the room where her father-in-law sleeps, even if there is something she wants, but sends a child to get it for her; and to smear the place where her father-in-law sleeps, she sends a young girl to do it for her.

If her husband's father is deceased or even his mother, she must not on any account approach their graves. This restriction will remain until she grows into an old woman who no longer has her periods, and only then will she be permitted to enter the cattle kraal, for the homestead will have become hers by that time [figuratively].

On no account is a young wife allowed to use the names of her father-in-law or mother-in-law, whether they are still alive or no longer living. The strongest oath that can be taken by a married woman is '*omamezala*' [parents-in-law], and no married woman, however bad, would tell a lie under such an oath; she would rather use some other oath. A married woman who swears by her parents-in-law when making false statements is regarded by everybody as evil, as a worthless person, and as less than a dog. And if it happens that a married woman, whether young or old, swears by the name of her parents-in-law, either the father or the mother, because of intoxication or thoughtless blundering, one would go to her home [the home of her parents] and claim a full-grown beast. And the father and the mother of the husband do not address the bride by her own name.[13]

When the bride is well and truly married, the boys of the home go out to hunt a buck to provide the skin breast-covering [*isicwayo*][14] for the new wife. A duiker should be sought, but killed with care so that its skin should not be disfigured by cuts and scars. The skin should be carefully pegged out, softened and tanned, and made into a breast covering for the new wife, with brass bead decorations along its edges and on the hind and forelegs of the skin.

The birth of her first child is reported to her people at home, for indeed this child is regarded as theirs, as it testifies that its mother arrived [at her husband's home] without defect, good and pure. This news brings great joy to her parents. After this it is no longer their responsibility whether their daughter has good or bad births, for indeed if the first birth is a failure and the child dies, it will be their responsibility to procure doctors to treat her by purging so that she may bear children normally like other women.

Chapter 17
RECTAL BLOODLETTING OF A CHILD

A woman having given birth to a child is required to remain in her room for a number of days, until the navel cord drops off. If a female child, the mother stays without coming out of her room for six days, and if a boy, for seven. After that she burns the birth litter. The burning of the litter refers to the woman taking the litter that was spread on the floor for her delivery, and disposing of it; it does not mean that it has to be burnt with fire. But she does leave her room by herself, without the child, to relieve herself or to visit the other houses, and this lasts for these few days. Only after the child becomes strong and she sees people continually coming into her room to see it, she daubs its face with wood ashes, and then she can take it out and visit the other houses with it.

After the lapse of three months since she gave birth, she shaves her head, and then, when the child has grown a little, whether it is a boy or a girl, a skilled person is sought to operate and bring about a good flow of blood from the rectum [*gweba*], a stalk of the *umlahle* shrub [*bridelia micrantha*] being used for the purpose. The operation on a male child differs from that on a girl, and he is operated upon again when he grows up.[1]

All the old people declare that a child who is not treated in this way can only grow up to be a useless person, and a person over-heated by blood, being inclined to go astray and get into trouble and become thoroughly immoral sexually [*ndinda*], because of the large quantity of blood that was never drawn off. For this reason, the custom of rectal bloodletting was rigidly applied to children to prevent them from becoming lecherous.

The father is not allowed to handle his child until the mother has shaved her head, so it is necessary for three months to pass before he can handle and play with it.

It was a matter of great fortune for a wife to give birth to a child just as her husband was leaving for war. He would enter the room of confinement fully dressed and armed for war, with all his weapons. On doing so he would address the child by name, some actually taking it in their arms, but others merely gazing at it, and then depart; for it is against our custom for a man to enter the room of a woman who has recently given birth [*umdlezane*] before the child's navel cord has dropped off. For this reason it is said to be protective treatment [*intelezi*] of great effect for a man to go to war straight from a room of confinement, for he would have magical protection [*amasithesithe*] from his enemies; it is therefore highly valued by our people.

Chapter 18
THE DEPARTURE OF THE ARMY

When the army leaves for war, all the men gather together to be sprinkled with protective medicine [*intelezi*] by the medicine man. After having been sprinkled, they may no longer sleep in their wives' rooms, and anyone who does so will destroy the effect of the medicine man's treatment. Therefore he fully deserves death, for having weakened and disgraced the king's army.

The wives of the man who have left for war would wear sprigs of wild asparagus [*iphunganhlola*, 'that which drives away evil'] on their heads, and continue to do so day by day. They would also wear their skin clothes inside-out, the soft inside without and the hairy outside within, which has the effect of hastening their movements. And when washing at the river they would at first avoid the water and not let it immediately touch their bodies. And their method of sleeping was to lie on their backs and cat-nap, not as usual, so as to wake up quickly.

And their husbands would observe these same customs as were followed by their wives at home. I am not including those who have fought and killed, for they do not eat the inner meat; and the medicine men treat them assiduously lest they should develop a form of insanity [*iqungo*] or become completely insane [*uhlanya*]. And so they also wear the wild asparagus worn by their wives at home. Only those who have killed an enemy [*izingwazi* or *izinxweleha*] avoid the inner meat, eating the outer meat only.

Their sleeping mats and pillows at home are folded and bound, and carefully placed in an upright position and not laid out on the floor. There is no noise or quarrelling in the home, all conversations being conducted in an atmosphere of friendliness and good humour. Even if the wives are not friendly disposed towards one another, they will leave their differences during these days, and resume them only after the return of the army.

Those who remain at the battle [on the battlefield, i.e. the casualties] are not reported, silence being maintained until the army returns home, and then only is it announced that 'so-and-so and so-and-so have remained at the battle'; and when this is heard, a great wailing is raised in the homes. All those who have killed [an enemy in battle] are now medicinally strengthened, and medicine men are sought to treat them, who will be paid for their services by the king.

PART III: ZULU HISTORY[1]

Chapter 19[2]
THE NTUNGWA TRIBES

I have already stated that 'those who went towards the west are known as the Ntungwa', referring to the Sotho tribes who are just as numerous as the Nguni.[3] But the Ntungwa have an intelligence superior to the Nguni, for they are a friendly and mutually compatible people among whom it is not normal to find trouble and disturbance as among the Nguni. They also differ in dress from the Nguni, who go about naked and do not care even if their children see their private parts [*amanya*, personal affairs].

The Ntungwa comprise many tribes, each with its chief, just like the Nguni. But their chiefs are not in the least like the Nguni chiefs, for they are a united and friendly people, unlike the Nguni.

Africa is a large country and so expansive that we down here imagine that we are in an ocean; and yet the nations towards the north and west have a country very much larger than ours.

Although I still want to explore the position of all the Ntungwa tribes, it is better for me to leave the description of the few [Sotho] tribes that I know and proceed to describe the history of the Nguni as I know it; and when I have dealt extensively with these matters that I know, I will go on to deal with the Ntungwa.[4]

Chapter 20
A KINGDOM FORETOLD

I have already stated that Malandela begot Ntombela, Ntombela Zulu, Zulu Nkosinkulu, Nkosinkulu Mageba, Mageba Phunga, Phunga Ndaba.[1] When Ndaba was still a boy who herded cattle along with the other boys of his age, he made a prediction through the song that he composed for himself and his age group [*intanga*] as follows:

Ndaba is a king! Oye! Ha! Oye!

But the song has since been changed and is chanted as follows:

Ha! Oye! Ji ji ji!

All the words used in singing it have been dropped.[2] It was composed by Ndaba while still a herd-boy, foretelling that there would come forth from his descendants one who would rule many clans. And he, Ndaba, begot Jama, Jama begot Senzangakhona, Senzangakhona begot Shaka, Dingane, Mpande, and other numerous sons.

[Extract from Fuze's Epilogue]
At that time the Zulu salute was not '*Ndabezithi*', it was '*Lufenulwenja*' [dog's penis], so that the remark was usually addressed to them: 'you of the unpleasant salute that is not used by the relatives-in-law'. This salute, '*Ndabezitha*', originated with Ndaba kaPhunga kaMageba kaNkosinkulu kaZulu kaNtombela kaMalandela kaMnguni, their origin [*isiqu*][3] [End of Extract].

The advent of Shaka was as follows. His father, Senzangakhona, used to herd cattle along with the other boys of his age, and it was the custom in those times for all boys of the same age-group [*intanga*] to come together to be circumcised in the several localities to which they belonged. And there was a place where Senzangakhona used to stay with the boys of his locality [*isigodi*], to which food was sent from their homes; and there was a clump of bushes where they used to stay and where they ate their meals.

One day there passed by a man of the Langeni clan of Makedama kaMgabi, searching for food [*thekela*, to visit neighbours for food in time of scarcity]. The Prince [Senzangakhona] and his small group of boys were eating at the time. The man was hungry, and when the Prince saw that he was hungry, he called him, and when he came forward, he saluted the Prince. He [Senzangakhona] then asked him where he came from and where was his home, and the man told him that he was one of Mbhengi of Nguga,[4] whereupon he gave instructions for him to be given food, and so he was given food, and he ate until he was satisfied. At this clump of bushes there was no lack of food, which came from the homes, and there was much meat because now and then a fine young beast would be slaughtered for consumption.

Chapter 21
SHAKA'S BIRTH AND CHILDHOOD

When he had finished his meal, the man took the path and went home. On arrival there he soon made the matter known to the girls and to everybody, telling them that he had met the Prince [*umNtwana*, royal child] of the Zulu chief by whom he was saved from starvation and who had given him food which he consumed until he was satisfied; and that he was a very fine person and indeed a son of a chief.

When the girls heard all this, they became enamoured of that Prince, kind and generous, who had helped one of their own people when about to die of starvation. And then their princess [*inkosazana*, chief's daughter], Nandi, said to that man, 'What about our going with you, for you to show us that Prince of the Zulu people who is so good?' The man agreed. And those girls of Nguga then went with that man and eventually arrived at that clump of bushes. And then the man went and sat down near the bushes where the Prince and his boy companions were sitting. They saw the girls, and they [the girls] were summoned. On arrival they were requested to stand over there. Then they were asked where they came from and whither they were going. Their princess, Nandi, replied and said she had come to see the son of the chief. She was then questioned as to why she wished to see him. She said she had come to see him because she loved him, and she wanted him to make love [*soma*] to her. All the girls were then invited to come forward, which they did, and stood in a line. And then the Prince saw Nandi, the princess of Mbhengi of Nguga. And indeed they came together right there, as desired by the princess. And what do you know? It was right there that the princess got pregnant.[1,2]

For a time it was concealed that the princess was pregnant, but eventually it became apparent to many that the princess was unwell.[3] When others enquired what was wrong with her, it was said she had '*ishati*', a bad body disease.[4] Messages were sent to those in high places in the Zulu clan. And then it was that Mudli, the son of Jama, began asking his brother, Senzangakhona, whether he knew anything of this matter [in which it was alleged] that Nandi, the princess and daughter of Mbhengi of Nguga was pregnant by him? It seems that Senzangakhona at first tried to deny it, for shame and for fear of his brother,[5] but finally admitted it.

And so it came about that the days passed until eventually Nandi gave birth to a son, Shaka,[6] at her home in the Langeni clan. The child stayed in the home of its mother, where it was well treated and nourished until it grew up.[7]

When the child had grown up to the age when he was able to herd cattle with the son of the Langeni chief, he [Shaka] was in the habit of tormenting him when they were playing with toy cattle made out of stones which the boys had picked up for making cattle, some making bulls, others oxen, and others cows and calves. Whenever they came to play with their stone bulls, the son of the princess [Shaka] was in the habit of annoying the son of the chief by breaking up his bull, for they used to make them fight by holding them in their hands. This went on for some time, until eventually the son of Mbhengi of Nguga got upset and reported this nasty trick which was being played by the son of the princess. And so it became a matter of concern to all the Nguga people, to see the son of the princess upsetting the son of the chief, and tormenting him.[8]

When the mother of Nandi heard this, she also became worried, hearing all the people in the home speaking critically of her daughter's child, saying that he had bad habits, and she realised that they would eventually kill him. And so she left, taking her daughter's child and departing with him for her former home where she was born, in the Mthethwa country under Dingiswayo, and placed him there in the care of the old woman who was her mother.[9]

And it was there that Shaka lived and grew up to become a young man, a warrior under Dingiswayo for whom he used to fight valorously. His heroism resounded throughout the country, and the fame of his heroism reached the ears of his father in the Zulu country. And so his father came, wanting to see his son who was a hero.

Chapter 22

SENZANGAKHONA'S VISIT TO THE MTHETHWA

Chief Senzangakhona kaJama visited the Mthethwa, paying a visit to Chief Dingiswayo kaJobe. It would appear that there was in his heart a desire to see his son whom he had never seen since his birth. He took his servants and royal girls [*umndlunkulu*] saying that he was going to court

SENZANGAKHONA'S VISIT

for a wife there, but really he was going to see his son, a matter which was not publicised.

When he arrived there, it was indeed good for Mbhengi of Nguga [Nandi's family][1] that there should come Senzangakhona, the father of Shaka, his great warrior,[2] especially as he [Senzangakhona] had visited him [Dingiswayo] in order to see him [Shaka].

Senzangakhona spent several days with the Mthethwa, and there was much rejoicing because of the visit of the Zulu chief. But the main business which was done there among the Mthethwa during those days, was to find doctors to medicinally influence [*thonya*, which is not to bewitch] the father, that he might be overshadowed by the son [overcome by Shaka's shadow or influence or *isithunzi*], so that he [Shaka] should enter into the chieftainship. Whenever he went to bathe with the girls and the servants, doctoring was done at the homestead. After a while he began to feel pain in his body. One day on his return from the stream, Shaka asked him for the gift of a spear,[3] but in doing so he already knew that the spear was Nomkwayimba's, the son of Senzangakhona. While Senzangakhona was still there, he felt that his body was no longer healthy. Another day when he returned from bathing in the stream, Shaka entered his room and asked for that spear which he had already heard was Nomkwayimba's; and he said to his father, 'Give me that spear, father'. 'It is not mine, my child', replied his father, 'it belongs to your brother Nomkwayimba'. Shaka then came out of the room and went into the cattle kraal from where he had come, and where he had been eating boiled ground-nuts together with the other young men. The chief did not stay very long because of feeling unwell. And so he took his leave and returned to his home in the Zulu country. And the sickness afflicted him until he reached home.

And it was about to happen that the son also followed behind him, leaving the Mthethwa and returning to the Zulu country.[4] And as soon as Shaka left for the Zulu country, Dingiswayo also left home on a visit to Zwide, the chief of the Ndwandwe, accompanied by a small body of servants as was customary. He also went on the pretext of courting, as Senzangakhona had done when visiting the Mthethwa. It was on this occasion that Zwide put him to death (1818). And from there began the series of evil events that brought about the many wars that have never ceased.[5]

Chapter 23

THE ARMING OF SHAKA

(AGAINST ZWIDE)

Shortly after Shaka's arrival at home, an alarming report was received to the effect that his 'father' Dingiswayo was no longer alive, having been killed by Zwide (1818). And it was shortly after his arrival at home that he killed his brother, Nomkwayimba.[1] At the time the chief was sick, and as soon as he heard that 'your son Shaka has arrived and killed his brother Nomkwayimba', he was so shocked at that report that he died immediately (1818).[2]

Shaka, being angered by the murder of his 'father' Dingiswayo, marshalled the Zulu and the Mthethwa and the Hlubi people to arms. It came to resemble the funeral hunt or ceremonial war [*ihlambo*, the washing of spears] for his father, Senzangakhona. The army sallied forth and made for the Ndwandwe country. But Zwide was very strong, and more fearsome than the other chiefs; therefore Shaka, whilst making an advance movement, wanted to draw the Ndwandwe army downwards [southwards, for the Ndwandwe lived to the north], and as he was doing all these movements, he was devising a plan to draw Zwide into the Zulu country. And what did he intend by this? Shaka knew very well that the Ndwandwe army did not depend on cattle on the hoof for food when it fought, but on rations of millet [sorghum] which it carried with it, and his intention was to harrass it until it became short of food and suffered from hunger. It was for this reason that he first advanced and then retreated.

And so he brought onwards the Ndwande of Langa [Zwide's father], who had a very effective army. In doing so, he brought it down from near Nongoma, where the magistracy now stands, but beyond it from Magudu, all that territory being under Zwide kaLanga, the great chief of the Nxumalo clan.[3] It advanced towards Mahlabatini where the Zulu country was situated. As for Shaka, he wanted to draw it towards the Mhlathuze river, so that it should fight at Nkandla and Nsuze, where the country is extremely broken. He had proclaimed to all the homesteads in the Zulu country that the foodstuffs should be removed, and that the homesteads should be abandoned and destroyed by fire.

And so the son of Langa brought his army forward until the whole of the Mahlabatini area of the Zulu country was occupied. And when the son of Senzangakhona saw the enemy, he arranged his own forces in inaccessible places. When he was about to launch the attack, he ascended a small hill known as Khomo near Sibhudeni. He mounted the Khomo hill and from there launched it and observed it.

There the two armies attacked one another, and there was the smell of war, and the dust rose up high. Well! Seeing that the Ndwandwe were so strong, what was the outcome? The Zulus were so enraged that their anger could only be quenched with water (Zulu saying), and they were fighting a fight of death. For in fact, before the clash, Shaka had given the order that the bundles of spears were to be abandoned, and that each man was to carry a short stabbing spear together with only one spear for throwing as the army was about to engage. No one carried three or more spears as was formerly the custom.

Just as the people of Mthimkhulu, wherever they went, never gave up but went on always,[4] so then the Zulus on this occasion: they seemed to be attached to the enemy with the strength of a marriage bond. The army fought with great intensity until darkness fell, and it was dreadful. For several days it fought with terrible fury. The horror continued until Shaka realised that he had mauled Zwide's forces considerably, and that they were hungry through not being able to get food anywhere, their own supplies which they carried with them being quite exhausted; and he thereupon devised another plan, and despatched several companies to go to the capital occupied by Zwide himself; and when they saw that the capital was no longer far away, they were to chant the Ndwandwe national war song so that there should be no alarm, and then enter the capital and seize Zwide.

Here fought Nomdidwa kaSojiyisa (Maphitha),[5] a mighty warrior, and Mvundlana kaMenziwa of the Biyela clan, 'he whose flaming walls answer to my call'.[6] 'He who was deprived of his oxtail ornament, Dlungwana of the Mbelebele regiment [Shaka himself], but eventually received it from Macingwane of the Ngonyameni kraal [Chief of the Chunu clan]'. Oh! Here the Zulus fought a great fight to demonstrate that they were exterminating the Ndwandwe people.

Chapter 24

THE NDWANDWE DEFEAT

And so those companies that were sent to Zwide's capital did what they were sent to do. Indeed, as they approached the Ndwandwe capital they chanted the Ndwandwe national war song, to announce that they had destroyed the Zulus. And it was then that the women of the place came out with shouts of praise and victory. And so the enemy was able to approach to very close quarters. 'What! It's Zulu kaMdlamfe!' [Senzangakhona's Zulus]. To their horror they heard shouts of '*Ngadla!*' ['I have stabbed']. 'Alas for my father's cow!' [their response]. And before they realised what had happened, there were many who had already fallen. When Zwide heard this, he jumped up and broke through the far end of the enclosure and fled.

When the army had been fighting for a few days, Somveli, son of Dingiswayo, asked permission of his 'brother' Shaka to go and see his children at home. Shaka consented, and Somveli departed and stayed away for many days. Shaka began to complain about this, and was always muttering, 'Hai, my "brother". What sort of a "brother" is this?' And some came to hear that Shaka wanted to put him to death. (For indeed this war was being waged in retaliation for the murder of his father, Dingiswayo, by Zwide). And so Somveli fled from home, fleeing from the wild animal who was his 'brother' who was about to kill him. There remained of his brothers Mbiya, the father of Mlandela, and all those who were with the army. (Mlandela begot Sokwetshata, and it was he who married Bathonyile, the daughter of Monase, the mother of Mbulazi [Cetshwayo's brother, Mpande's son].)

Hau! And the Zulu army continued with its work of destruction.

And so the Ndwandwe nation came to be completely scattered. Many collected their belongings and made their way north. On the way Somaphunga kaZwide turned back and returned to the Zulu country. There he bore his son and heir, Mgojana, and his brothers, Mankulumana and Hlokolo and others.

But as for Shaka, he could not put down his shield but continued to attack other clans, wishing to subject them to his rule. It was thus that there arose Shaka's praise: 'Isidlukuladlwedlwe [long-armed robber who robs with violence] who destroys with his shield ever ready on his knees'.

His chief councillor was Ngomane kaMqomboli of the Mthethwa clan, the lesser one being Mdlaka kaNcidi of the Langa clan. His main attendent [*inceku*] was Mxamana kaNtendeka[1] of the Zibisi of Mahlase, and there were other officers and headmen, great and small. His footrest was Ngqengelele of the Buthelezi clan, who arrived from his place as a person with unpierced ears [*isicuthe*], and whose body was used to spit on whenever the king wished to expectorate, or to rest on when he lay down.[2]

And so Shaka ruled and became a king, as foretold by his grandfather, Ndaba, that it would be a Zulu kingship. He wished to fulfil this prophecy, and so attacked all those who opposed him, but those who submitted, he left and ruled through them.

All the Nxumalo clan left except for Sothondose kaMalusi who was one of them. Among those who left was Soshangana kaZigode kaManukuza kaNdwandwe, Zwide's kinsman through a common ancestor. Soshangana made his way north towards the country of the Mnyembane, now ruled by the Portuguese. And there was wild confusion amongst the people, who began to lift their ears and say, 'What sort of a king has now arisen?' And he conquered everywhere.

Chapter 25

THE NGWANE CAMPAIGN

It was not long before Shaka attacked the great chief of the Ngwane, Matiwane kaMasumpa, wishing to conquer him so that he should be under him. But Matiwane did not consent to be ruled by Shaka. And so was fought a great war, the Ngwane having been very powerful.

The war lasted a long time, until Shaka introduced a new method hitherto unknown, the use of a short spear for stabbing at close quarters, with only one spear for throwing at the enemy as it approached. And then Matiwane was defeated and became a wanderer in his flight. But in the end he returned to the Zulu country to seek the mercy of the king, saying, 'The clod is weary, you of Senzangakhona; accept me'. And the request was pleasing to the king, and he agreed. But after a time there appeared Zulu plotters who informed against him and said he was still seeking the chieftainship, and made false accusations against him. He was conducted to a large donga, and there the great chief of the Ngwane was put to death without having done the slightest harm, his only fault being that he had been received kindly by the king;[1] for which we Zulu people will forever live in shame until our dying day.

And that donga became famous, and whenever a person was condemned to death, he was taken there, and the expression came into use, 'Take him to the place of Matiwane [the place of execution]'. And even now that donga is still known, for Dingane cast many Boers into it.[2]

Mpambani, the chief of the Khambule and the Ncube,[3] who are known humourously as '*amaZilankatha*', when he saw that the wild animal Shaka was aroused, collected his people and made his way south, finally arriving at the Mpolweni, a tributary of the Mngeni. He then addressed his people, describing to them all the methods of warfare, and telling them they were weary of war and no longer wanted it. After thus speaking to his people, he dressed himself in full war dress, armed himself with his shield, and said, 'Let me show you how a battle is fought.' So saying, he threw himself into a large pool, after which many others committed the same extraordinary act. Then those who still had command of their senses prevented the others from following on and throwing themselves into the pool. The Khambule are numerous in Swaziland, and some have gone down to the Cape Colony, being scattered throughout the country.

Chapter 26
THE ATTACK ON MACINGWANE

It was a matter of common knowledge that Macingwane kaLubhoko of Ngonyameni [the place of the lion] was an evil monster who killed his own children, and put others to death without mercy. He also was sufficiently powerful to conquer other clans. But when Shaka appeared, he began to be hindered. He had been in the habit of fighting Senzangakhona and defeating him in the throwing of spears, and then with shouts of 'Hoiye' the fighting stopped. But when Shaka appeared, it was different and no longer resembled the playful fights of former days.

Macingwane was indeed powerful. It was he who destroyed Mpongo kaZingelwayo of the Ndlovu clan, and vanquished Lembede kaNdima of the [closely related] Bayeni family in a dispute. But after a while there appeared another bull, a young bull against which this old one could never contend. Macingwane quarrelled with Shaka, and they fought a great and fearful battle which ended in the complete defeat of Macingwane, and his dispersal.

By this time the white people had arrived at Thekwini [The Bay, later Durban], Messrs. Fynn (Mbuyazwe weTheku), Ogle (Wohlo), Popham (Febane kaMjoji),[1] and Cane (the father of Nanise), who had come by way of the sea. Mbuyazwe had already arrived in the Zulu country on a visit to the king. And in that campaign when Shaka was in pursuit of Macingwane, it was he [Fynn] who accompanied him

MACINGWANE

and travelled with the Zulus as far as Pondoland. There Shaka left him with a regiment, to serve as the caretaker of that country, as its government. And when he returned they composed these praises about him: 'Mbuyazwe weTheku [Fynn of the Bay],[2] the black-tailed finch which comes from Pondoland. But Shaka experienced a setback in Pondoland. He retreated back to the boundary of the Mpondo country, and established his rule there. He returned with his main army, leaving Mbuyazwe as the government of that country (1828). He [Fynn] once resided at the king's place for several months, paying homage to him. He was also present at the death of Nandi, the mother of Shaka, whilst still paying homage to him (1826).[3]

To these white people Shaka gave girls from his harem, who became their wives. They bore them many children, now comprising several clans, and those clans are still known by the surnames of their fathers. They are distinguishable by being white, but they are black in all other respects.

That ferocious creature, Macingwane, who used to kill so many people including his own children, also experienced the pangs of death, having fled as far as Ensikeni [a mountain in East Griqualand] at Mamangalahlwa ['Mother I was thrown away', i.e. the back of beyond], to avoid death at the hands of Shaka who was pursuing him. It seems that he had forgotten that he had long been exterminating others, including his own children.

Macingwane kaLubhoko was terribly cruel. He murdered Ndabezimbi and Mqayana, his sons, along with many others, killing them because he saw that they would become men and contend with him. And the one who married Masijula the mother of Zimema, would also have been put to death if Macingwane had been still in power, and not wandering over mountains as a fugitive from Shaka.[4]

Shaka had many regiments: the Wombe (his own age group), the Siklebe, the Mbelebele, and many others that I am unable to enumerate.

Here is his war song which was sung when cowards were about to be put to death:

Ho! Ho! Pick out the cowards!

And all cowards were cruelly put to death when this song was chanted. The man was seized, his arm lifted, and then stabbed under the armpit like a goat, as he was told, 'Just feel the spear which you tried to avoid'.

All the people would be astir when they heard that the great warrior [*ingqwele*, leader and champion] had arrived today, and they would applaud and praise him saying:

> The blade that vanquishes other blades with its sharpness.
> He who roars like thunder as he sits, the son of Menzi.
> The rock piles of the Nkandla range,
> Protecting elephants in stormy weather.
> Mbelebele's fulminating voice,
> Causing disquiet in every home,
> Until every home is turned upside down.
> Shaka, a fearful name I dare not utter.
> The long-armed robber who robs with violence,
> Who destroys always in a furious rage,
> With his ever-ready shield on his knees.

Yes indeed, but I cannot quote them all [his praises] lest I fill this book with them.

He spoke as he pranced [*giya*] and chanted [*chwaya*] and said, 'Zulus, they must go forth and die in their tracks, for it is a convulsion of the sky and the earth. O! O!'

And it was heard that the destroyer of men was speaking.

Chapter 27

THE DISPERSAL OF THE QWABE

I have heard of no serious quarrel, only a scattering consequent upon Shaka's acts of destruction. But what is known is that Senzangakhona was merely a yearling bull to the Qwabe, and he was subject to the Qwabe. It was this that give rise to the statement made by the Qwabe chief, Phakathwayo, with regard to Shaka, saying of him, 'Eya! What is this stumpy little stick, which, whilst partaking of maas with a platter in the one hand and a mash of mealies in the other, is approached by a dog and butted by its head?'[1] This was said by Phakathwayo because he despised Shaka, and as an insult to him. But we well know that as long as fighting was done by throwing spears at one another, the Zulus were subject to the Qwabe in importance, they were not equal.

QWABE DISPERSAL

It is said that on the occasion when the son of Senzangakhona was marshalling his army to attack Phakathwayo, he gave the order, 'Do not kill him, but seize him and bring him to me'. But because of the great powers of kingship which were in Phakathwayo, he was so shocked on finding that the Zulus had closed in upon him that he died before they had even touched him.

The whole country was in a state of restlessness for fear of Shaka. It was at that time that Nqetho, Phakathwayo's brother, fled and made his way westwards, putting up piles of stones for luck as he went, which are never passed without a stone being picked up and added to the heap, as is the custom even now. Many people do not know who started these heaps, and so I now inform them that they were started by Nqetho, the Qwabe chief, when fleeing from Shaka.[2] He who passes a cairn of stones [*isivivane*] is required to pick up a single stone and throw it over his shoulder backwards on to the heap[3] before proceeding on his way. By so doing he is asking for good luck.

At that time the country was greatly disturbed by refugees, but some remained behind with their heads bowed low, finding it hard to abandon their homes. They who lacked courage fled. And there was one Sonyangwe kaKhalimeshe of the Zulu clan,[4] who collected his people and fled during the night into the large forest of Ngoye. There he remained in hiding with his people. It was laid down that no fire was to be lit in any circumstances, and if a beast was slaughtered it was to be eaten raw without being boiled or roasted, for if a fire were to be lit, they might be detected by the Zulus and killed. In consequence they came to travel mostly by night and concealed themselves by day. Eventually they crossed the Tugela and all the other rivers, finally settling at Khwela (Otto's Bluff) where they remained for a few years. The Mngeni river was known to them as the 'Msonganyathi' [the surrounder of the buffalo]. Eventually they moved on to the Mzimkhulu river where they are to be found today. They are known as the Bhaca because they hid themselves [*bhaca*] from their own people, the Zulus. Even today raw meat, unboiled and unroasted, is a great delicacy among the Bhaca; they rate it superior to either boiled or roasted. If you did not let a Bhaca eat his meat raw, but presented him with cooked meat only, you would be stinting him.

Not a single person was able to live in peace during those days of disruption by Nodumehlezi ['He who thunders as he sits']. His praises with which they praised him when he danced a solo spectacle [*giya*], the great warrior and son of Senzangakhona, were foreseen by his great-grandfather, Ndaba, that he would give rise to one who would be a king over all the others.

Here is Shaka's war song:

> He conquered every country,
> Where can he conquer now? He!
> He! Eya Eee!
> He vanquished chiefs,
> He vanquished nations,
> Where can he conquer now?

Chapter 28
THE FLIGHT OF MZILIKAZI

Everyone knows that Mzilikazi kaMashobana was very powerful, but when attacked by Shaka, all that came to an end and he was overcome by 'the bird that consumes all other birds'. But he made an attempt to fight. Even in flight Shaka pressed him with the army for a great distance.

It happened that while Shaka was in the midst of his assembly addressing them, the long crane feather fell from his head-dress to stand quivering on the ground,[1] whereupon he shouted [his father's praises]:

> Now I have him, assembly of Mjokwane kaNdaba,[2]
> He who defies orders, He who ignores advice.
> A conqueror speaking with tears of rage,
> Like Phiko of Bulawini.
> The buffalo overlooking the fordable drifts,
> Like the hunter at the place of Mamfekane.
> Mjokwane's beautiful eating mats,
> Which were used by comely maidens.
> Consumer of a wife, the mother of Sukuzwayo,
> Consumer of Sukuzwayo and his son.
> He consumed Mabebeta of Nokokela,
> He consumed Msikazi of Mdimoshe,
> And what did he intend to do at Masamlilo's
> Where crowds of people were drinking?

> He who ate two sticks of sugar-cane at Sondombana's,
> And only one intestinal beetle emerged.
> Ravenous consumer of Maqanda and Nsele,
> Who ravenously consumed the groundnuts of Mudli,
> even the husks.
> He who did not go in accordance with the councillors,
> He was like Vimba of Mangwekazi.

When Shaka praised his father in this way, his whole army thrilled and trembled, and the people were roused to anger, as if they saw the enemy right there, for them to fight and die fighting. After shouting these praises, he would repeat the great national song of his grandfather, Ndaba: 'Ndaba is a king! O!', whereupon the people would boil with rage, fit to die with anger.

On other occasions they would suddenly find a green snake [*inyandezulu*] in their midst.[3] Then the whole army would beat its shields and shout the salute, '*Bayete*', for whenever the Zulus have occasion to shout that salute, they arm themselves even in the heat of the day, even now.

The Zulu army pursued Mzilikazi as far as Mashonaland, turning back after a great distance. It was there that Mzilikazi was able to save and fortify himself. The Zulus turned back in 1826.[4]

Chapter 29
THE DESTRUCTION OF NOMAGAGA

Nomagaga kaNsele was the chief of the Khuze clan, who begot Mmiso who begot Khukhulela, the father of Msikofili,[1] who occupied the country to the west of the Mzinyathi [Buffalo river], where the village of Pomeroy is now built, near the hills which are thereabouts. While the Khuze were innocently living there, they were suddenly overwhelmed by a host of an army early one morning. The army had intended to fall upon them at dawn, but they got lost on the way, for they did not know the way and got lost, until they were helped by a cock that crowed towards dawn, indicating that the chief homestead of the Khuze was situated near there. You will have heard these praises of Shaka: 'He who approached Nomagaga during darkness, opposed by a rooster'. This means that the rooster roused the people who were about to be killed unawares, being still asleep.

The army came upon them in the early morning in an unexpected onslaught, but the Khuze fought in spite of it. Many people were killed, and it was here that Khukhulela was wounded as a child.

Cattle were bred here in such large numbers that one could steal to one's heart's content. It happens that if you breed too many cattle, you are slandered even by one of your own relatives, so that you should be killed and he who remains inherit your estate, for you are one of his relatives.[2] This was the original reason why all the people killed off their fowls, because of the fact that they attracted the army. The people used to breed fowls in large numbers, calling them *inswempe* [partridge] and *inkwalindanyana* [pheasant]. The name '*inkuku*' for a fowl originated from its habit of saying '*kuku kuku*' when calling its chicks, and so the people called it '*inkuku*' because that is what it says.

But I have no idea where our people found the fowl.[3] Again, those fowls which were bred by the people were not the same as these we see today. They were very much smaller, being bred to be slaughtered for the treatment of children suffering from colds and fevers [*umkhuhlane*]. A child suffering from *umkhuhlane* was given its broth to sip, with good effects. I now see that the white people who come to this country do the same as was done by our people in olden days.

Well, sirs, I have nothing new to say, for everything is the same and everybody is the same. In the olden days our people supported their cooking pots with three stones, and here now are the white people with their pots with three legs. That which is three is perfect in its strength, just like 'The Father and the Son and the Holy Ghost'. The first post is firmly embedded, but the second adds strength to the first; and the third so strengthens the other two that they become firmness itself. And it is the same with court testimony. If the first witness speaks the truth, which is then supported by a second, and then by a third, the evidence is firmly substantiated.

Chapter 30

THE STRENGTHENING OF ZULU POWER

And such were Shaka's upheavals in South Africa. He arrived unexpectedly, and he arrived when Zulu power was not great in Zululand, being less than many other powers which were greater than it. He came and raised up the power of his people so that it became stronger than all the others that had been strong, and they who had been above his father and grandfather he humbled and lowered. It was a most astonishing feat. And yet it was the great announcement foretold by his great-grandfather, Ndaba, that he alone would be a great king, for from his progeny would unexpectedly appear the one who would rule the whole of South Africa.

Only one power did Shaka not disturb, and that was that of the Embo, because he regarded Zihlandlo [its chief] as his younger brother [*umnawakhe*] It was only he whom he allowed to build a royal enclosure [*isigodlo*] and to rule as he wished, because he was as his younger brother. For this reason many members of other clans were to be found among the Embo.

Zihlandlo and Sambela, his brother, were very great friends, Zihlandlo having the greatest respect for him and regarding him as a chief greater than himself, notwithstanding that Sambela was his next younger brother by the same mother and father, Gcwabe kaKhabazela kaMavovo, children of a Swazi dignitary. Their friendship bound them firmly above and below, only their heads being apart.

If a person thinks and looks at the unexpected activities of Shaka, he cannot conclude that he was merely the progeny of Senzangakhona and Nandi; he can see clearly that he was a special product appearing from above, who arrived here expressly for the purpose of bringing unity to the country instead of disunity, and rule by one person instead of everyone doing as he pleased. These words which I speak are supported by the fact that Nandi never became the chief wife [*inkosikazi*] of Senzangakhona, and that when she became pregnant and gave birth, she did not live with him as a wife with her child, and so the child belonged to its maternal grandmother. And its father did not live with it, so that it became a child of fathers who had not begotten it. And when the father began to long to see his child, it was to begin to bring death upon himself when he was not yet due to die.

Just consider Nandi's longing, longing to meet Senzangakhona without even having seen him. Consider also their meeting and the fact that as soon as they came together Nandi became pregnant with Shaka! They never came together again, only once there in the clump of bushes. I trust that even a child cutting its first teeth would realise that this was a deed designed for the rapid advent of the owner of this country of South Africa.

In my opinion Zwide did not act of his own volition when he put Dingiswayo to death. I maintain that Zwide, who was a very powerful chief, was motivated by the intuition as to what would happen, and so killed Dingiswayo without the slightest guilt, because his removal would enable all these things to be brought about. In relying on his own great power, he brought about his own downfall, not knowing that all human power comes from One only, God indeed.

Chapter 31
THE MARRIAGE AND DEATH OF NANDI

Nandi, the princess of Mbhengi of Nguga, the great chief of the Langeni clan, on seeing that her child was growing up whilst she was still living at home as an unmarried woman [as a girl], left and went to marry Gendeyana, a man of importance in the Qwabe clan, where she gave birth to a daughter, Nomcoba, and a son, Ngwadi, at the Wambaza homestead.[1]

She did not consider going to marry Senzangakhona by whom she had a son.[2] She remained with Gendeyana after she was married to him, until Shaka became the Zulu chief, when she returned to her son with the daughter, Nomcoba; but the son, Ngwadi, remained behind and lived at the home of Wambaza and became the head [*umnumzane*] who controlled it, even though his father was no longer alive.[3]

Shaka had no wives as his father had done. He had only a harem of girls [*umndlunkulu*] not wanting to produce progeny lest his sons disputed with him and killed him before he could complete his chieftainship. He did that which was done by the chief of the Mthethwa when he put Tana to death and Godongwana (later to become Dingiswayo) [who escaped]; and that which was also done by the Chunu chief, Macingwane, who killed Mqayana and Ndabezimbi, and the others saved themselves, I think, by refusing to eat [poisoned food]. But what we have heard as a firm report is that although Shaka did not beget, nevertheless there was a girl of the Cele clan who gave birth to a son.[4] But that child was kept in constant concealment so that it should not be seen by the king, for he would have killed it. For a time Nandi was able to conceal the child, but eventually it was discovered; but Nandi arranged for it and its mother, the Cele girl, to escape. When Shaka became enraged because his mother had hidden the child from him, he stabbed his mother, but she did not hasten to die. After the son had stabbed his mother, he then suffered great sorrow, seeing the evil that he had done, and grieved greatly. The incident was hushed up, that the king had stabbed his mother on finding her playing with the child born to the Cele girl, a member of the harem.

But Mbuyazwe weTheku (Mr Fynn) denies most emphatically that this happened, and asserts that she was ill with dysentery. We do not know which is the truth, but a person could doubt, perhaps, and ask the question, 'But is it likely that the Zulus would have revealed to him, a white man, the secret of what actually happened?' In my view I see that he did indeed stab her.[5]

[THE ORIGIN OF THE DISPUTE BETWEEN MBULAZI AND CETSHWAYO]

One of the harem girls was suspected by the king of being pregnant, and she was given to his brother, Mpande, with the request that he propagate for him as he was in a position to do so. And so it came about that Monase, Mpande's chief wife and the mother of Mbulazi, Mantantashiya, Mkhungo, and Bathonyile [a girl], was from Shaka's harem. For some special reason which is unknown, the king allotted her [Monase] to his brother to bear children on his behalf. It was this that led to the dispute between Mbulazi and Cetshwayo.

When Mpande became engaged to Ngqumbazi kaMbhonde of the Zungu clan [the mother of Cetshwayo], Shaka sent a message to Tshana [the father of Mbhonde and the grandfather of Ngqumbazi] to request on behalf of his younger brother Mpande, that he may marry this girl. And on his consent, Shaka paid the lobolo cattle on behalf of his brother Mpande.[6] And so now you know the way in which the Nxumalo princess Monase was married, and that she had been Shaka's concubine, and that he finally allotted her to his younger brother Mpande, to whom she bore Mbulazi, Mantantashiya, Mkhungo, and Bathonyile [a daughter].

When these children grew up, Cetshwayo, son of Mbhonde's daughter [Ngqumbazi], and Mbulazi, son of Mntungwa's daughter [Monase], their father [Mpande] began to talk freely, disregarding his previous statements and bringing out statements hither to unheard, to the effect that 'Mbuyazwe[7] is the greater', being born to the wife of his elder brother Shaka. But this was not accepted by the Zulus. Even the Boers, they who installed Cetshwayo[8] as king, knew him whose ear they had pierced and marked, for when Mpande returned home to the Zulu country after fleeing from Dingane in 1840, escorted by the Boers, he was asked by them to point out his heir amongst all his children. Thereupon Mpande pointed out Cetshwayo, and they cut his ear and made an ear-mark. But the king had forgotten all about this, and when questioned by those who answered him and denied him, he replied, 'Are you not aware that I bore Cetshwayo when I was a mere commoner? Do you not understand that this nation belongs to Shaka? No! Mbuyazwe is the king, who is the son of Shaka'.

But some Zulus denied this statement of the king's, and maintained that he had not been in earnest when he said that the heir was Mbuyazwe, who was the son of Shaka. They said that the king wanted those of his sons who were now men to quarrel and kill one another, so that there would remain Mthonga, the son of Nomantshali, the wife whom he loved dearly. For sometimes as the king was talking, he would remark to the others that Mthonga was his heir, whom he had fathered as a king; and that those whom he had fathered as a commoner, before he had partaken of the medicines of kingship, could not be come kings.

Chapter 32

THE DAUGHTERS OF JAMA

Jama's principal daughter was Mkabayi [Mnkabayi], who was senior to them all, followed by Mawa and Mmama, who were possibly twins. But Mkabayi was senior to them all, and whilst Senzangakhona was still a minor, the Zulu nation was ruled by her, she being the ruler rather than Senzangakhona. Her home was among the Qulusi [a section of the Zulu people], the home of the princess. Even after Senzangakhona had attained manhood and she had handed over to him to rule for himself, she nevertheless continued to be his elder sister and to advise him on matters concerning the Zulu nation. But Mkabayi was a person with a violent temper, often putting people to death. Even at the present time the Qulusi section of the people still exists, and the Zulu kings rule over it and appoint headmen to control it.

As to her younger sister, Mawa, it was she who crossed over [into Natal] during the reign of Mpande, crossing over into European territory [*esiLungwini*] for some reason which is unknown. She crossed over with certain others, such as her headman Mangena kaNokuphatha of the Nkwanyana clan, who had a district of his own in Zululand. After Mangena left Zululand, the Zulus composed this song about him:

> We hear that Mangena is bearing a pot of water.
> They beat him with a whip on his stomach,
> And he crawled on hands and knees until sunset.
> Cattle! Eya! He!
> May they be collected throughout the land,
> For he has spoken.

Mangena came down and settled at Umvoti, his heir being Bobiyana who was enlisted by Bishop Colenso at Ekukanyeni on his arrival from England in 1856, sent out by the Queen to enlighten the country of Natal and to be its Bishop.

[REFUGEES FROM ZULU AUTHORITY]

Mangena, by the way, was one of the elders of the Zulu people who fled and came here to European territory [*esiLungwini*] on account of certain matters which were not satisfactory to the Zulu authorities. There were many who arrived here and complained that they were being killed for no reason whatever, and yet the person making such a statement was an evil criminal with many faults. One would say, 'It is alleged that I practice witchcraft', which was in fact true, he being a witch of the very worst type. And as soon as he had settled down, or shortly afterwards, he would begin to commit the evil practices for which he had been driven out. It was not that the dignitaries and the elders and the common people were fleeing because of false accusations, for we now know that they were all driven away because of their serious criminal faults.

Among the dignitaries [*izikhulu*] who came here saying that they were escaping from death, there were not many who came here without fault. Sogweba kaMasekwana kaMenyelwa of the Ntuli clan, whose brother was Mbuzo who remained behind at the back of Qudeni mountain and eventually died there, whose elder brother was Sogweba, the chief of the Menyelwa clan, abandoned his chieftainship in Zululand where he was a commander in the Thulwana regiment, the regiment formed from Cetshwayo's age group. This was before the great dispute between the Princes [Cetshwayo and Mbulazi] (1856).

We know Dikida kaMgabashe, Mazungeni kaMtezuka of the Khumalo clan, Madumu of the Ntuli clan, Khanyana kaZiweweni of the Mkhize clan, but we do not know what led them to flee from Zululand.

Chapter 33
THE DEATH [AND BURIAL] OF NANDI

Of all events that occurred in Zululand, there was none as tragic and as serious as the death of Nandi, the mother of Shaka. It is said that when Shaka received the news of the death of his mother, the Queen Mother [*indlovukazi*], he came out of his house with his shield, in full dress, and stood for a while and then laid down his shield. Then he stood silent for a time, and then tears began to flow copiously. There was a long silence while he sobbed, and then he suddenly gave a loud scream: '*Maye ngomame*!' ['Alas for my mother']. Wo! And there was heard a great death wail from all the people there in the home, crying out, '*Maye ngomame*!', while others cried, '*Maye babo*!' ['Alas indeed'], and as they repeated it the homestead shook with emotion, which lasted throughout the night.

And on the following day the death wail continued as people arrived from all directions to take part in the lamentations. And on that day the wailing lasted until dark. Just realise the size of the country [population]! From the earliest hours the people continued to arrive and lament, until the king gave an opportunity for a rest from lamentation and ordered through his headmen that the people were to be silent and rest for a while. And so silence was maintained for a short time; and then the wail was raised again by streams of mourners from other areas, the people arriving with loud cries of lamentation. And when their eyes became dry of tears, they put snuff into them, because there were spies moving about looking for those who were not shedding tears, and killing them.

That came to an end, and then a period of mourning was observed that lasted several months. You will realise that at the burial of the body there was great grief, because the queen was not buried alone but interred with her servants, male and female – those who lived with her preparing her food and at tending to her requirements. She was buried with a large number of people, and they were buried alive and not dead.

And so! A year passed with people unable to visit their houses, for anyone found sleeping in his house would certainly die, for why should he go to sleep in his house when there was still mourning? When was he purified? A woman found pregnant was instantly put to death along with her husband.

On the day of purification, the chief councillor, Ngomane kaMqomboli, announced to the vast assembly of people who had gathered together, 'Indeed, today the nation has completed its mourning

ROYAL RESIDENCES

for the Queen Mother [*indlovukazi*] who has now become a benevolent spirit to watch over the Zulu nation. Everybody should now return to their homes and beget, and eat their maas [lead a normal life]'.

And all the people dispersed and returned to their homes. Then came the time for cultivating crops, and the cultivation went on as in previous years. The crops ripened, and then came the time to observe the first fruits ceremony, and everything followed the course of former years.

Everyone who escaped that convulsion congratulated themselves, for people were put to death quite innocently. It was simply a matter of luck to him who was protected by his ancestral spirit.

Chapter 34
ZULU ROYAL RESIDENCES

Here are the names of the Zulu royal residences: Nobamba, Siklebeni, Bulawayo (or Gibixhegu), Mbelebele, Dukuza, Khangelamankengane, Ekukhethekhetheni, and others that I do not know well.

Nobamba was the home of Senzangakhona, as was also Siklebeni. Bulawayo was named after the capital of Mzilikazi kaMashobana of the Khumalo clan, who was driven out by Shaka and fled towards Mashonaland. The name Gibixhegu [Oust the Old Man] is a reference to Mzilikazi, because his capital in Mashonaland is still known as Bulawayo.[1]

Dukuza and Kangelamankengane belonged to Shaka. Dukuza was situated in Bhodwe (Port Natal),[2] and is known as Stanger today, that very town. It was its owner's favourite residence, and it was where his brothers put him to death. Khangela was situated near South Coast Junction, now known as Congella – they still call it by its original name given by Shaka. The word '*khangela*' was probably intended to mean that it was where a watch was kept on the vagabonds [*khangela amankengane*]. The vagabond that caused Shaka a great deal of trouble was Mnini, the chief of the Thuli clan. It was he who caused great trouble to the king because he would not consent to the appropriation of his cattle. When the Thuli saw that the lion was approaching to rob them of their cattle, they concealed them in the thick coastal bush [*uthungulu*] which abounds along the Bluff [*isibubulungu*], seeking suitable places to conceal them. Shaka then built the establishment which he named

'Khangelamankengane'. But the Thuli refused to part with their cattle, and finally succeeded, for the Thuli were the only people never to be robbed of their cattle by Shaka.

One of the most important things that Shaka did whilst living in this residence was always to rise early and proceed to the beach to watch the action of the sea. On arrival each person was required to throw his stick into the sea to ascertain who were witches, for that of a witch never returned. The owner of the stick that did not return was in consequence killed on the spot on the grounds that he was a witch [*umthakathi*].

The truth about water is this: If a person has been bereaved of a relative, whether a wife, mother, father, child, or other blood relation, water will not spare him, it will take him. For this reason, if a person has lost a relative, it is not safe for him to approach water in flood, or if not in flood, water in a deep pool.

It was from the sea that Shaka learned the technique of controlling soldiers when he set them to fight in battle, from the example of the waves in their action. Every day he went to watch them and all the movements made by the waves of the sea.

[SHAKA AT THE HEIGHT OF HIS POWER]

At that time Shaka was the ruler of the whole of South Africa, there being no chief who dared to touch him. And there in Thekwini [Port Natal] he had white subjects who came from Cape Town, who were with Fynn and Ogle and the others. His powers of sovereignty were full to the brim of the basket, and he ruled in a manner never known by his father Senzangakhona, and his grandfather Jama, and his great-grandfather, Ndaba; nor by his ancestor Phunga, nor by his ancestor Mageba, nor by the ancestor of his grandfather, Nkosinkulu, nor by Ntombela, nor by Malandela. It was the first time that there had been a government to unite the whole country of South Africa under a single ruler like Shaka. And it was for this reason that all people were said to be Zulus. Nevertheless there were a few who were inclined to raise their hackles, but such an attitude soon brought about self-critical regrets. Only one man was wise, Sobhuza [the Swazi king], who, on seeing all this, submitted and paid lip service [homage with the tongue] to the Zulus whilst preparing his caves as places of refuge. Another was Makhasana, the Tembe chief, who, on hearing all this, also submitted and paid lip service. He became a servant to the Zulus by trapping civets for their skins, and by killing ostriches and elephants. Elephant tusks, ostrich feathers, civet skins and other skins, were conveyed to the Zulus. Blue cranes were also killed and their feathers plucked. All this was a token of homage to the Zulus. But in addition to all this, the Tonga [the Tembe-Tonga], being a clever people, worked diligently to search for medicines, so that if a person treated them badly, they would retaliate with magical spells, and he would die immediately.

The Zulus invaded the Tembe country on two or three occasions, robbing them of their cattle, with the result that in the end the people, realising they were being attacked for their cattle, abandoned cattle altogether and took to breeding fowls only, and the cultivation of crops, mealies and monkey-nuts and other foodstuffs. And so the Tembe country became peaceful with people no longer being attacked and killed for nothing.

Chapter 35
SHAKA'S ATTACK ON THE NYUSWA

This attack on the Nyuswa was not an act of aggression in itself, but the result of the king's annoyance. The senior chief of all the Ngcobo [of which the Nyuswa is a branch], Mapholoba kaMbhele, had two sons, Sihayo and Mgabi. When their father died they disputed the inheritance. The Ngcobo clan was a large one and comprised several sections. There was the senior one known as the Nyuswa, and the junior one [*isizinda*][1] known as Ngongoma.

The dispute between the two sons of Mapholoba was of course very serious, and at the outset the Qadi section, the senior in rank and in origin, and that of Tayi of the Langeni section, and that of the ancestral home of Mavela, united in supporting Sihayo of Mapholoba's chief homestead, Enkumbeni, and disowned Mgabi, being unanimous in support of Sihayo. This trouble came to the ears of Shaka, and he mobilised his army and went to arbitrate. But the Ngcobo were not fighting, they were just disputing. And this was the origin of Shaka's praises as follows:

> He who gazes to the south of the Dungele,
> And the cattle of Sihayo followed him,
> And there followed those of Mafongosi,
> Which were milked by one of Mavela's yokels.

> There was no dispute among the Nyuswa,
> Only a dispute over castor oil plants in deserted sites,
> They saying *ntete*, *ntete*, wait for the skin parings.

The slander that the dispute was over castor oil plants arose because no cattle were involved. The Dungele were a clan, otherwise known as the Dunge. And the assertion that 'the cattle of Sihayo followed him, and there followed those of Mafongosi, which were milked by one of Mavela's yokels' was another slight or slander.

The chief of the Ngongoma section, Bofungana kaMavela, was the chief of the original ancestral home [*isizinda*], and he bore Mafongosi, who bore Siphandla, the father of Mbozane who died recently. Mavela was the son of Mashiza kaNdaba kaNombika kaGasela kaNgcobo, the senior chief of the original family home, being one with Xonxo who begot Sanimuse, who begot Mdunane, who begot Dindi, who begot Sokebi, who begot Dlomo, who begot Nonyanda, who begot Mahawule, who begot Madlenya, who begot Hemuhemu, who begot Langalakhe. The members of Langalakhe's family are now separate and known as the Fuze, and those of Mbozane as the Ngongoma, whereas in truth they both belong to the Ngongoma. The term 'Fuze' is a general one for all the Ngcobo subclans, but more particularly for the *isizinda* section, because it was Ngcobo's ancestral home.

This clan (the Ngcobo) is friendly and respectful towards its various sub-clans. Notwithstanding their large number, it is recognised by all that Mqedi kaDeliwyo, the grandson of Dubuyana kaSihayo kaMapholoba, is the only chief of them all. Even the Shangase clan knows that Mqedi is their real chief. The division of the great house of Ngcobo is firstly the Nyuswa, followed by the Qadi, and then the Ngongoma. The Langeni clan under Madoda kaBhacela kaThondolozi kaTayi kaBhebhe comprises just a section of Mapholoba kaMbhele's large family, without being actually separate from it even though it may appear to be so now.

By now there have been further additions to the Ngcobo tribe, so that they seem to be independent clans, but this is not so. They are all one people under Chief Mqedi kaDeliweyo. There are the Mgangeni under Kadupi kaNomazocwana kaNdela, and those of Ngada kaVelemsuthu, who are known as the Ngathi of the most junior house of Mapholoba. There are also those of Swayimana kaZiphuku kaSinqila, a scion of the house of Mapholoba; and those of Sotobe kaDikwayo, who was forever disputing with Dubuyana, and who today has his own section like the

NATAL AFFAIRS: SHAKA

rest. Finally there are the Shangase, the section under Mkhetshana, who was the younger brother of Ngcobo by the same father and mother.

> Far distant is the tribe of Nyuswa and Ngcobo,
> Contesting with the Zulus,
> And it will vanquish them!
> The elephant that drinks boiling water.

Even now the Ngcobo are increasing daily, and we do not know where it will end.

Chapter 36

MATTERS ALREADY RECORDED

[BY BISHOP COLENSO]

Now I am going to tell you about matters that I have read in the book written by Sobantu [Bishop Colenso], *Izindaba ZaseNatal* [*Natal Affairs*] (1856), dealing with early history.

[And Fuze reproduces the first twelve sections dealing with the Cape: the Portuguese discovery, the Dutch settlement, the British occupation, the frontier wars, the Xhosa self-inflicted famine; and in the first part of the twelfth section, a geographical description of Natal: 'The Queen's Country of Natal extends from the Umzimkhulu to the Tugela along the sea coast, and from the sea coast to the Drakensberg. Beyond the Tugela is the country of the Zulus, under Mpande the son of Senzangakhona.' He lists the six 'counties' of Natal, the main towns and the principal rivers.]

Chapter 37

SHAKA

(AS TOLD BY THE WHITE PEOPLE)

Izindaba ZaseNatal 12[1]
'Now let us relate the history of Natal. Seventy years have passed since the birth of Shaka (1787), dating from the time of the writing of this

book (1856). His father Senzangakhona was the son of Jama, Jama of Ndaba, Ndaba of Mageba, Mageba of Phunga. Senzangakhona had many wives and children. But Shaka as a child lived with his mother's people in the Mthethwa clan.[2] When Senzangakhona died, Dingiswayo, the chief of the Mthethwa, installed Shaka at the age of thirty years to be the chief over his own Zulu people. Many of the Mthethwa joined him, recognised him as their chief, and entreated him to assist them in fighting an enemy against whom they were engaged, the Ndwandwe. He agreed and summoned an army and attacked that clan, and killed its chief, and compelled its people to submit to his rule. This was the beginning of his undertaking to fight every clan. He attacked them, killing their chiefs and many of their people. Those that survived submitted to him. Day by day he extended his rule.'

Izindaba ZaseNatal 13
'Shaka had an army of fifteen thousand men, always on the alert and armed for war. He distinguished his regiments by the colour of their shields. He arrived courageously and told the army: No throwing of flights of spears — stab at close quarters and shout *Ngadla* [I have eaten, devoured, destroyed].' [Colenso gives Shaka's war song,[3] and a number of Shaka's praises.[4]]

Izindaba ZaseNatal 14
'But Shaka was a man without pity. There was a certain white man (Isaacs) who visited him and recorded this matter: [the slaughter of a large number of children: an extract from *Travels and Adventures in South-East Africa*].'

Izindaba ZaseNatal 15–18
'Whilst Shaka still ruled, Mbulazi[5] (Mr Fynn) and a few other Englishmen arrived. These Englishmen came to settle in Natal. Mbulazi visited Shaka frequently, and advised him in many matters. He was present at the time of the death of Nandi, the mother of Shaka. And here is the account of it, as described by Mbulazi:' [the death of Nandi, apparently from dysentry; Shaka's reaction; the lamentations and the executions,[6] and the burial, from which he was debarred: an extract from *The Diary of Henry Francis Fynn*].

Izindaba ZaseNatal, 19–23
[Continuation of Fynn's account: his visit to Dukuza to witness the

purification ceremony a year after the death of Nandi: an extract from *The Diary of Henry Francis Fynn*].

Chapter 38
DINGANE
(AS TOLD BY THE WHITE PEOPLE)

Izindaba ZaseNatal 24
'But notwithstanding that Shaka was so powerful, he was killed by his brother Dingane. The army had gone to make war at a far distance. Shaka remained behind at his capital, Dukuza. He was seated in the cattle kraal towards the upper part, talking to his headmen and watching the cattle returning in the afternoon. Then came his two brothers, Dingane and Mhlangana, with an official [*inceku*], Mbhopha, and others, saying that "We have just returned from a hunt". When they had come close to the king, Mbhopha said to those present, "Do not worry the king with your lies". He went amongst them and disturbed them and dispersed them. He spoke a few words, and the king also spoke briefly to his brothers. Mbhopha then rushed forward and stabbed him in the back. The king tried to escape, but his brothers pursued him and stabbed him to death with spears. (Sept. 28, 1828.)

'But others say that he was first stabbed by Mhlangana, for Dingane used to complain at the constant killing of people. They came together and prepared a plot to kill him, and chose Mhlangana as the one who was to stab him. Mhlangana, in determining to stab him, said he would select a particular place for the wound where he would stab him to instant death. He chose the place below the armpit, but he stabbed him in the arm.'

(If you find some sections in brackets, you must understand that they have been written by me, M.M. Fuze, and not by the white people, for there are some matters that conflict.)

The words of M.M. Fuze
(The true story of Shaka's death is as follows. The army left on a campaign known as the 'clean sweep' ['*khukhulelangoqo*'] for operations at the Bhalule [Olifant's river]. His brothers, in agreement, remained behind and did not go on that campaign, because of their dissatisfaction and disapproval of their brother's policy of killing people. Having come together over the matter, they approached Mbhopha kaSitayi, who

lived with the king, sharing his food, being a member of the Zulu royal household. They promised him that if he agreed and killed Shaka, they would apportion him a certain part of the Zulu country to be his own territory over which he would rule as chief.

Whilst these negotiations were under consideration, Mkabayi the king's father's elder sister, who also condemned the bad conduct of the son of her younger brother, pleaded with Mbhopha with words of delusion to give him courage, promising him great benefits if he would prevail upon himself to stab the king with a spear. And so like a fool he agreed to do it, for the sake of becoming a chief and ruling over a part of the Zulu country. And so he committed that act of evil, and killed the king, which, in turn, brought about his own death.

After they had killed Shaka, they buried his body in an empty grain pit. All this happened in the absence of Mxamama kaNtandeka of the Sibisi clan, his main attendant [*inceku*] and praiser [*mbongi*], he having been sent away on some mission. On his return he found the king no longer alive, having been killed. He lamented with fury and cursed both Mhlangana and Dingane, comparing them with dogs, and entreated them to kill him. He flung himself on the grave and begged them to kill him. But they would not kill him, and it was not until he cursed them in the vilest terms that they killed him. It was this Mxamama who whenever he observed the vultures flying overhead, would praise the king with the remark that 'Your birds are hungry and desire food', so saying because he wanted people killed.

And this fellow Mbhopha who had killed his king through being made a fool by the royal princes who had promised him great things, did in fact receive the reward promised him. A large tract of country was carved out for him, and he received many cattle. But after the passage of two or three months he was put to death. It was said that as he had the evil courage to strengthen him to kill a king of such greatness, he should be put to death because he would surely repeat such an act in future.

After this, a dispute arose between the two princes, Mhlangana and Dingane. Then the sister of their father was approached, Mkabayi, and she secretly indicated Dingane [as successor], the son of Bhibhi, whom she said to be the chief wife. She then devised a plan and directed all the princes to go and discuss the matter at the stream. But Mkabayi had already made arrangements with the men that they were to seize and kill Mhlangana and spare Dingane, when they got to the river. And so this was done in accordance with the command of Mkabayi.

DINGANE

As soon as Dingane assumed the kingship, he killed off all his brothers except Mpande, the son of his mother Songiya, whose body was bad in the leg,[1] and Gqugqu, who was still a small boy and not yet a young man.

One day after he had disposed of his brothers, he assembled a regiment to attack Wambaza, the great residence of Gendeyana of the Qwabe clan, with instructions to kill Ngwadi, the son of Nandi by Gendayana. But Ngwadi had already heard everything, as well as the death of his brother Shaka, and had already mobilised his home force. A battle was fought, for Ngwadi had a powerful force, but eventually Dingane's regiment forced its way through the fence and went in and exterminated Ngwadi and his force.)

Izindaba ZaseNatal 25
'Dingane reigned in the place of Shaka. He started to kill. He killed his brother Mhlangana and all Shaka's relations. He summoned Mbulazi (Fynn) and other white men who were at Thekwini [the Bay at Port Natal], but they were afraid, thinking that they might be killed seeing that they were the children of Shaka. And they refused to go to him. Dingane got angry and dispatched a regiment to seize their cattle; it killed a few blacks, but the whites fled. Dingane then said, "Come back, I will do nothing to harm you". And they returned and asked for their cattle. Dingane agreed saying, "Yes, if you return five black chiefs who have run away from me": They refused, and he refused to give up the cattle. He then sent spies to spy out the country in search of those chiefs. And the army went out twice, advancing inland and returning along the coast. Dingane removed the eyes of those spies, because the army had gone out on their advice and returned with nothing.[2]

Time went by. Many people dispersed by Shaka began to return to their country in Natal, and they submitted themselves to Mbulazi (Fynn) and Febana (Farewell), and the others. These white men were held in very high regard by the black people at that time. Even now the followers of Fynn still swear by him when taking an oath.'

The words of M.M. Fuze
(It was at this time that Zihlandlo and his brother Sambela, the sons of Gcwabe kaKhabazela kaMavovo, were killed. They were killed for no reason; they were killed because they had been friends of Shaka.

Here is a matter which is associated with that incident. There was a youth employed by Zihlandlo as a servant. He was of the Ngcobo clan, and his name was Magwaza, alias Thuphana kaMatomela kaThoko kaDileka kaDindi. He had been adopted by the Embo people [Zihlandlo's people] when his people were dispersed at the Umvoti when Shaka sent Manjanja kaNhlambela to attack Matomela at the Umvoti. When the enemy had killed his uncle, Mkhaliphi, Matomela, who was the head of the family, ordered his people to follow Mahawule kaNonyanda, a chief of those parts who was setting out for the Manyiseni towards the Tugela. His people tried to persuade Matomela to go too, but he refused, saying that he did not want to leave his home, and that they should go and take care of Thuphana (his son). So they left him behind in the old home, still alive, but he was finally devoured by wild animals. While they were on the journey, Magwaza (Thuphana) escaped and crossed the Tugela and arrived among the Embo people, where he was adopted by Bhambada kaShabase kaMavovo, who took him to Zihlandlo, who appointed him as his milkman.

One day when Magwaza was sent on an errand at sunset, he met a person on the way who divulged to him that the Zulu army was going to attack the Embo people the following day, and kill Zihlandlo. Magwaza naturally passed this information on to Bhambada and to the chief. But who could possibly believe that the Zulu army would kill Zihlandlo, Shaka's 'brother'? But what had been heard by Magwaza was true. It was now the day on which he was to be killed, because he did not believe what was said – as for Magwaza, he saw that it was true and fled during the night – the next morning the homestead was surrounded by Dingane's army to kill the friend of Shaka. It killed both Zihlandlo and Sambela. Zihlandlo was killed in the Dimane homestead, and Sambela in the Kwanini homestead.)

Izindaba ZaseNatal 26
'Capt. Gardiner arrived (1835), a great scholar whose knowledge amazed the people.[3] On one occasion he went to the Zulu country on a visit to Dingane. He sat with Dingane in the open space [*nkundla*] and showed him many things, the products of the white man's knowledge. He strongly entreated Dingane to invite a teacher to instruct his people in the things of God. Dingane refused at that time to allow his people to be taught. He said, "Go and teach the people at the Bay first". He then made an arrangement with Dingane, whereby . . .' [the 'treaty of extradition' between Gardiner and Dingane, which Bishop Colenso condemns].

DINGANE

Izindaba ZaseNatal 27
'This dark and dangerous agreement soon brought forth its fruits of evil.' [The return of refugees to Dingane, who ordered them to be killed.]

Izindaba ZaseNatal 28–30
'Dingane agreed to the Rev. Owen living near to his capital of Mgungundlovu, and teaching his people.[4] He began to teach them (Oct. 10, 1837), . . . but at the end of four months (Feb. 6, 1838) a most terrible thing happened which terminated the teaching. I refer to the murder of Piet Retief and his followers to the number of sixty men, treacherously murdered by Dingane.' [Colenso relates: the entry of the Boers into Natal, the first visit to Dingane, the recovery of the cattle from Sigonyela, the second visit to Dingane, the signing of the document prepared by Owen, and the invitation to the entertainment on the following morning.] 'Dingane spoke pleasantly to Piti [Piet Retief] and to some of his leaders, and entreated them to stay a while and drink beer. They seated themselves and drank beer, after which they were entertained with the singing and dancing of a national song and dance [*inkondlo*]. Dingane then rose and said, "*Hambani kahle*" [Farewell, a good journey], and then entered the opening to his private apartments [*isigodlo*]. As he was about to pass through the opening, he tossed his blanket in accordance with a prearranged plan he had made with his people. Then tumult arose, and the soldiers surrounding them closed in. The Boers tried to get away but the Zulus seized them and he [Dingane] shouted "*Bambani abathakathi*" [seize the wizards]. They beat them with sticks. The Boers drew their knives and fought hard, killing some, but they died one by one until all were dead. Their bodies were dragged over to Matiwane's hill. One single Boer escaped, and he went off and reported to the others what had happened.'[5]

Izindaba ZaseNatal 31
'Owen was not present at that time. Dingane had invited the Boers in the morning at a time when Owen was in the habit of reading the book of God and praying alone. At first he wished to go with them, but then he changed his mind saying, "No, it is better that I conform to what I normally do". He sat down and read the book and prayed to God. Here is his account of that event: "Feb. 6, 1838. Oh! What a day of grief! I am trembling as I write this account." [An extract from *The Diary of the Rev. Francis Owen.*]

Izindaba ZaseNatal 32
[Dingane allows Owen to depart.]

Izindaba ZaseNatal 33
[Dingane dispatches ten regiments to massacre the Boers in their encampments.]

Izindaba ZaseNatal 34
[The Boers consolidate under the leadership of Piet Uys, and set out to attack Dingane.] 'They came to a certain narrow passage [*umngcingo*] between two small hills at Taleni. At this spot they first caught sight of Dingane's force, but it retreated slightly, doing so purposely in accordance with the king's instructions, to allow the Boers to approach the narrow passage and enter into it, thinking that they were pursuing the Zulus who were afraid. And so it happened: the Boers entered the narrow passage, at which stage a body of Zulus cut across at the back of one of these small hills, unobserved by the Boers, so that one force was blocking the back and the other the front. The Boers were hemmed in without room to retreat to reload their firearms. On realising that they had no room to fight, they all advanced in force, killing a number of Zulus by this movement, found an opening and got through. But their leader, Piet Uys, and twenty of his followers, and his son of whom he was very fond, got into difficulties at a spot where the horses could not get through. They were set upon by the force and surrounded. Piet Uys was already wounded, and he said to his followers, "Go on, I am already dead". Some did so and escaped, but the father and his son remained behind and fought to the death.'

Chapter 39

BOERS AND BRITISH AGAINST DINGANE

Izindaba ZaseNatal 35–36
[The first attack against the Zulus by the British settlers was successful in that a large number of cattle was captured. It was a small-scale operation which did not venture across the Tugela, and the cattle were rounded up from homesteads inadequately attended because of the disturbances, in the Ntunjambili (Kranskop) district. The second attack was undertaken on a larger scale altogether: 12 whites, 30 coloureds and several hundred blacks. Bishop Colenso's account may well be

transcribed from a Zulu eye-witness narrator:] 'On the evening of the third day the English force arrived at the Tugela. Funwayo kaMpopoma of the Luthuli clan and his men were to go out and investigate. They crossed the Tugela and at the home of Kude they arrested two spies of Dingane's and shot them, and then returned to make a report. Then there was a great dispute among the whites. Some said, "Let it advance at once" [presumably the British force], and others said, "Let us wait until it arrives" [presumably the Zulu force]. Finally they decided on advancing. They crossed the Tugela and climbed a hill and arrived at the home of Zulu kaNogandaya at Ndondakusuka. They surrounded this homestead early in the morning as it was getting light. There was one of Dingane's regiments there, and they fired at it with guns. The people who were in the huts saw bullets entering, and hung on to the roof structures, but the huts collapsed with the weight of the people. Then the shooting was directed towards the upper parts, and the people were shot down. The whole homestead was destroyed, the people killed and the huts burned. But one of them who was about to die uttered his final warning words, "Kill me right now, but the great elephant is coming, and it will trample you underfoot".

And very soon the great elephant unexpectedly appeared to check the situation with the power of its army. But Dingane was not there in person at the time, only his headmen, Madlebe kaMgedeza, Zulu kaNogandaya and Nongalaza kaNondela. These headmen together with the veterans were posted on a small isolated hill from which they could see everything that was about to happen, and advise the army, which consisted of ten thousand men. The Zulu nation was angry over the seizure of its cattle at Ntunjambili (Kranskop), and also the burning of the Ndondakusuka homestead before its very eyes, and it was thirsting for revenge. In consequence they fought with a fierceness which was quenched only by death. Even when wounded they crawled forward with their spears to throw them lying down in an effort to kill. It was no wonder that the whites fought with determination, realising the danger. They were in a position near the homestead, the English and the coloureds armed with guns being in the front, and the blacks armed with spears being behind them.

The first regiment of Zulus attacked at the run. They were shot down like mown grass. They halted, trembled, retreated and scattered. Others arrived from other directions. The white force divided, one section advancing in one direction and the other in another. One body fought with great courage for a short time, and scattered the regiment attacking it. After that it fled towards the Tugela drift. And then the Zulu leaders said, "Oh! Could they be on the run?" This greatly encouraged the Zulus, who now appeared from all directions and surrounded that other small bodyguard which remained behind, and overwhelmed it and exterminated it. Many were killed, being blocked by the drift; many threw themselves into the Tugela and were drowned. Twelve whites died,[1] and all the coloureds except for a few. Many blacks were killed, only those who fled first being able to escape. They reached Thekwini [the Bay at Port Natal, now known as Durban] singly, all with the same report: "You see me, the only survivor". And such was the battle of Dlokweni.[2, 3] It was here that Mpande, who was a headman under Dingane, became famous, for it was he who had doctored the army.'

Izindaba ZaseNatal 37
'After a few weeks Dingane's army arrived at Thekwini [Durban]. All the whites there went to live on the island in the middle of the bay [*ichwebe*].[4] During the day they stayed there, but at night they went into a ship that was there. For fifteen days they lived in this way, watching the black army wildly destroying everything belonging to the whites. Household furniture, clothing, dogs, cats, fowls, everything they seized and destroyed: they pillaged Gardiner's house and all his property, and then passed on to Mlazi to Adams Mission, where they threw a burning brand onto the roof, but it did not burn.'

[Colenso gives a short account of the Battle of Blood River:] 'The Zulus attempted three times to break through the defences. Then Potolozi [Pretorius], the Boer leader, ordered two hundred men to ride out on horseback through an opening at the back of the encampment, and advance on two sides and hem the Zulus in the middle. They acted accordingly and struck the Zulus as if they had been a swarm of bees. About three thousand were left lying there. Of the Boers only three were killed. Such was the battle of the Ncome [Blood river], Sunday, Dec. 16, 1838.'

Izindaba ZaseNatal 38
'Dingane fled in great fear. He burnt the whole of his Mgungundlovu capital, and took to the forests near the Mfolozi with the remainder of his army, and there remained in concealment for a long time. The Boer

force advanced forward and reached Mgungundlovu whilst it was still burning.' [They found and buried the remains of Piet Retief and his followers, and returned with five thousand cattle.]

The words of M.M. Fuze
(Whilst the king was still in hiding, he sent Bhongoza of the Ngcobo clan, a great spy, to proceed with courage to the Boers encamped above the Mthonjaneni spring, he himself being down in the thornveld with his army, cattle, women and children. And so the son of Ngcobo, with great courage, went up to them in the high lands. Dingane meanwhile set his army in order, and made arrangements for his cattle and women. The headmen instructed the soldiers to adopt a sitting position, and to hold their shields in such a way as to resemble cattle.

When Bhongoza arrived among the Boers, they regarded him as a spy, and questioned him as to the whereabouts of Dingane and his army. He replied saying that he was in hiding in the thornveld with his women and cattle. They asked him how many regiments he had with him. He denied the existence of regiments, saying, 'They no longer exist, for, as you saw at the Ncome [Blood river], you wiped them out. He is now living only with his household, women, children and cattle.' 'Are you not leading us into a trap, Bhongoza?' And Bhongoza swore most emphatically that he was not. The Boers then armed, bound Bhongoza with a rope, and said, 'Come and show us where Dingane is to be found'.

When they had armed, they took Bhongoza along with them with a rope fastened round his neck. And what do you know? As soon as they appeared at the Mthonjaneni spring, they saw down below them a large number of cattle and people. The Boers then asked Bhongoza, 'What is all that, Bhongoza?' 'Those are all the cattle, and the rest are members of the household, women and children, for all the men were exterminated at the Ncome'. And so they went down. As they began to get down to the thornveld, Bhongoza slipped his halter and escaped. And then he was heard by the Zulus shouting, 'They are within, men of Mjokwane kaNdaba',[5] and with that there arose thunderous roars from all sides. And it was then that the Boers began to shout 'Where is Bhongoza? Where is Bhongoza?' But whom could they question, for where was he? He had long since fled and joined his own army.

Oh! Now they [the Zulus] remembered them, stabbing them at close quarters. When the Boers saw that they could do nothing against such a powerful force, they discharged their guns and advanced forward without fighting. It was here that one of the Boers cried out in exhaustion, 'Go on, fellow horsemen, I died down below'. They [the Zulus] went on stabbing them and pursuing them towards the Mfolozi. And there lay in waiting the umHayi regiment. But they nevertheless went on towards the Mabedlana hills. They were those who made for the Nhlazatshe mountain, pursued by the Zulus as they went.)

Izindaba ZaseNatal 39
[Dingane attempts to negotiate with the Boers, but they cannot trust him.] 'They [the Boers] were therefore unable to disperse and cultivate the land, and it was necessary for them to be always on the alert.

'At this time (December, 1839) a dispute arose among the Zulus, for Dingane had two brothers whom he had not killed. The senior was Mpande, and the very much junior was Gqugqu, still just a boy. Mpande was a grown man, but the people used to say he was not very bright, merely a "nonsense" [*isinonseyana*!]. Dingane directed that he be killed, but the chief councillor, Ndela kaSompisi kaNkobe of the Ntuli clan, objected, saying, "No, King! This thing is worthless, and you will gain no fame by killing it. Let it be." And Dingane desisted. But Mpande was in his own way a clever man.[6] People began to tire of Dingane, and some said it would be better to be ruled by Mpande and co-operate with the Boers and other races. Dingane heard this, and decided definitely to kill him [Mpande]. But his army had gone out to attack the Swazi king, Sobhuza, and Mpande decamped with a large following. He crossed the Tugela at Dlokweni, and established himself around the Umvoti. He then sent messengers to the Boers to seek their assistance. At first they said, "It is a deceitful trick of Dingane's to catch us." But he [Mpande] was able to convince them that he was speaking the truth. They combined with him on the understanding that they would protect and strengthen Mpande, and in return he would help them. This crossing over of Mpande is known as the "severing of the cord" [*ukugqabuka kwegoda*].'

The words of M.M. Fuze
(The truth of the matter is as follows. When the Boers had harrassed the Zulus so greatly after Dingane's defeat at the Ncome, Dingane began to seek a stronghold of safety. He therefore sent his army to attack the Swazis in an attempt to secure their cave strongholds. At this

stage Mpande had become wary and had ceased to pay respectful visits [*khonza*] to his brother as he had always done. He began to remain at home in his residence of Ngqakavini (later known as Mlambongwenya), where, according to Zulu custom, he said that he was sick; but it was a pretence, he was not really ill at all. Dingane remained silent for a time, until he realised that he [Mpande] was not sick but lying and planning to desert. He contrived a means of tempting him, in accordance with Zulu custom, and sent two of his servants, Ncagwana and Mathunjana, directing them to take forty heifers to Mpande which he would find most attractive when he saw them, and for which he would then be obliged to thank the king at his residence, where he would be killed. Accordingly, the two servants conveyed the cattle to the Prince Mpande. On arrival with the cattle, they divulged to him that they were not a gift but a device to tempt him so that he should be killed. Those two servants were apparently tired of Dingane's wickedness in destroying harmless people, and therefore did not conceal from Mpande that it was a plot to kill him.

When Mpande heard this, he did not fear or delay to speak and send messengers throughout the Zulu country to announce that 'the country is full of horses' [presumably Boer horses], and that the people should come over to him and flee straight to the Boers. Well! What would happen now? Seeing that Dingane's army had gone to Swaziland, few men remained behind in the homes. There was a stampede of people, for they were weary of the war of fire of the Boers which had exterminated them with muskets. They went over to:

> He who crossed afterwards
> Of the house of Shaka;
> The swallow that gets lost in the sky,
> He who appears in his feather head-dress
> Between the English and the Boers.

For who could prevent him, seeing that the whole of the Zulu nation was at war in Swaziland? But even there in Swaziland Dingane's army was unable to dislodge the Swazis from their caves, and failed.

In such circumstances the army demanded to return, and soldiers began singing a song on their arrival there:

> We know of the Zulu who departed in our absence,
> You did not tell them by the way,
> You did not tell them while we were away.[7]

This was a great national chant with Dingane's soldiers.)
    On the arrival of the soldiers, Dingane sent his army to turn back all those that it came across who were on their way, not yet having crossed the Tugela. Here is the chant of Dingane's soldiers:

> Ah! He-he!
> Iya! He-he!
> Iya! Iji! Iji!
> We will not see them,
> He is among the enemy.

They were sent to bring back all the people, to frighten them but not to kill them. Only one person killed the king's people contrary to this order, and it was Mxakaza of the Hadebe clan, the father of Mhalaza. He defied Dingane's order that the people were not to be killed but only to be brought back. But Mxakaza, a most evil villain, used to say to each person he found on the way, 'I pass two ribs and stick it in', as he stabbed with his spear.)

Chapter 40

THE DISPUTE BETWEEN MPANDE AND DINGANE

Izindaba ZaseNatal 40
'And so it was. The Boers collected four hundred mounted men under their leader Potolozi [Pretorius], and Mpande marshalled his army amounting to four thousand men under the command of their leader, Nongalaza kaNondela of the Nyandwini clan. That army invaded the Zulu country to the Maqongqo (January 1840).[1] But the forces were not together: Mpande's went by itself and the Boers' went by itself.
    But the Boers did an evil thing at that time. Whilst assembling their forces at Mgungundlovu, an emissary from Dingane arrived, the headman Dambuza,[2] along with Sikhombazana, his servant. They came and delivered a message from Dingane with reference to a reconciliation. But the Boers arrested them both, and questioned them

severely. They admitted that they had been sent by Dingane to see what they [the Boers] had arranged with Mpande. They took them to the Mzinyathi [Buffalo river], and there conferred with Mpande. Mpande said "This man, Dambuza, it is the one who plotted the murder of Piti [Piet Retief] and his followers, and it was also he who advised that I should be killed." The Boers said that he should be killed. In doing so they broke all the white man's rules, killing such a person who was an emissary from another ruler. Dambuza died bravely, denouncing them who were killing him, saying, "You are doing wrong now, even if you are white people." And he continued, "But it is of no consequence to me if I should die; but I do plead for this youth who accompanies me, Sikhombazana, for he is only my servant and goes where I tell him." Nevertheless they were both killed. That was a very wicked deed, and a disgrace to both whites and blacks.

A few days after this killing, Mpande's army fought Dingane's. The battle was fought with fury. Many of Dingane's soldiers defected to Mpande, and in consequence Dingane's army was defeated and fled. The Boers followed Dingane, pursuing him across the Black Mfolozi and beyond the Pongolo.'

The words of M.M. Fuze

(In his flight Dingane eventually reached the uBombo range and established himself there in the forest. One day his cattle despoiled the field of a local resident, a member of Nhlongaluvalo's family, Nhlongaluvalo being the father of Sambane of the Nyawo clan; but this person was sympathetic and forgave the king. After a while they again trespassed into that field, completely eating it out. The man reported the matter to the king. And Dingane sent people to examine the extent of the damage, and they found that they had indeed completely finished it off. The king consequently felt sorry for the man who had suffered, and gave him four heifers as compensation for the loss. He then added a condition, saying, 'You may take the heifers, but I will retain the stubbles [stem stalks] for my cattle'. Wo! The man became angry with unquenchable wrath on hearing the king's arrangement that he was to be given four heifers only and that the cattle-licked stubble was to belong to Dingane. He immediately ran off to report to the Swazis that Dingane was now alone, all his soldiers having gone back to Zululand to fetch their effects. Oh! The Swazis rejoiced exceedingly at this. They armed and travelled through the night, being led by that man of the Nyawo clan who was to show them where he [Dingane] was encamped.

And so the Swazis arrived during the night. Well! Seeing that the king was living in a temporary shelter with only his household and a small body of men that had remained behind, who slept by themselves at a considerable distance from the shelter where the king slept with his household, in the middle of the night Dingane's Boer hound [*igovu*], one of the king's dogs that slept beside him, began to bark, barking because the Swazis had arrived.[3] When they had surrounded the hut, they stabbed him with their spears. Then the king ran out and fled into the forest. By the time the small company that had remained behind with him woke up, the vagabonds had long since run off. They searched for the king during the night, but he was not to be found. They searched until dawn. The search continued the next day, the Zulus being watched by the Swazis as they did so, when the Swazis were heard to shout out that the king was over there in the forest. And so the Zulus made for the forest, to the spot indicated to them by the Swazis. They found Dingane lying down wounded. They carried him to the shelter and examined the wound with which he had been inflicted. And then they inserted their own spear into the wound and enlarged it, whereupon he expired. They then dug a grave and buried him, and all returned to Zululand. For he, when about to pass away, said to them, 'I am now dead. Go and return to Mpande and pay homage to him. But there is one thing that is painful to me, and it is that our people will always be maligned at Songiya's [Mpande's mother] as evil-doers'. So saying he passed away.[4]

But Dingane was more evil than his brother Shaka. He killed one of his father's sons [Shaka] because he said he was troublesome, continually killing people who had done no harm, and constantly attacking clans, so that there was neither peace nor rest. But after he had spoken thus and killed Shaka, he became a greater torment than Shaka. This person with an evil heart killed all his brothers after killing their king, despite the latter having left him in comfort, not wanting to kill one of his father's sons, out of respect; not wanting to force him [Dingane] to take part in campaigns such as the last campaign, the 'clean sweep' [*khukhulelangoqo*].

Dingane, because of his wickedness, after killing off all his father's children, went on to kill Ngwadi kaGendeyana, killing him because he was Shaka's brother, born of the same stomach as himself [the same

DINGANE'S CHARACTER

mother]. He killed Zihlandlo kaGcwabe of the Embo people, killing him because he had been friendly with Shaka, who had permitted him to have an enclosure [*isigodlo*] with a harem [*umndlunkulu*] like himself. He killed him along with his brother, Sambela.

Dingane, although a person in form, had the heart of a dog and the nature of a witch [*umthakathi*]. He killed Dube kaSilwane, the Qadi chief, for no reason whatever other than that he excelled him in a dancing competition in which they were both participating. After he had excelled him, as his attention was directed to the leg rattles [*imifece*] and he was thinking that the chattering of the leg rattles was like the syllables of speech, as soon as the handsome blue-grey monkey [*isimango*] of the Qadi clan began to dance, Dingane stabbed him, thus causing the death of the son of Silwane. This evil man considered that seeing he [Dube] had excelled him in dancing, he [Dingane] would now deprive him of his chieftainship, and excel him there.

Dingane was truly like a poisonous snake. Even when in flight with his household from his brother Mpande, as he was crossing the Pongolo, one of his servants looked towards where the harem was crossing, for which he was condemned, and Dingane said, 'You are looking, what are you looking at? Take him away', and so he was put to death.

Not a single good act was ever committed by Dingane, in contrast to those I am now about to narrate about Shaka.

When a certain man who had been condemned was about to be put to death, Shaka asked him, 'seeing that you are about to be put to death, what beautiful thing are you leaving behind on earth?' And the man said, 'sir, I am leaving the king, and I am leaving my small child as it is beginning to laugh, and I am leaving a young calf as it is beginning to frisk and frolic'. On these words Shaka said 'Release him!'

On another occasion, Shaka, seeing his people's fondness for snuff, gave a heifer in calf to two retainers and instructed them to take it as they travelled around asking for snuff on the way. To the person who did not make excuses and apologies [*landula*] when asked for snuff, but who simply gave it without comment, they were to give the heifer to be his own. Those two men travelled around until the sun was about to set without finding such a person, finding only those who even if they had snuff began to *landula* before giving it. After they had travelled far they came upon an old woman who, as they were still requesting it, without a word simply handed them a helping of snuff. They then said to her,

'This is your beast, drive it and go home with it'. She was astonished to get a beast knowing nothing about it, and she thanked them with the greatest of thanks.)

SHAKA'S CHARACTER

(Even though we may condemn Shaka for having a lust for killing people, we can say with conviction that he was a clever man who liked to act intelligently. He wished to co-operate with the white people, having seen the products of their knowledge. I feel sure that had he not been killed, our life would have been different for us, because he ardently desired to associate himself with the white people in respect of all their works of wisdom.

On another occasion, Shaka asked whether there was anyone present who could contend with the sun by shouting at it until it set. 'Anyone who can do such a thing I will give that beast in the cattle kraal'. One man came forward saying that he could do it. The following day dawned brightly. And indeed as the sun emerged, the man shouted with a loud voice, 'That sun! That sun indeed!', and continued all day shouting in this manner. As it started to set, he had long since come to an end.

It was Shaka who coined the famous expression, 'Dough is often nibbled as it is moulded'.[5] He also said that a man should strongly masticate his boiled mealies in order to wake up fresh and strong in the morning; and that he should not eat moist and finely ground food only, otherwise the body does not get strong. I maintain that the Zulus did well to extend the wound inflicted on Dingane by the Swazis, so that he too should feel the spear as he made his great brother Shaka feel it. He who gives pain to another, even to him will others bring pain.)

Chapter 41

THE ESTABLISHMENT OF BRITISH RULE

Izindaba ZaseNatal 41–47
'On the death of Dingane, the Boers gathered on the banks of the Mfolozi (Feb. 14, 1840); they fired their guns, and proclaimed and installed Mpande as king of the Zulus. That was done by Potolozi [Pretorius]. Mpande gave them thirty-six thousand head of cattle and they went away with them, in terms of the compromise.'

[After the withdrawal of forces from Port Natal, the re-despatch of British troops under Captain Smith by land from the Cape (May, 1842); the unsuccessful attack against the Boers encamped at Khangela (Congella); the Boers capture the Point and its military stores, and besiege the Fort, bombarding it daily with cannon; Dick King's ride to the Cape for reinforcements, and their arrival thirty days later by sea; the relief of Durban and the raising of the British flag. Bishop Colenso's account of the birth of the British Colony of Natal describes an event that did not concern the native inhabitants, and Fuze has no comments to make.]

Chapter 42

WICKED RUFFIANS

[BRITISH RULE IN NATAL]

Izindaba ZaseNatal 47 (cont.)[1]
'But there were certain blacks who did an evil thing at that time. The commander of the regiment that had arrived by ship said, "All blacks are to search for cattle and horses and bring them to my regiment". A few blacks went out and killed three Boers who were not fighting against the English regiment. They went to their homes where they found some women and tore off their clothes and exposed them, treating them very roughly and cutting them with spears, and drove them out of their homes. Such an act was very wicked, and those people committed a very disgraceful deed.'

The words of M.M. Fuze
(These ruffians were Funwayo kaMpopoma of the Luthuli clan and his people, who committed that disgraceful deed. They killed Derek and his two sons, and performed a very filthy act by stripping the married women stark naked, and sticking them with spears and driving them out of their homes to starve.

Such acts of violence are an indication of a person's character, for what sort of person is he? And so it was. Even a person who did not know Funwayo or who had never set eyes on him, would soon see that he was a person of no worth, a mischief-maker and a doer of bad deeds. He was a ruffian all his life. He had his own area adjoining that of his brother Nondenisa kaMabhangwini of the Luthuli clan. Nondenisa's area still exists under the control of his grandson, Mdungazwe kaMakhongolo, but that of Funwayo was cut up and abolished. And his son, Ndlela, since deceased, was also a person of no worth, being a scoundrel just like his father, and greatly addicted to liquor. He deprived his brothers of everything by his acts of robbery. Ndlela's son committed an act against the law, as a result of which his chieftainship came to an end and he was placed under the control of others.)

Izindaba ZaseNatal 47 (cont.)
'The Queen ruled over all the land of Natal. Some of the Boers were content under her rule and are still here. Pretorius and many others determined to depart. They again surmounted the Khahlamba [Drakensberg] and met their own people who were living there below the great river [Vaal river] and who were independent at that time, having left the Queen's territories.

After a time it was reported that those people wanted Mpande to attack the English in Natal. It was also reported that they were oppressing the black people with whom they lived. The English Queen said, "Those Boers are my subjects, even though they have left my territory. I will not permit them to rule themselves and act in this way." She sent an army with an officer, and it fought the Boers and defeated them, and the Queen ruled over that country. Pretorius and some of his people crossed that great river [Vaal river] and settled beyond it and ruled themselves. The Queen left them alone there, and even now the Boers rule themselves there (at the time of publication of this book by Bishop Colenso in 1856).'[2]

Izindaba ZaseNatal 48
'The country below the great river was occupied by a large population of Sotho people before the arrival of the Boers. Before the arrival of these black people, in ancient times that country and other countries thereabouts were occupied by Bushmen. These diminutive people cannot be educated because they do not associate with other people. They have no cattle and no cultivated lands, and they live by stealing people's cattle and on buck which they shoot with poisoned arrows. They do not live in communities, and if separated by only a river, they cannot understand one another because they speak a language of clicks. They live in caves in the mountains, in which they paint pictures of cattle and people mounted on horses and other such things, but these caves have now been abandoned.'[3]

Izindaba ZaseNatal 49
'The Queen has since abandoned that country below the great river [Orange River Sovereignty, abandoned in 1854]. Recently there was fighting between the Boers and Mshweshwe (Moshesh), and the Boers were defeated. They then invited the Queen's High Commissioner at Cape Town to come and reconcile them with Mshweshwe (Moshesh), which he did, but I do not think they will live in peace permanently.'

Izindaba ZaseNatal 50
'The Queen by her word confirmed what had been done by her officers in respect of the affairs of Natal. She appointed Somtseu (Shepstone) to be an official to advise the Government on affairs relating to the black people. She gave instructions in the strongest terms that the officers were to act justly, so that all her people should live happily under her rule.'

Izindaba ZaseNatal 51
'It is well that the black people should know that the Queen will certainly not allow them to be treated unjustly, deprived or despised, or to be driven forcibly from the lands on which they are settled by her permission.'

Izindaba ZaseNatal 52
'The Queen wants her black people to be taught the trades of the white people, so that they may have a stake in the country like the white people.' [Bishop Colenso explains the reasons for taxation.]

The end of *Izindaba ZaseNatal* by Bishop Colenso.

Chapter 43

THE ZULU KINGS

Accounts of the sons of Senzangakhona kaJama kaNdaba kaPhunga kaMageba kaNkosinkulu kaNtombela kaMalandela kaMnguni.[1]

Senzangakhona's eldest son was Shaka, born under unusual circumstances [*umhlola*][2] if one studies carefully the story of his birth, which was brought about by the desire of Nandi, the chief daughter of the Langeni chief, the desire for Senzangakhona as a boy still in the seclusion of circumcision, the ardent desire that he should come together [*hlangana*][3] with her, although they did not know each other, never having seen one another before, with the result that she became pregnant with Shaka, as the maiden daughter of an important chief, Makedama kaMgabi [alias Mbengi] of Nguga [his residence].

And the name which they gave him was also significant, because it meant that he would violently disturb [*shakazisa*] all the tribes.[4] His mother, Nandi, having desired Senzangakhona so passionately, her love for him came completely to an end when she got pregnant; the love between Senzangakhona and Nandi completely cooled down, and there was no further interest between either of them. Both being members of chiefly families, they could do as they pleased without hindrance by anyone. Is it not right that one should study intently the significance of that incident? And understand the meaning of his name? And what he would do on earth?

Shaka as a grown man had a good, strong, well-built body; he had good buttocks, well shaped but not large, unlike Mpande who had very large buttocks. He had a large body, but it should be borne in mind that he was a man of war and not sedentary. He was brown in colour, unlike Mpande who was black, and as a king, glossy with good food. He did not get stout like Mpande, but remained muscular and powerful. Both Shaka and Mpande were of the same size as Dingane; the one who was tall was Mhlangana.

Having described about Shaka to the last detail, it would be right to think about the names of Dingane, Mpande and Mhlangana, and their interpretations, for all three are quite clear. The name Dingane means that he would suffer from want [*dinga*] and that he would not die in the country of the Zulus. It means that he would have bad habits which would make him a wanderer throughout the country, and in the end come to a country which was not his own, where his bones would be buried. On the other hand the name Mhlangana means that his grave would be in a reed swamp [*umhlanga*], in an open place and not at home.

Finally the name Mpande indicates that he would be the root [*impande*] of the Zulu nation. It tells us that if he had not existed, the Zulu royal house would never have been here. And why? Because it was only he who produced progeny. All those that I have enumerated have no child to greet them in the land.[5] And why? It was deliberately done – there is no other reason.

'FIRST FRUITS'

> And so he [Mpande] entered into the kingship:
> The tall column of smoke
> Which appears with his feathered head-dress
> Between the English and the Boers.
> He who crossed afterwards,
> Of the line of Shaka;
> The swallow that lost itself in the sky.

[The rest of this chapter, subtitled 'The Reign of Mpande', constitutes Chapter 46 in this edition; the greater part of Fuze's Chapter 46, 'Offences for which the penalty was death', which is quite out of place, has been transferred to Chapter 14.]

[Extract from Fuze's Epilogue]
Senzangakhona, whose name means 'we do so for a reason', begot Shaka who would violently disturb [*shakazisa*] all the tribes, and Dingane who would be in want [*dinga*] and die in the uBombo range, and Mhlangana who would be killed in a bed of reeds [*umhlanga*], and many others; and Mpande whom he said would be the root [*impande*] of the Zulu royal house. He [Mpande] produced Cetshwayo who would be slandered [*cetshwa*], and he [Cetshwayo] produced Dinuzulu whose name means that the Zulus would be made tired and exhausted by him. Dinuzulu begot Maphumuzana and Nyawana, saying about them that 'I have found the feet [*inyawo*] that will walk for me, and the one who will give me rest [*phumuza*] from the burden I have borne for so long'. Thus a name reflects its owner like a person's shadow.

Chapter 44

THE FIRST FRUITS CEREMONY

All the Zulu kings celebrated the ceremony of the first fruits [*umkhosi*]. The month to celebrate it was Ngcela (December). The *umkhosi* started at the beginning of the new moon. On that day all the regiments assembled and not a single person remained at home except the sick, old women and children, and perhaps old men who were helpless and unable to walk. During the celebrations the moonlight was very bright.

No one would eat the new crops until that day, the day on which to start doing so because the king would have already done so. Should there be anyone who had eaten the new crops before the king, he would

'FIRST FRUITS'

be fit for death because he would be overshadowing the king, and casting an evil influence or shadow [*isithunzi*] over him. Even if it was a bad year with however great a famine, no one would dare to kill himself by doing that.

That day of the *umkhosi* enabled the emaciated to get food and recover from their emaciated state. No one is hungry on that day, and when they return from the *umkhosi* they will be able to feed on green mealies and sugar-cane as they please. There is one thing in particular that they refrain from eating before having partaken of the medicines of the first fruits ceremonies, and that is the pumpkin. Meat is not wanted by anyone, having surfeited even the dogs. Beer is now as plentiful as the water used for scraping skins.

Such was the system of government of the Zulus, that at the *umkhosi* the king gave details of all matters concerning his administration; the regiments that have been given permission to marry and the particular regiment of girls that has been allotted to them in accordance with the wishes of the king and his advisors.

When the king tastes the first fruits [*ukweshama*], the medicine men set out to procure the wild gourd [*uselwa*] from other places, together with the medicines required for the ceremony. The medicine men treat the king by making him sip medicine from his fingers [*ncinda*]. He rises before the sun; by the time it emerges he has long since been waiting for it. As soon as it appears, he menaces it with his battle axe [*imbemba*], attempting to sever it into two, but before doing so squirts at it [*chinsa*] with the powerful medicines of kingship.

The soldiers are then ordered to seize a savage bull, and when they have done so, they force it to lie down: and then the king comes and gives it a blow with his axe [*imbazo*],[1] and the soldiers shout 'Ji!' three times. The meat of that bull is not boiled, but all of it is roasted in the cattle kraal and smeared with charred medicines [*insizi*] by the medicine men. These strips of meat [*imibengo*] blackened with sooted medicines, as soon as they are roasted on the embers, the medicine men throw them into the air to be caught before falling to the ground, and the young men share them among themselves. They are not eaten if they fall to the ground; otherwise all that meat must be eaten.

The following morning all the soldiers are given an emetic to drink as soon as they get up, because of having eaten that meat. They are now required to vomit in one place into a large container, and as soon as they have vomited into it, the medicine men take it and mix it with their medicines in accordance with their knowledge, and use it to make the national coil [*inkatha*] to be kept in one of the royal residences such as Siklebeni.

Should there be a severe drought, the headmen and elders meet together and go to the capital to confer with the king about it. One day the king will summon the nation, select a number of oxen from the royal herd, and proceed to Emakhosini [the place of kings] where Senzangakhona, Jama, Ndaba, Punga and Mageba are buried, and there propitiate the ancestral spirits and offer praises and represent the nation. All those oxen are slaughtered. And after that no one need lack for rain, because no matter how dry it may have been, it rained whenever the kings were propitiated.

It sometimes happened at the *umkhosi* ceremony, when there was a full attendance and the Zulu kings were mentioned, that a large green snake [*inyandezulu*] would suddenly appear standing straight up in the air. And when the Zulus beat their shields and saluted, '*Bayete*', it would disappear and be seen no more.

The *umkhosi* ceremony cannot be held without first going to Emakhosini to request *ubukhosi* [the essence of kingship which pervades the place],[2] so that it may be brought back by strong young men and conveyed to the capital. Sacrifices of cattle, prayers and praises must be offered at Emakhosini, for if this were not done, the *ubukhosi* could not be carried because of its weightiness, even if there were twenty young men. No one can force the office of the Zulu king and become the king without the permission of the people, after they have first sought the consent of the Zulu kings where they repose.

During the time of Dingane's reign the *umkhosi* was celebrated to its fullest extent. When it was held, the whole nation was assembled. The people would come district by district, and Manyosi kaDlengezele of the Mbatha clan would arrive with the people of his district, a very tall fellow with a shiny countenance and long spindly legs, and with a stomach right out there. He would arrive provided with beer contained in large vessels; and meat and maas and ground nuts and all the delectable foods. If a hungry person approached him with salutations, he would be given an ample supply.

But Manyosi was not only an important person, but also an expert at composing songs, and also an orator. Many of the songs sung were composed by him. His main occupation was as a gluttonous eater of food, being able to finish off a whole goat alone. When a goat was slaughtered, it was boiled until it was so well cooked that the bones fell away from the flesh, leaving the meat by itself. When his servant took it to him after it was cooked, he gave him water to wash his hands, and after that he ate. When the food was placed before him, he repeatedly put his hand into the pot and took helpings of meat, now cooked to a messy mass. He would consume the whole animal, leaving only the ankle bones and the head. After this the servant took a large pot of beer, lifted it up, and held it for him to drink. He would drink while the servant held it in position, and only when the dregs remained would the servant remove the pot from his mouth; and after he had eaten, Manyosi always lay down flat out.

On the occasion when 'the cord was severed' [*ukugqabuka kwegoda* between Dingane and Mpande] and people realised that Manyosi was now deserting Dingane, they said when talking alone among themselves, 'Hau! Even Manyosi has deserted Dingane now and follows Mpande like the rest of the people. Wo! *Sobohla Manyosi*!' [It will subside, Manyosi!], referring to his large stomach which could consume a calf as a python swallows a bushbuck even with its skin. This very same Manyosi eventually begot a son whom he named Sobohla, a sarcastic comment on the remark that people used to make to him, saying '*sobohla Manyosi*!'

[The rest of this chapter is transferred to Chapter 46, 'The Reign of Mpande'.]

Chapter 45

MPANDE'S GOOD CHARACTER

Mpande was a very good man, and no other of the sons of Senzangakhona ever equalled him in goodness, for he behaved with humbleness and not arrogantly like the rest. His name means that he was the root [*impande*] of the Zulu nation. He was born a good person, without the wicked heart of his brothers.

There was one brother, the next in order of birth after Mpande, who remained behind [on the battlefield] on the occasion when Shaka went to war against Soshangana kaManukuza, the great chief of the Nxumalo clan, [the brother] who died before he had taken a wife, but he had his own home, Mfemfe. That brother of Mpande's was Nzibe. He was the son of Songiya,[1] a princess of the Hlabisa clan. When Mpande was given permission to marry by his brothers, he married Nozibhuku, a girl of the Nxumalo clan, and installed her in the Mfemfe home where she bore him Hamu, whom he appointed Nzibe's heir. That house still exists to this day.[2]

This prosperous and fruitful king, Mpande, on assuming the kingship, built his capital at Nodwengu, which had two entrances. His chief councillor was Masiphula kaMamba of the Mgazini clan of the Zulus. This headman had a violent temper, without pity for anyone, and if anyone committed a fault he was instantly put to death. Owing to his violent temper he came to be feared even by the king and by all the royal children. One day Masiphula in a rage killed his own son, Ziyankome, on suspicion of having slept with a girl of the royal household [*umndlunkulu*], for no one was allowed to have relations with these girls. Because of that son of Masiphula having been a companion of the same age [*intanga*] as the royal children, it caused great grief to them all, even to the king, but they could do nothing to Masiphula.

This headman liked killing people, and of course he was greatly feared, even by the king and all the royal children, for he was like a wild animal. On the occasion of the king's demise,[3] Masiphula wanted to follow the custom observed by Shaka when Nandi died – to bury people alive in the grave and to kill people to accompany the king. But he was unable to do so because there was now Cetshwayo, who when he heard the rumour that Masiphula ardently desired to do so, sent word to Masiphula to the effect that, 'People are not to be killed, for how will we rule if all the people are killed off'. This message pricked Masiphula, for he had yet not killed people; although I cannot positively assert that there was not a single person laid down as a sleeping mat for the king, from what I know of that fellow Masiphula!

The Nodwengu king [Mpande] naturally did not want to kill a single person as far as he was personally concerned, for he loved all his father's people. One thing was painful to him: when he killed his only remaining brother, Gqugqu, who remained with him when Dingane killed off all the sons of Senzangakhona. Gqugqu was spared because he was still a very small boy, and Mpande escaped because of the pleadings of Dingane's chief councillor, Ndlela kaSompisi, who said to him, 'sir, why kill this idiot of your father's?', saying so because Mpande had a growth on his leg which prevented him from walking properly.

The killing of Gqugqu happened in this way. He also had a home of his own and a following who paid allegiance to him. It happened one day, while he was paying his respects [*khonza*] at the king's residence like all of them, as he was sitting in the assembly he sneezed, and his followers exclaimed, '*Thuthuka Mageba*' [Good luck Mageba], according to the custom observed when the king sneezed. This was taken as an indication of a dispute arising between him and his brother Mpande, and he was put to death. For the word '*thuthuka*' is not used to any member of the royal house but the reigning king, being similar to the word '*bayete*'. Even though Mpande put Gqugqu to death, it brought no joy to his heart to kill the only surviving son of his father, of the so many begotten by Senzangakhona. Well! Seeing that he was not an absolute ruler but subject to the influence of others, it could not have happened that Masiphula kaMamba would have maintained absolute silence, he who liked to kill people so much! Gqugqu suffered death on this narrow pretext.

Chapter 46[1]
THE REIGN OF MPANDE

[Extract from Fuze's Chapter 43]

The formation of his regiments indicates the cycles of his reign, the king of Nodwengu [Mpande's capital], and the number of years of his reign. He began to rule on Feb. 14, 1840, on the day when he was installed by Potolozi [Pretorius], the Boer, on the banks of the Mfolozi, and continued until 1872, when he passed away. This shows a reign of thirty-two years.

His first regiment was (1) the Sangqu (maShishi), followed by (2) the Ngulube, then (3) the maPhela. And then he formed (4) the Thulwana (maMbhoza) from the age group of his own children. Then followed (5) the Nkonkoni, then (6) the Ndlondlo, then (7) the Dlokwe, then (8) the Mbonambi (Nkonyan'ebomvu), then (9) the Nokenke (the Zulu nation being split [*kenkesile*] at the time when there was trouble between his sons. After the Nokenke he formed (10) the Khandampemvu (Nqak'amatsh'ezulu), then (11) the Ngobamakhosi at the time when there was unity between father and son, the son having grown up and the father grown old.

There are also many female regiments, but I am not as well acquainted with them as with those of the men. There are those of Shaka, Dingane and Mpande, and those of Cetshwayo. There are the Ngcoshe, Nkehlela, Khwani, Mvuthwamini, Sitimane, Ngcugce, Thiyane. There are many regiments of girls but I am not well acquainted with them.

MARRIAGE BY ORDER

Regiments of girls were formed for the purpose of marriage by order [*juba*] to those of the men; and at the time of marriage by order, it was the king who decided which female regiment the male regiments should marry. No young man could marry as he wished without the king's permission. And no girl could marry in accordance with her own choice even if she was in love with that young man. As females mature much sooner than males, it caused great sorrow for a girl to be parted from her lover when girls were allotted to an old regiment, which the king had ordered to marry. It was this evil rule that caused the downfall of the Zulu nation, because of the arrival of other races which were watching and prying with the intention of destroying the Zulu kingdom, the European territories [*esiLungwini*, particularly Natal] harbouring large numbers of people who had fled with their sweethearts and who were now desirous of living together with their friends. It was this that brought about the downfall of Zulu rule.

Since its introduction by Shaka, it lasted until the overthrow of Cetshwayo by the white people in 1879. The trouble began when Cetshwayo was defied by the Ngcugce regiment of girls, which when about to be allotted in marriage to the Ndlondlo regiment, refused and said, 'A single string of beads does not meet' [Zulu proverb: it is unsuitable, if not impossible], so saying because their lovers were to be found in the Dloko and Nokenke regiments. It was an astonishing thing for girls to dictate to the king, before he had made his decision.

[Extract from Fuze's Chapter 44]

When the girls were allotted in marriage [*juba*] to their respective male regiments, many girls married themselves to the same person because of not wishing to marry undesirables whom they did not like; and in consequence some men of good standing [*abanumzane*] used to produce large families in a day [in no time!], and establish much larger homesteads than other people. But some insignificant nonentities [*abafokazana*] were unable to get even a single girl in marriage.

Concerning the lobolo for a girl married by order of the king, it was not a great difficulty for the father of the girl that she could marry a man before he had produced the lobolo cattle. And why? Because when a girl threw herself upon a man whom she did not know and whom she had not met, the father generally called for the cattle after the girl had given birth to a child by that man, the father receiving one or two cattle, and eventually six or possibly ten, a long time after the girl had become a married woman.

It was not a treasure [*igugu*, here in the sense of a value or a matter of great concern], that the lobolo cattle for a girl should be ten [as laid down in the Natal Native Code]; in the majority of cases it was only six, which was regarded as sufficient for a child's head [and Fuze is referring to times a hundred years ago!]. It was good for people to meet together and come to terms between themselves [as to the number of cattle].[2]

At times if a girl gave birth to children without lobolo the father of the girl would come and carry away one of the children as a replacement for his daughter, an arrangement acceptable even to the husband, who might then produce the cattle and recover his child.

Chapter 47
THE REIGNS OF THE ZULU KINGS

At the outset, before the account of the years of the reigns of the Zulu kings who were responsible for forging this great nation together, it is right to remember that all kings are supported by God, and it is He who appoints and supports them. If sovereignty is not supported by Him, it is dead, and authority non-existent. Also if a king rules without the realisation that he is a servant, a mere headman to represent his people to God, his kingship is non-existent and dead, because God will soon bring it to an end.

Shaka, who moulded the sovereignty [*ubukhosi*] of the Zulu nation, ruled for only ten years.[1] For when he defied the Owner of all peoples for whom he ruled his people, his rule was terminated and God roused his brothers to kill him, advised by their father's sister, Mkabayi, who said that Shaka had exterminated his father's people, killing them for nothing and for no reason. And so Shaka died at the end of those ten years. And Mkabayi installed Dingane in his stead.

Dingane succeeded to the position of his brother Shaka. But he committed acts even graver than those of his brother. He said he killed his brother because he behaved like a madman towards his people, but he went on to do things far worse than those by his brother; and so, having ruled for only six years,[2] he was condemned by God who brought his years to an end, and he died. In his place He appointed his brother Mpande.

Mpande succeeded to the position of his brother, Dingane. He, Mpande, endeavoured to respect God, knowing that the people he ruled did not belong to him, but to his father [Senzangakhona], saying so as if he knew that his father was responsible for them to God.[3] Mpande ruled until he was given milk to drink,[4] having ruled for thirty-two years,[5] ruling well.

Mpande was followed by his son Cetshwayo who succeeded at a time of disturbance and disorder, on account of a dispute having arisen between Mpande's two sons: Mbulazi, son of Monase daughter of Mntungwa of the Nxumalo clan, one of Shaka's concubines from his harem [*umndlunkulu*], given in marriage by him to his brother Mpande to beget for him; and Cetshwayo son of Ngqumbazi daughter of Mbhonde of the Zungu clan.[6] Mpande in his old age said that he well knew that Shaka had provided the lobolo for him to marry Ngqumbazi and said that she was his chief wife, but by the time his sons grew up, he had forgotten the action of his elder brother, Shaka, and that his heir was Cetshwayo of the house of Ngqumbazi; and he began to recollect a statement to the effect that his heir was Mbulazi, who was the son of Shaka's concubine. He also forgot what had been said by the Boers who had installed him, who questioned him when he was on the way to attack Dingane, as to who his heir was. He pointed out to them Cetshwayo, and they then cut his ear and made a mark by which he could be identified.

This is how this dispute between the princes began. Cetshwayo himself tried with all his power to dissuade his brother Mbulazi from quarrelling, but there was Mantantashiya, Mbulazi's younger brother, who did not agree at all that there should be no fighting, and who finally spoke privately to Mbulazi,[7] saying, 'You are afraid'. It was painful to Mbulazi to be called a coward. And so they fought. The iziGqoza [Mbulazi's faction] were defeated, beaten by the uSutu [Cetshwayo's faction]. Many of the royal princes died on that day, and it caused great grief to the king, and he hated Cetshwayo. That was the end of the remark, 'Makhasana [Mpande] is satisfied, who saw his rams butting one another'. This remark was greatly resented by the whole of the

Zulu nation, as it led to the belief that it was the king himself who had set his sons on to fight.

At the time of his passing, the king was no longer kindly disposed towards Cetshwayo, because he had killed his children at Ndondakusuka. According to the habits of people, when the king reached old age and was living with his young wife Nomantshali who bore Mthonga, because of living with her he no longer associated with his old wives. Here arose a rumour that Nomantshali was a witch [*umthakathi*] who possessed love medicine that seduced the king from his home and family,[8] and transformed him into a fool. It was said that Nomantshali possessed evil medicines with which she could cause beards to grow on the married women [the king's wives], even a forest of hair. This accusation of the king's wives was eventually accepted even by the king's children, which strengthened the conviction that this wife was a witch. From this conclusion of the royal family arose the suspicion that since the king was now under the spell of Nomantshali, he now wanted to nominate Mthonga as his successor after him. This talk caused strained relations between Mthonga and Cetshwayo. Now the Prince (Cetshwayo) developed a hatred towards his mother [co-mother], Nomantshali, and wanted to kill her.

One day the Prince, in his hatred of his junior mother, Nomantshali, sent Bhejana kaNomageje of the Cebekhulu clan, his servant of the same age as himself, and others, to fetch Nomantshali from Nodwengu and bring her to him. And so Bhejana and his body of men went to Nodwengu to fetch the king's wife. On arrival he reported his business to the king, who expressed astonishment at who could demand that Nomantshali should leave the king and go to him. When Bhejana told him that she was demanded by Cetshwayo, he protested strongly against such monstrous events. Following these protests, Bhejana's men rushed at the woman and seized her with their hands and ordered her to leave with them, but the king held on to her and refused to release her. They then snatched the king's sugar-cane that had been placed in the house, and came out and ate it. They stressed that they were adamant about the king's wife. After a time the king spoke and said to them, 'Allow her to rest a little, and I will release her and hand her to you to take away'. So they quietened down for a while, and then he allowed her to go, and they took her away and then put her to death.

The king then cursed the Zulu nation saying, 'O! O! Cetshwayo does this to me! O! He has brought down the canopy of heaven upon them to entomb them all. They will have cause to remember the foolish iziGqoza,[9] for not one of them will remain alive on account of what they have done to me!' And so when Cetshwayo came to the fore, he was faced with this curse. In addition, his father had been in communication with the whites, condemning Cetshwayo as a bad man; and the whites believed Mpande and now regarded Cetshwayo as a man with a most violent temper. And the coming here of the whites to request the installation of Cetshwayo as his father's successor, was arranged by the Zulu nation in consequence of the unsatisfactory situation in which Cetshwayo was placed. There was also a rumour current among the Zulus that Mbulazi did not die at Ndondakusuka, where the battle of the dispute was fought. There were those who declared most emphatically that he was taken under the protection of the white people, and that he was still alive. It was for this reason that it became necessary for the white people to come and install him (Cetshwayo). It was not because the Zulu nation was unable to install its king for itself.

For these reasons the accession of Cetshwayo to the position of his father was not fortunate, and he had to contend with a dangerous atmosphere. No sooner had he succeeded and reigned for five short years, than in the sixth he was destroyed by the white people.[10] For even his installation by them, as subject to the conditions imposed by them, was not legitimate; it was simply a device to ensnare him. And there were interfering whites[11] with a sweet tongue, who were in the habit of approaching the dignitaries of the Zulu nation with attractive talk of what they could do for themselves if they agreed to demolish the royal house, saying that they could all rule as chiefs [independently] and no longer be subject to the rule of one man only, who oppressed them mercilessly.

At that time Hamu, the son of Nozibhuku, the daughter of Sotondose, the chief of the Nxumalo clan, was starting a dispute which no Zulu person could understand, for had not Mpande taken his [Hamu's] mother of the Nxumalo clan in order to restore the house of his [Mpande's] brother, Nzibe, at the Mfemfe residence where he [Nzibe] had been the head? The Zulu people were therefore at a loss to understand Hamu's claim, for not until all the sons of Mpande came to an end in the succession of birth in the house of Songiya [Mpande's mother], could Hamu come in.[12]

Chapter 48
THE REIGN OF CETSHWAYO

This king was good natured and well behaved, and loved all his father's people. When Somtseu (Shepstone) arrived to install him in his father's place, this son of Sonzica warned him very seriously not to kill people. But Cetshwayo personally was very fond of his people, and concerned himself very much with them. And it was for this reason that the Zulu people sided with him at the time of the dispute between him and his brother, Mbulazi. Even the chief headman, Masiphula, who was possessed of a terrible temper, supported Cetshwayo because he had more confidence in him than Mbulazi. Mbulazi was very proud of being a royal prince, whereas Cetshwayo always showed respect towards dignitaries, addressing them all by their surnames.

The maMbhoza (Thulwana) regiment on its formation had great prestige, as it contained many members of the king's family – it followed the second [third] regiment formed by Mpande after his accession. The first he formed was the Sangqu (maShishi), followed by the Ngulube, then by the maPhela, then by the Thulwana (maMbhoza, Injobo kaShikana), the age group of the king's sons, Cetshwayo, Mbulazi, Shonkweni, Mantantashiya, Ziwedu, Siteku, Dabulesinye, Somklwana, and also Hamu. This regiment of the king of Nodwengu [Mpande's capital] attained great distinction on its formation because it was the regiment of the royal princes who were of the same age as the prince who would eventually succeed to his father's position.

This regiment had some very bad habits from the time of its formation, which troubled the people. Whenever it met a man travelling no matter where, it would detain him and demand that he perform the sex act with his wife[1] before going on. It was a most evil practice in the country, but it was not done if Cetshwayo was among them because they respected him, he being the senior of them all. Their chief officer was Sogweba kaMasekwana kaMenyelwa of the Ntuli clan. He also did not like what was being done by his regiment, and it was not done when he was present, or if the Prince Cetshwayo was present.

A bad report became current concerning Sogweba, which caused him to flee and cross over here into Natal, having heard that the king was angry with him and sought to put him to death. And so he fled with all his following, after which Mnyamana kaNgqengelele kaShenge of the Buthelezi clan was appointed in Sogweba's place, to become the general of the Thulwana regiment.

When the Zulu dignitaries heard of such bad habits of the maMbhoza regiment, making fools of men by forcing them to dance and play children's hopping games, and also to sing the songs of their wives at the time of consummation of marriage, which was wicked, they reported to the king, expressing amazement and saying that the practice would bring about the downfall of the nation. The king ordered it to stop, and it was stopped immediately.

The food for the princes was served in separate vessels, the maas in one dish, the meat in another, and all the food for the princes. When it was served and taken to them, Cetshwayo, to show his disregard for them [his superiority], would leave and go to the stream to bathe, accompanied by his servants, and his brothers would have to wait for his return before they could eat. It seems that he was their superior in strength also, when they wrestled.

Cetshwayo did not begin to rule on the death of his father, he began when his father was still alive, at the time of the enrolment of Thulwana regiment. He was king over his brothers before he was installed as king to rule over the Zulus. For even they who had been iziGqoza who had fought for Mbulazi, as soon as they returned to Zululand became uSuthu loyalists altogether. For there were many important people who had been iziGqoza who had remained in Zululand, not having crossed over [after Ndondakusuka] into Natal, because they did not wish to be ruled by a white government.

There were many occasions on which friction arose between Somtseu and Cetshwayo when he was still prince and not yet king. The first of which I know was the occasion when Somtseu visited Mpande to request that the princesses, sisters of Mkhungo, be allowed to go to their mothers, Monase and Masala, the mother of Sikhotha, who were living near Pietermaritzburg under Ngoza kaLudaba of the Majozi clan, Somtseu's chief headman. One day [on the occasion of this visit] Somtseu, accompanied by Ngoza and Zashuke (a headman under Ngoza and a son of Mbeswa of the Ngubane clan), together with the followers of these two headmen, went to see the Zulu king, Mpande, to assist these princesses, Bathonyile and others, for the king to agree to send them to Natal, where their brothers were, Mkhungo and Sikhotha. Ever since Somtseu's arrival the king had been very pleased. Somtseu therefore went up to the royal enclosure [*isigodlo*] to speak to the king, accompanied by Ngoza. Well! Seeing that the king does not live alone but always surrounded by attendants, as Somtseu was discussing the matter he had come about, assisted by Ngoza on some points (because these royal ladies were living at his own residence), the attendants were conveying every word to the Prince Cetshwayo.[2] And so it happened that one day Cetshwayo summoned his uSuthu supporters before Somtseu.

Now just listen! The Zulus arrived, the mighty warriors of the maMbhoza regiment, dressed in full regalia, together with the Prince who was wearing a feather head-dress [*ubuthekwane*] similar to the one he wore at the battle of Ndondakusuka. And the maMbhoza fellows performed their dance. The king was seated in his small wagon which was pushed by hand. All the dignitaries were gathered together, including the chief counsellor Masiphula, and Ntshingwayo kaMahole of the Khoza clan, and Sekethwayo kaNhlaka, and many other prominent persons.

As the maMbhoza began to reach the climax and to shout, 'Iya! Ehe! Cover them with dust! Insignificant little fools! Subdue the enemy!', the Zulus began to approach Somtseu and his retainers, wanting to repeat the Piet Retief affair of Mgungundlovu. Now Mpande's praises were heard.[3] 'Gxoboshe [the pulveriser], he who was late to cross of the house of Shaka, the swallow that gets lost in the sky, the tall column of smoke that appeared with a feather head-dress between the English and the Boers.' Mpande shouted to stop it. 'Hau! Hau! What's this, Ndlamvuzo [Cetshwayo]! What are you doing?' Cetshwayo did not reply to his father, he only exclaimed, 'I could die here and now completely!' And the maMbhoza responded, 'We could all die completely!' It was then that Masiphula shouted to stop them, and to express astonishment. He was followed by Ntshingwayo who also shouted to restrain them, and by other dignitaries. And then the maMbhoza stopped and stood completely silent.

It was then that Cetshwayo questioned Somtseu, saying, 'What was your object in going to see the king in the royal enclosure? What did you go to discuss?' Somtseu narrated the matters he had discussed with the king. And when Somtseu had spoken, the Prince said, 'Hail I have heard what you have to say, and I wish Ngoza to come out in the open, for him to tell us what he was talking about in the enclosure'. As Ngoza was about to come out into the open to speak, Somtseu turned him back and refused to allow him to speak. He realised that it was a pretext to kill him.

The situation now became very serious, as the maMbhoza began to infiltrate among Somtseu's people, so that each would have a victim to kill. But the Zulu headmen called for order, realising that it would be a repetition of the Piet Retief affair. And it was then that the son of Sonzica [Shepstone's father] came out with 'Ha! You son of Mpande! Do you imagine that I am here alone? What are you thinking of doing to me? The death wail that would mourn for me will come from yonder (pointing towards the north as he spoke). Do not imagine that I am travelling alone.' The Zulus were brought suddenly to a stand of complete silence, and those who had infiltrated among Somtseu's people began to move out. This was the saving of them. They were surprised to see the Zulus moving away from them, not yet knowing the reason. As the Zulus moved away, one man of Zashuke's group had soiled his trousers, and it was running down his legs.

Approximately I should say it was the year that Mshukangubo was killed by Sidoyi kaBaleni kaNongcama, the chief of the Enhlangwini Dlamini, during the troubles of 1858.

When Cetshwayo was installed as king in 1872, Somtseu attended accompanied by a small force of whites and his headmen. He returned with two hundred bullocks presented to him by Cetshwayo.

But what was painful to Cetshwayo at that time was the action of Somtseu, who, after returning home from the installation, proceeded onwards to attack Langalibalele, in spite of the fact that he had warned him [Cetshwayo] not to shed blood. It was this which made Cetshwayo ask, 'Why should my Father, after coming to warn me not to kill, leave me and proceed straightaway to kill the old man who is my "father"? He should allow Langalibalele to come to me and not to be driven into exile.' Those words of the Zulu king found no way into the heart of Somtseu. He went on to kill Langalibalele in 1873.[4,5]

The fact was that Langalibalele himself was frightened and did not want to go to Zululand, on account of the trick played upon him by Dingane when he summoned his elder brother, Dlomo, and then killed him for no reason. It was this that made the son of Mthimkhulu [Langalibalele] go and eventually reach Mshweshwe's brother, Molapo, and hide himself in Basutoland, in the belief that he [Molapo] was the most suitable person with whom to seek refuge; whereas it was he who when Langalibalele reached him, handed him over into the hands of the whites, and Langalibalele suddenly and unexpectedly found himself under arrest, thinking that he was hiding with a friend, whereas he was seeking refuge with a wild animal.

Chapter 49
CETSHWAYO'S FIRST FRUITS CEREMONIES

Even though Cetshwayo died in disgrace, he was not so much at fault as to deserve it, because of his good character and government. Even in the matter of killing his junior mother, Nomantshali, he did not think he was doing wrong, because he believed the report that was current throughout the Zulu nation that she possessed magic medicines obtained from the Tongas. Nomantshali did indeed do strange things which had never been done previously among the Zulus, for on one occasion when the king was unable to attend the first fruits ceremony [*umkhosi*], she came forward to represent him, dressed like a king [*inkhosi*, pl. *amakhosi*] and carrying a small shield, to represent the Zulu nation.[1]

As far as I am personally concerned I could swear to it that Cetshwayo was a good man who loved all his people, but he disliked favouritism and partiality, and would accuse a wrong-doer openly, preferring not to act unpredictably. The acts committed by his brother, Hamu, of killing people in temper and for no reason, indicated that his brother had designs on the kingship. But such claims were puzzling,[2] for how could he have them seeing that all Mpande's own sons were still alive?[3]

All first fruits ceremonies held by Cetshwayo were celebrated at Nodwengu, his father's capital, doing so to demonstrate to the people that he was still Mpande himself, and that they had no cause for disunity. For indeed it is customary for each chief to hold the ceremony in his own residence. Cetshwayo's capital was at Ulundi, but he did not celebrate there. One only was held at Mlambongwenya, the home of his grandmother, Songiya [Mpande's mother], which was the residence next in rank after his father's.

The junior regiment, Ngobamakhosi, had no quarters at the capital, Ulundi; they were quartered with the Thulwana regiment only, together with other regiments. Whenever the Ngobamakhosi was at the capital, it had to share accommodation with its seniors, the maMbhoza (Thulwana), who were men with wives. Therefore, when a wife visited her husband of the Thulwana, a junior of the Ngobamakhosi would have to sit outside and wait whilst the iMbhoza [a member of the maMbhoza regiment] discussed private matters with his wife, and eventually there developed a rift between the maMbhoza and the Ngobamakhosi.

For these youths of the Ngobamakhosi would call out to the men of the Thulwana when it was dark and now time to sleep, 'Hurry-up, old chap, we want to come in and sleep'. Matters remained as such for some time, until these men complained that they were being treated with disrespect by these youths. And so eventually there arose a quarrel between the maMbhoza and the Ngobamakhosi, and they began to hate each other.

One day shortly before an *umkhosi* celebration, Hamu, the king's son, quarrelled with Sigcwelegcwele kaMahlekehleke, the commander of the Ngobamakhosi, disputing these very regimental matters, for Hamu was an iMbhoza and Sigcwelegcwele an officer of the Ngobamakhosi. They quarrelled violently, and Hamu accused Sigcwelegcwele of treating the maMbhoza with disrespect. They quarrelled violently, both of them, and finally threatened to get even with one another at the *umkhosi* celebration. Well, then, seeing that Hamu was a royal prince and Sigcwelegcwele also a man of rank, a commander, what was to happen? It was perfectly plain that nothing would be right at this *umkhosi* ceremony.

And indeed it was that *umkhosi* of 1878 that was so disastrous. When the Ngcugce regiment of girls was ordered to marry into the Ndlondlo regiment, it refused saying, 'A single string of beads does not fit the neck' [Zulu proverb; it is not fit or right], so saying because it wanted to marry into the Dlokwe regiment where the girls' lovers were. This became a very serious matter to the king, because such a thing had never happened to the Zulu kings, that a king should be defied by a troop of girls.

On the day of the *umkhosi*, the two regiments, Thulwana and Ngobamakhosi, sprang at each other. It had already become evident that they would fight, having been indicated by Hamu, son of a king, and Sigcwelegcwele kaMahlekehleke, commander of the Ngobamakhosi. A fierce fight ensued. But the youths of the Ngobamakhosi were stronger than the men of the maMbhoza, and generally got the better of them. When Hamu saw what was happening, he called out to the maMbhoza, 'Do not beat them with sticks, stab them with spears'. As soon as this was said, the men were saved, and they cut down the youths with their spears. The situation became very grave, and it was clear that Hamu's business was to advance his claim [to the kingship].[4]

Although it was the young members of the Ngobamakhosi who had been stabbed, the people were greatly enraged because of the many casualties on both sides, a matter that caused great pain to the whole of the Zulu nation. When Sigcwelegcwele heard that he was being condemned by all the elders and his death being demanded, he fled into the bush and remained there for some time. But when the king realised that this was a conspiracy to kill Sigcwelegcwele, he sent word to him to look after himself carefully. At that time the Zulu nation was in a bad way. And there was also the unfortunate affair of the Ngcugce girls.

And so one day the king sent some servants to give a fright to the daughters of Sigwili, who had remained at home without paying the slightest attention to the proclamation of the king that they should wed. But those servants killed those girls, notwithstanding that the king had given no such order. Now listen, for it was loudly reported in Natal that Cetshwayo had killed off all the girls in Zululand, an utterly false statement, for it was only those two daughters of Sigwili that were killed, and not by the order of the king.

This was the year that Gebhuza (F.E. Colenso, Esq.), son of Sobantu,[5] visited the Zulu king, wishing to see him and hear for himself on the spot these matters which were being spoken about the Zulu king. (Gebhuza was in fact a lawyer). Gebhuza made this visit shortly after the fight between the two regiments, which was such a serious affair. According to Hamu, the number of warriors of the Ngobamakhosi stabbed and killed by the Thulwana approached 800 or more. This caused strained relations between Hamu and his brother, the king. It was resented by the king also because he saw that it was these soldiers killed by the Thulwana who would fight for him in the European war which was about to be launched against the Zulus (for indeed he had already heard about it). As for Hamu, he no longer met the king, and he eventually committed the act of deserting to Natal, secretly inviting and encouraging the whites to come and kill the king, even though he had not the slightest claim against him.

And so one day when Hamu had firmly resolved to kill the king, he approached Nkabanina of the Hlabisa clan (an iMbhoza with whom he used to eat), and tried to induce him to kill the king, cutting short for him a spear into a dagger [*isinqindi*] with which to stab him, as Mbhopha had done to stab Shaka. But it distressed Nkabanina to kill his cousin, for of course, Mpande's mother, Songiya, was born in the Hlabisa clan. When Hamu saw that it was impossible for Nkabanina to commit this evil deed, he fled from Zululand into Natal.

Chapter 50
MAGEMA'S VISIT TO ZULULAND

On the 15th July, 1878, I Magema M. Fuze, left Ekukhanyeni with my brother, Ndokweni, and Nani Mncube kaMashiwulani (who was an iMbhoza of the Msiyana clan), and Mbungumbu kaFunwayo of the Mayaba clan of the Hlubi tribe, who was living with the Hlubi at Ekukhanyeni.[1] The four of us left in the afternoon and set out for Zululand, very desirous to visit the Zulu king, Cetshwayo.

In the course of our journey we were very desirous to pass by my father's home to the south of the Mzinyathi [Buffalo river] and below the emaHlabo mountain. After passing by there, having seen our relatives – our mothers and brothers – we crossed over to the other side of the Mzinyathi and made for the home of Matshana kaMondisa, chief of the Sithole clan.[2]

On our arrival at Matshana's, as soon as he heard that this Magema was the son of Magwaza who lived at the drift recognised by the Government as the Mzinyathi drift [river ford], he was greatly pleased, because of what happened a few years previously when his cattle crossed over into Natal during the winter when the water was low, and the herd-boys of Magwaza suddenly saw a large herd of cattle which they recognised as Matshana's. On hearing the account from Magema, Matshana gave him a three-year-old steer, saying that it was a gift to his father to thank him for what he had done during his lifetime, in driving back his cattle after they had strayed unknowingly into Natal. The beast was driven to the home of Magwaza in Natal.

We remained at Matshana's home for about three days, during which we were well treated. There were two princesses [*amakhosazana*] married to Matshana: Bekiwe, who swore by the king when taking an oath, she being the younger sister of Shingana [a son of Mpande], and her sister. They treated us with great kindness, being delighted to meet people who had come from Sobantu and who were on their way to the king, their brother [in Zulu kinship] at Ezinhlendleni. The work which they were doing was making eating mats, having girls working under them.

On the fourth day after our arrival at Matshana's, we left and went forward to the king in Zululand. We slept several nights on the way, and then arrived at Ezinhlendleni, in a large tract of thorn country, at the Nhlungwane river where the water is unpalatable, and was it hot!

We arrived accompanied by two elders, Mfunzi of the Xulu clan and Nkisimane of the Luhlongwana clan, emissaries employed by the king in communications with Sobantu.[3]

On arrival, for we arrived in the morning about the time of 10 o'clock, when the cattle were beginning to disperse after the slaughtering, our presence was reported to the king by the chief officer, Siwunguza kaSilawane, the brother of Gawozi, an important man of the Mpungose clan. We had already been questioned about where we had come from, where we were going to, and what was our business, and then we were presented with a massive joint of beef and given a room for our accommodation. The king was there at Ezinhlendleni, where a residence was in the course of construction, to be known as Mayizekanye, later to be changed to Olandandlovu. The meaning of these two names can be readily understood. The one, 'Mayizekanye', means, 'It doesn't matter, let it come even though we don't want it' [referring to *impi*, army or war]. That name was quickly changed, because when it was heard in Natal, it caused great concern. It was then said to be 'Olandandlovu', which means, 'It is from here that the elephant is fetched', the elephant of course being Cetshwayo. For at that time it was well known that the white people were about to invade Zululand, to fetch the king, and to abolish Zulu rule.

At Ezinhlendleni we stayed for ten days, and then left on the next day. I saw the king and spoke to him two days after my arrival. Cetshwayo was a pleasant person with a good presence, handsome, concerned for all his people, and extremely kind in his speech. I recall the days I spent there at the home at Ezinhlendleni, when cases were brought before him of quarrels among his subjects. He tried them justly, and in the majority of cases reconciled the disputants, not wanting them to quarrel, and brought them together by directing that each should produce a goat to be slaughtered, and that each should come to the same homestead and eat it together.

On the day when I bade him farewell, he directed his two emissaries, Mfunzi and Nkisimane, to accompany me and see me safely to my home in Natal, and to pay his respects to his Father, Sobantu. He said they were to go with me by way of Gwadi's place where there were some sheep belonging to the king, and that they were to select two ewes which they were to drive and deliver to my mother. They travelled by the way of the official, Makelekehlana of the Dladla clan, where there were some cattle belonging to the king, and there Makelekehlana presented me with a bullock which I slaughtered. So that I should not hunger on the way, the emissaries sought out food for me from the king's stock, to provide me with food until I reached the country of Natal.

While I was speaking with the king in the cattle kraal, he said to me, 'Do you know that the white people are coming here? But we Zulus will not run away from them. As for me, I do not pay homage with this little island of Senzangakhona's, I pay homage only on my own account to the white people. I know that that will be the day when the country is torn to pieces.' I first heard from the king on that day that the white people were about to invade Zululand.

And so we came away and returned to Natal, travelling according to the king's instructions. We returned by the way we had come, calling at my father's home at Mahlaba to the west of the Mzinyathi, where we had previously crossed. Our mothers, for joy, slaughtered a beast for the king's emissaries, Mfunzi and Nkisimane. We stayed there a few days resting, and then went on with my mother's two sheep which she had been given by the king, making for Pietermaritzburg and Ekukhanyeni and home and Sobantu.

Chapter 51

THE EUROPEAN INVASION

It was not long after this that a serious incident occurred in the household of Sihayo kaXongwa of the Ngobese clan, he being a man of rank. Two of Sihayo's wives were caught committing adultery, but Sihayo himself was not at home at the time, being at the capital with the king. When the women realised that they had been caught committing an offence for which they would be put to death, they fled and crossed the Mzinyathi into Natal, the boundary between Zululand and Natal. But as they fled they were followed by Mehlokazulu kaSihayo and his people on horseback, in a rage because his mothers had been caught committing a base act during his father's absence. As they started to set foot on the boundary of Natal,[1] Mehlokazulu had arrived and put them to death on the spot [*khona lapho*, right there], and gone back. Well! As he was killing them, the Natal Government spies posted at the drifts saw it all, and it was reported immediately. And then relations became strained and difficult between the Zulus and the Government, in accordance with those words the king had spoken to me: 'The white people are coming to Zululand, but we Zulus will not run away from them'.

PRELUDE TO WAR

The European invasion of 1878 [1879] was not brought about because Mehlokazulu killed his mothers on Natal soil, but because it had already been decided to destroy this savage government adjacent to an enlightened one, because the Natal Government feared that one day it would be suddenly and unexpectedly attacked.[2] It seems that the white people had in mind the events and bad deeds of Dingane.

But Cetshwayo on his part was a man of good character who would never have committed acts like those of Dingane. And why? Because he was strongly critical of the action of Dingane in taking Piet Retief unexpectedly by surprise, after he had recovered his cattle from the Molefe Sotho chief, Sigonyela, and of all the evil acts of Dingane in killing the king, Shaka, and all his brothers, killing them by surprise treacherously. Cetshwayo abhorred such behaviour, and he never killed a single one of his brothers.[3] He liked them all, and respected them. Even as regards his brother Mbulazi whom he fought at Ndondakusuka, he [Cetshwayo] did not wish to quarrel with him, but eventually did so because of his persistence, he [Mbulazi] being encouraged by his brother, Mantantashiya, who was a scoundrel and who very much wanted to fight, notwithstanding that he saw that the Zulu nation had moved to one side [in support of Cetshwayo]. Eight royal princes died [in that conflict].

Following the killing of the two wives of Sihayo, the High Commissioner at the Cape, Sir Bartle Frere, ordered the king to send Sihayo and his son Mehlokazulu to him to investigate the case and ascertain why Mehlokazulu had committed such an unheard-of act as to come and kill people on the borders of the country of Natal. When that message summoning Sihayo was received by the king, he gathered together the Zulus and asked them what they had to say in the matter. The Zulus divided into two opinions, the majority saying that it was not right for Sihayo to be sent to the white people; but many of the leaders thought that he should be sent to them. Then the king assembled the regiments and asked them for their views. They all objected unanimously, saying that it was not right that Sihayo should be handed over to foreigners, because no subject of Natal had been killed, only those of Zululand. It then became clearly apparent that the white people were determined to wage war against the Zulus. And such was the position.[4]

At that time the whites were continuously negotiating with the leaders of the Zulus, promising them that if they agreed to support them in abolishing Zulu rule, they [the whites] would give them chiefdoms

BRITISH INVASION

and each chief would rule for himself, thus doing away with the people being ruled by one man who would always be putting them to death. The Zulu leaders at that time were in constant communication with the authorities in Natal.

The Government was insistent in its demands for Sihayo and Mehlokazulu. At that time Sobantu was defending Cetshwayo, and demanding to know what wrong he had done that he should be attacked. But there was no longer a loophole for the Government to act otherwise, because it had already decided to invade Zululand.

The month of December [*Ngcela*] came, and the last year was completed. In the year 1879 [1878] the British army mobilised to cross the sea and proceed to Natal and head for Zululand. In November [*Lwezi*] it crossed over into Zululand.[5] And then it began to fight and to kill the people of Sihayo, for this happened when only the old men and women were at home, the young men having assembled at the king's capital. As soon as it attacked the people, the news reached the king's capital that the European army had invaded Sihayo's country. At the same time it also crossed the Tugela at Dlokweni [Bond's Drift].

When this happened Cetshwayo dispatched two columns, one with many troops to the Mzinyathi and the other to Dlokweni. All the forces directed to the Mzinyathi in the direction of Sihayo's country were placed under Ntshingwayo kaMahole of the Khoza clan, and the headmen under him, Vumandaba kaNteti of the Khumalo clan and others. The headmen in command of the column proceeding to Wombane at the Nyezane river were Phalane kaMdinwa of the Mkhwanazi clan and Mabilwana ka-? of the Mdletshe clan.

At the time of darkness at the new moon [*inyanga ifile*, dead moon] by which time the European army had passed through Sihayo's country and camped under a very small and very steep hill known as Sandlwana, on the day of the death of the moon, they having heard that the Zulu army was on the way to meet them, rose early and made in the direction where the Zulu army had camped a short distance beyond a small hill known as Mashushana. When the whites saw it [the Zulu army], they did not hesitate but immediately opened fire. And it was then that the Zulu army arose, listen to me! and moved forward with great speed. In fact the whites were there to provoke the Zulus to fight. When the Zulu army arose, it made with great speed towards the white army, and when it saw the white army advancing, it retreated rapidly, for the whites were all mounted on horses. There were the Dlongwas (the Hlubis of

Mbunda), the Ngwanes of Ncwadi kaZikhali, and some Christian black people from Edendale, together with the whites, all mounted.

It [the Zulu army] went away from there, and proceeded past the small hills of Mashushana, and came into view of Sandlwana towards the west. By then the soldiers had formed up beneath Sandlwana. When the Zulus came into the open, there was a volley from the whites below Sandlwana, and they fired the cannon four times. Then the Zulu warriors lay down, and then rose and rushed forward at great speed. A commander who was encouraging his men, standing on a prominence to the east of Sandlwana, on seeing his men lie down when the cannon thundered, shouted, 'You did not say that you were going to lie down!'[6] When the warriors rose, they entered the tents of the soldiers, and there they stabbed the soldiers who were then exhausted from firing their guns. There they killed and destroyed the European army that was there.

While this was happening, a large section of the army had made its way towards Mangeni, where old men and invalids, women and children were hiding. After they had mopped up there [at Sandlwana], the Zulus crossed over into Natal to account for the whites who were hiding in a building at the drift of Jim Rorke. The whites in the building amounted to about thirty only,[7] but they fought until dawn the next day against the Zulus, who were determined to get in and kill them. But they [the Zulus] had disregarded the king's orders that they were not to cross over into Natal, and so they withdrew and returned to Zululand, in accordance with the king's orders which had been advised by Sobantu, who had said, 'since I know that the white people are determined to defeat you in the end, it would be best for the king not to cross into Natal, so that I will be in a strong position to defend him [answer for him], for you will never succeed in defeating them'. So Sobantu advised the emissaries from Zululand, Mfunzi and Nkisimane, who had been sent to him when the war was in progress.

The Zulus died in heaps there, killed by those white men in the building. They went on killing them until dawn, and in the early morning the Zulus withdrew defeated, leaving behind heaps of dead on the ground. The other column that had proceeded to the Nyezane river was blocked by the whites at Wombane for four weeks. At the end of those weeks, there arrived a large force under the command of Lukhuni (Sir Evelyn Wood). It broke through from the upper side and established itself at Nkambule at Dudusini.

Chapter 52
ZULU DEFEAT AND DESTRUCTION

At the end of those four weeks 'Jininindi, fearless black one with the heart of a lion' [a praise of Cetshwayo], mobilised and directed his army to the European army at Dudusini. He placed it under the command of Mnyamana, his chief councillor, and he warned it not to attack the whites in their encampment, but when they were outside. It then went and made for Dudusini where the European army was encamped.

On the following day it fought. The Zulu army ignored the order of the king that they were not to attack the whites where they were entrenched, and attacked them in their defences at dawn after having surrounded them. The whites resisted them and shot at them, and the Zulus failed to effect an entrance. Other forces from other places heard what was happening and came forward, but they all failed. After a time the Zulu army broke and fled.[1]

After the whites had driven off the Zulus, they came out of their defences and followed them, making for Mahlabathini with the object of capturing the king. When they came near to the capital, the king sent a message to them expressing a wish to tender a fine of certain white cattle known as 'Inyoni kayiphumuli'. But the Ngobamakhosi regiment refused to give them up, saying, 'The white people will be able to eat them only after we have all perished', and they killed them all and ate them. And while the whites were bathing in the Mfolozi river, Zibhebhu kaMaphitha shot at them and killed a number, but they replied, 'Even though you shoot us, we will come to you tomorrow'.

And on the morrow Lukhuni (Sir Evelyn Wood)[2] directed the army to the capital where the king was living. The Zulus met it there, and there was a fierce battle. But the prowess of the Zulus was of no avail there, and they were scattered. The king disappeared into the thorn country with a small body of warriors, which was later sent back because it was feared that their presence would lead to the king's tracks being soon perceived. The king went on with Mkhosana kaZangqwana of the Zungu clan, who was a headman, and with a number of servants, and with his household. He made for the Ngome forest in the area of Mnyamana kaNgqengelele, the chief councillor, and entered his residence which was in the forest, and stayed there in hiding.

The white people sought for the king for a long time, but the Zulus refused to disclose where he had passed by or where he was in hiding.

Eventually the general, Sir Garnet Wolseley, arrived. He entreated Mnyamana and the other headmen to inform him where the king was in hiding. And then Mnyamana, realising that it was useless to continue concealing the king, disclosed where he was, and then sent the information to the king that he had told the whites. The white people then went to that homestead in the forest, when they had heard that the king was living there. On finding him, they took him and the people with whom he had been staying, and brought him to Mahlabathini.

One day the Zulus gathered before Sir Garnet Wolseley, and the king spoke about all the matters which he wished to address to his people. He directed Zibhebhu to guide the family and the Prince Dinuzulu. On the day on which he was taken away, Sir Garnet Wolseley addressed the Zulus as follows: 'You see him today, and you see him for the last time; you will never see him again'. And Jininindi [Cetshwayo] was taken away and taken into a ship and taken across the sea and deposited in Cape Town.

At that time Sobantu was protesting strongly, asking on behalf of Cetshwayo what wrong he had done to the English that he should be so punished, seeing that he had never crossed [the Tugela] to attack them. And so the Zulu affair was discussed, now in the hands of the high authorities in England. In the end Cetshwayo was vindicated, and it was found that he had done no wrong. He asked for permission to go to England to see Queen Victoria. He was allowed to go over together with a few of his headmen. He summoned Phosile kaManyose of the Mbatha clan and Ngobozana kaVukuza of the Mpungose clan, for Mkhosana kaZangqwana of the Zungu clan was already with him in confinement at the Cape. Gebhuza kaSomtseu (Mr H.C. Shepstone) was taken to act as interpreter when he spoke to the high officers; also an attendant to cook for him and one to dress his hair. He went overseas[3] and saw Queen Victoria and Prince Edward and the dignitaries who rule England, and all the important people. And they were also greatly pleased to meet the Zulu king. It was said that he was to return to his country and rule his people as he had previously ruled them.[4]

When the king arrived at the Cape he found Somtseu kaSonzica there to meet him, having come from Mgungundlovu (Maritzburg).[5] It was here that he was delayed, and meetings were held to induce him to agree to the land between the Mhlathuze and the Tugela being retained by Natal.[6] The king objected to this. But the whites insisted, saying that unless he agreed to this, they would never return him to Zululand.[7]

RESTORATION

When he saw that many days had passed with the whites still insistent, he simply had to agree, though not with his heart, but he hoped that he would be able to make further representations when he arrived in Zululand. And so they brought him back to Zululand.

On reaching Zululand he sent Mfunzi and Nkisimane to report to Sobantu that he had arrived in Zululand. The message which Sobantu delivered to those emissaries was as follows: 'I am very grateful; I hope to come and see him during the winter. But I say to you, be always on the alert and do not think that those who brought about the downfall of the king are satisfied. They will continue to destroy him. Be careful and watch after your own interests, for only a bird can build its own nest'.

In fact these words of advice came to pass exactly according to the mouth of Sobantu. Regarding the promise that he would go and see the king in the winter, he made it at a time when the king was about to pass away (for the king was restored in the spring). As to the warning that they should watch after their own interests, he spoke the truth that they would destroy the king unawares, he being under the impression that having been restored by the Queen, the matter was settled; but it was not so with those who were digging game pits for him to fall into.

Chapter 53

RESTORATION AND EXPLUSION

Somtseu was sent to convey the king back to his home. All the people of Zululand rejoiced seeing that their king had been restored by the Queen. It was a great pleasure for them to see Somtseu arrive in Zululand, and there was joyful celebration amongst the people.

After Somtseu had departed, having brought back the king, all the dignitaries came forward, and the king's capital was constructed. There was a military force that had been sent out by Ndabuko and the uSuthu loyalists to go and attack Zibhebhu kaMaphitha of the Zulu clan.[1] That expedition was a grudge of hatred between the uSuthu and the Mandlakazi. Its despatch was not told to the king, it was hidden from him. When he heard of it, it had long since left. He sent to recall it, but by then its vanguard had already reached the Mandlakazi homesteads, and there was nothing to be done about it. That expedition engaged the Mandlakazi at Msebe, and the Mandlakazi routed the uSuthu who were there, only a few escaping.[2]

And subsequently, the son of Maphitha with his lopsided little head-ring advanced on Cetshwayo's capital, Ulundi, which had recently been built but not quite completed. Well then, who was aware of it?, seeing that there was a large number of people gathered together there, rejoicing to see their king restored by the white people, after having given up hope of ever seeing him again. Here were gathered all the Zulu leaders who were the pillars of the nation. Beer was not in question, being brought continually by the women. Meat was not needed by anyone, being plentiful. And this force was not anticipated by anyone.

A woman happened to go out to relieve herself, and whilst there she saw Zibhebhu's force advancing with speed on Ulundi – indeed it was very early in the morning. When she returned she shouted and raised the alarm: 'Here is the Mandlakazi army coming!' As soon as the men came out they saw it. Ah! Here is the army coming indeed! The king, on hearing that this was the truth, dispersed his servants to collect the soldiers together in one place. But where were they?, seeing that some young men had already risen when it was still dark to escort their sisters back to their homes, who had brought the food the previous day. Others were still asleep, drunk from the beer brought by their sisters. Hau! It was terrible beyond description.

At this stage the king dispatched Godide kaNdlela of the Ntuli clan, who was the headman in charge of the Bulawayo residence, to collect the soldiers to form up in one place in their companies, and if possible for the whole army to come to him, because the king wanted the whole army, once assembled, to retire into the bushveld so as to be in a better position to fight; but it became difficult to do this because the Mandlakazi were now at close quarters. As Godide was arranging his force, the Mandlakazi were already there, and they stabbed him and he died. At this stage the uSuthu were numerous, and they tried to make a fight of it, but by now the whole of the Mandlakazi army had arrived, and the uSuthu broke and fled.

When the king saw that all was lost, he mounted a horse but it fell with him. He again mounted it, and it nearly fell, and so he left it, picked up his arms and went off. When Hayiyana kaMaphitha saw that the Mandlakazi were near, he called to his boy bearer [*udibi*] saying, 'Bring those weapons, boy, bring them here. This is what we desire, to die with our king'. He called for a pot of beer and drank, and then went out armed, hearing the Mandlakazi now nearby.

EXPULSION

The Mandlakazi killed all the dignitaries, about forty men who were the pillars of the Zulu nation. Those who were not there were Mnyamana kaNgqengelele and Ntshingwayo kaMahole. A man among the leaders who fought fiercely was Vumandaba kaNteti of the Khumalo clan, who stabbed the Mandlakazi until they lay in heaps, until they finally overcame him by showering him with a flight of spears, and he fell, the great warrior of Nteti.[3]

The king, after leaving his home, went away and entered a small bush and sat down beneath it. But here were the Mandlakazi following and killing the fugitives. On seeing the king under the bush, they who were still searching, they threw two spears at him, both of which struck him on the thigh. It was then that the king was heard to exclaim, 'Miserable menials, you stab me with spears in my father's country?'. Then they realised that it was the king, and replied, '*Ndabezitha*! (Your Majesty!] We did not know it was the king, we thought it was Ziwedu'. They then approached him and gave him the salute, '*Bayete*!', and sat down. They were two of Somfula's following, one being a servant. By then the king had withdrawn both the spears from his thigh. They sat there for some time and then went back.

As soon as they went back, the king got up and went on. He proceeded onwards until he came to a place where he had herded as a boy, a shallow valley where there was an underground hole in which one could hide, and he remained there until dusk. There he was surprised to meet another fugitive, a man whom he knew well. He, on seeing the king, went to the home of a retainer to obtain a fat bullock, which he slaughtered and prepared a meal for the king. He also obtained a newly woven unused sleeping mat, and prepared a sleeping place for the king.

On the following morning it was reported to certain people that 'the king is here!'

When it became known that the king was still alive, having escaped from the Mandlakazi, the Nkomonophondo regiment belonging to Zwekufa of the Cube clan, mobilised to go and fetch the king. They took him to their old stronghold of the days of Dlaba, the father of Zwekufa, at Manziphambana in the Nkandla forest, where Dlaba had successfully defended himself against Shaka. The Cube camped outside the stronghold and surrounded the king, and loudly announced, 'It is fitting that the Mandlakazi come and take the king now'. And so it was, and the king stayed there in the stronghold among the Cube, who required the Zulu people wishing to see the king to apply for permission from them.

Well then, seeing that Malimati (Sir Melmoth Osborn) was now at Eshowe as the Government's Resident Commissioner, he began sending messages to Sigananda of the Cube clan, requesting that the king be allowed to come to him at Eshowe. But the king did not consent to go to him. The matter remained as such until the arrival of Mr Grant from Durban, requested by the king from Sobantu, saying that he [Sobantu] should find him [the king] a clever European to come and advise him in his affairs and write letters for him if he so wished, seeing that even Zibhebhu had Europeans to advise him.[4] (Zibhebhu had the sons of Mr McAlister assisting him in writing letters and also helping him in the dispute with the uSuthu. Those Europeans were even with the Mandlakazi army when it went to destroy the king at Ondini.)

Chapter 54
THE DEATH OF CETSHWAYO

The arrival of Mr Grant as advisor to the king was a help to Malimati [Sir Melmoth Osborn] in his attempt to persuade the king to come to him at Eshowe. Well then, the king having been persuaded by his adviser, left Nkandla and went to Eshowe. He was placed in the residence of Keke, a member of the Zulu clan by birth, and he lived there at Keke's place.

And so the king lived in that residence with people who served him loyally, but in great distress because he was not in friendly relationship with Malimati,[1] for indeed the king had not expected that he would be under the control of a man like Malimati who was in league with Zibhebhu who had brought about his downfall.

While he was living there, and on the occasion when Malimati slaughtered a beast for him, he began to suffer from stomach pains;[2] and it was then that his doctor who was looking after him, Mbombo of the Nxumalo clan, provided him with the medicine [*amakhambi*, herbal remedies] to be used as an enema at the stream. When he came back he was informed that the daughter of Qetuka [Cetshwayo's wife] was in pain, and he told Mbomba to go and help the wife [*umlobokazi*, new wife]. She then gave birth to Nkongolozana, whose name was later changed to Manzolwandle.[3]

CETSHWAYO'S DEATH

The king's illness became severe, and when he felt that it had got the better of him, he summoned those with whom he lived and charged them saying, 'Mortal illness has now overcome me. Over there is my son, Dinuzulu, whom I am leaving behind to be reported to the Queen. I leave Dinuzulu to rule for me as I have ruled for Mpande, Mpande having ruled for Shaka, Shaka having ruled for Senzangakhona, Senzangakhona for Jama, Jama for Ndaba, Ndaba for Phunga, Phunga for Mageba.[4] It is well that Dinuzulu should take up arms against Zibhebhu, and I will also be there in the midst of the battle, and we will defeat him'. After a few more slight words, the king passed away [*goduka*, go home] to rest in peace from his great tribulation which was a surprise to him, as he had not expected to see it from the day of his birth.[5]

After the king had departed, his body was kept in the room where he had passed away [*khothama*, bow down]. The house was sealed and plastered with mud so that no smell was apparent to those going about outside.

Then differences arose between Malimati and the uSuthu people [Cetshwayo's supporters]. Malimati wanted the body to be buried right there, but the uSuthu refused, demanding that it be taken to Mahlabathini to the other kings. Owing to these differences a quarrel arose between them. (The body had been placed in a short coffin and arranged in a sitting position, in accordance with Zulu custom).

When the day approached for the removal of the body, the uSuthu sent word to a Christian convert whom they knew, Hlabangana, who owned a wagon, and borrowed it from him to transport the body. When the wagon arrived, Malimati had already assembled his force of traitors [*amambuka*]. A fight took place, but the traitors were routed, and the uSuthu drove them into a pool of the Amatikulu river where there were many crocodiles. But realising that it was a long way to Mahlabathini, they came to the conclusion that it would be better to bury the body at Nkandla, where it would be among people who would respect it and give it great care. And so they transported it with the wagon, and buried it at Nkandla near the home of an important man there, Luhungu of the Shezi clan, who with his children have watched over it even until today.

Chapter 55
THE BIRTH AND CHILDHOOD OF DINUZULU

During the days of Mpande's reign while Cetshwayo was still a prince [royal child], some years after the battle of the dispute between the royal princes which was fought at Ndulinde hill at Ndondakusuka, and at which Mbulazi and eight of his brothers were killed, Mpande put Msweli to death, an elder of the Nzimeleni clan. (I am unable to give the reason for his death because this execution was not a weighty matter. All I know is that the king gave orders that none of Msweli's children were to be killed).

And so it was done: Msweli was put to death and all his children were brought away. Among them was his daughter, Somakoyisa, a short stocky girl, pretty too, with a light complexion. On arrival she was taken to the upper part of the royal enclosure [*isigodlo*], but the Prince Cetshwayo fell in love with her and eventually sought the king's permission to marry her, and the king consented.

But there were the daughters of men of higher rank than Msweli whom the Prince had already taken in marriage for the purpose of producing progeny. Among them was the daughter of Sekethwayo kaNtuzwa, an elder of the Mdlalose clan, who had been installed as the chief wife over all the others. Now when these wives gave birth, they either usually lost their children or produced daughters only. On the Zulu people expressing astonishment and wonderment at the cause of this state of affairs, the diviners were approached and asked what was the cause. The diviners gave a cause which none had expected. (The people had expected it to be the work of witches). They reported that, 'This is the work of the Zulu kings, who say they know that among the royal Zulus progeny is not wanted. Senzangakhona had many children, but Dingane killed them all. After that there was Mpande who had many children, and there they were being killed off completely at Ndondakusuka. The Zulu kings say that in future there will be born one prince only, so that there will be no more quarrelling and killing.' (So reports Nyosana kaMadwala.)

Hau! The words of the diviners caused great surprise to the Zulu people, and were likened to a portent [*umhlola*]. After a period of peacefulness, the daughter of Msweli became pregnant and bore a son. They named him Mahelana-who-comes-from-Ondini. At that time the Prince was living below the Mhlathuze at Ndlayangubo in his Ondini-olubomvana residence, not yet having built Ondini [Ulundi] in the Mahlabathini area, which he built when he was king. The people used to go and pay their respects to the Prince at Ulundi, doing so less frequently to the king at Nodwengu. At the time of Mpande's death in 1872, Mahelana was about five or six years of age. Therefore his grandfather had already seen him, but Mahelana's eyes were still too young for him to see his grandfather.

The child grew up until he reached an age when it was fitting for his father to give him a name, and he named him Dinuzulu, saying 'This one is wearied by the Zulus'.[1] And Dinuzulu grew up to become a strongish child.

After him the daughter of Majiya gave birth to a son who was named Nyoniyentaba. He was the second of Cetshwayo's children who was born and lived, after the others who had been born and immediately died.

When Dinuzulu was still a boy of about ten years, and Nyoniyentaba one or two years, the European army invaded the country and destroyed the nation. It was at that painful time that the Zulus began to weary of their king. For when Cetshwayo gave this name to his son, he was giving expression to his very own feelings. And indeed the Zulus promoted and completed all that which had been predicted by Cetshwayo in naming his son Dinuzulu, and in the end they sold him to foreigners because of their weariness of him. If I say they became weary of him, Dinuzulu eventually became wearisome even to his 'grandfather' Mnyamana kaNgqengelele, who, even when the king [Cetshwayo] was removed by Sir Garnet Wolseley and chieftains appointed to control the country after the king,[2] and it was said that he was appointed, objected, saying, 'My chieftainship is finished, which I used to have to rule the Zulus, and that which you now offer me I do not like'. But after a time even he rose against the son of Cetshwayo, Dinuzulu, and in the end his son, Tshanibezwe, hated Dinuzulu to the extent of trying to bring about his death. (I well remember when the Judges came to Eshowe to try the case of the Princes Ndabuko, Shingana and Dinuzulu, when it was alleged that Dinuzulu had killed a young son of Mnyamana's named Madweledwele; and Tshanibezwe kaMnyamana lied to bring about the condemnation of Dinuzulu).[3]

Chapter 56
THE DEFEAT OF ZIBHEBHU

When the king, Cetshwayo, was passing away at Eshowe, in a farewell message he said, 'I am now going, but I am not the first to whom it has happened. I am leaving Dinuzulu. In my rule I have ruled for Mpande, and he ruled for Shaka, and he for Senzangakhona, and he for Jama, and Jama for Ndaba, and Ndaba for Phunga, and Phunga for Mageba.[1] You are to report to the Queen that I have left Dinuzulu. And I say to you, Dinuzulu, as soon as you have buried my body, mobilise the Zulu nation to attack Zibhebhu and fight against him. You will defeat him, for I will be in the midst of my army.' When the king had finished his words, he passed away.

At the time of the death of Dinuzulu's father, Dinuzulu was a boy of about thirteen or fourteen years of age, clever and with the qualities of the young of the Lion. And so it happened that as soon as the king was buried, Dinuzulu rushed off and hurried to the Boers. Well! The Boers were very pleased about this, because they had already been entreating the king [Cetshwayo] to allow them to help him with a force to fight Zibhebhu. When Dinuzulu arrived among the Boers, they assembled and took him and mounted him on a white horse, and appointed him king in his father's place, and he was accorded the royal salute, '*Bayete*'. And the Boers spoke [in justification] saying, 'You all know that his grandfather, Mpande, was appointed by us'.[2]

No sooner had a few days passed than the son of Cetshwayo mobilised the army, summoned the Zulus and the Boers, and made straight for Tshaneni where Zibhebhu was in position. He stationed the Zulus in front, and the Boers followed behind. And there the Zulus fought with Zibhebhu.[3] When the Mandlakazi effectively forced back a horn of the uSuthu, the Boers fired heavily on the Zulus, firing indiscriminately on both the uSuthu and the Mandlakazi. Then 'the calabash and its contents were shattered', and there was utter destruction.

In spite of the strength of the Mandlakazi ['great strength'], the uSuthu drove them back with a long thrusting horn. As the entire stock of the nation's cattle were now in the possession of the Mandlakazi, the uSuthu recovered them in one fell swoop, and killed the people in wholesale slaughter.

Well! Seeing that cattle were no longer known to the Zulus, being all completely in Zibhebhu's possession, they appropriated them even to the scraggiest. It was then that Zibhebhu and the remnant of his followers fled and made for Nyoni to the west of Eshowe, and which had long since been annexed to Natal. And here Zibhebhu established himself with his people, the uSuthu having captured the whole of the Mandlakazi territory.

Owing to the large number of the nation's cattle which had been in Mandlakazi possession, no distribution of them was made, each householder [*umnumzane*] helping himself, the king's sons helping themselves together with the Boers, not to mention Mnyamana and Ziwedu. As for the emissaries, Mfunzi and Nkisimane, who were in the habit of being sent to Sobantu at Ekukhanyeni and to the Government, they also received their share. All the uSuthu loyalists possessed stock on the day. And remember that they had all become poverty stricken!

And so Zibhebhu departed with his people (the few that had escaped being killed), and established himself at Nyoni. After the passing of a few years, he applied to his chief, Malimati [Sir Melmoth Osborn] for permission to return to his former territory. Because Zibhebhu was very acceptable to Malimati (far more so than Dinuzulu), he summoned them both to attend his office together one day [at the magistracy], and informed Dinuzulu that Zibhebhu would be returning to his country. But Dinuzulu, on hearing this, objected most strongly in front of Malimati, within the sight and hearing [eyes and ears] of Zibhebhu, and said he disagreed absolutely that Zibhebhu should come and reside next to him, because he had killed his father. But he [Zibhebhu] insisted on returning to his territory. Because Zibhebhu was a great thing to Malimati, he was given the permission. It was then that Dinuzulu became as enraged as a fire that has to be extinguished with water [Zulu saying], and they parted hostile towards one other.[4]

Well! As Zibhebhu was now puffed up with importance, his small regiment of youths known as 'Inyon' emhlophe' [White Birds] also swelled with encouragement, and he was determined to return because he thought that he could now check the uSuthu. And so he returned to the abandoned sites of his homesteads as he desired.

But Zibhebhu was unable to stop his wrongdoings. And so it happened one day that a number of Zibhebhu's young men quarreled with those of Nkowane kaMsongane, and one of the Mandlakazi died. When this was reported to Malimati, those of Msongane were punished and those of Mandlakazi exonerated.[5]

Chapter 57
THE ZIBHEBHU DISTURBANCES

Being accustomed to doing evil things, Zibhebhu set out early one morning to go and attack the home of Msutshwana of the Mdletsheni clan and a member of the Mbhoza regiment, wishing to kill him. Msutshwana, being unawares, was taken completely by surprise and killed by the troop. The alarm was raised and a message sent to the Prince Dinuzulu to the effect that 'Your "father", Msutshwana, has been killed by Zibhebhu'. Hau! That was a wicked thing for Zibhebhu to do, by killing a man who had not quarrelled with him in any way. Mamonga woSuthu [Dinuzulu's praise-name: 'the core of the uSuthu'] got angry to the point of extinction by water [Zulu saying], recalling what he had said to Malimati, that this man Zibhebhu was a bad character, with a love for fighting and killing people, and that it was not right that he [Malimati] should bring him [Zibhebhu] near him [Dinuzulu] because it was he who had killed his father.

At sunset [*selibantu bahle*, when people look their best], Mamonga woSuthu mobilised his army. Zibhebhu, in doing these evil things, had taken up a position at Ndunu, a hill beyond today's Nongoma magistracy (at that time it was the camp of the Nongqai [Zulu sepoys]). The uSuthu had encamped among the small hills at Ceza (a mountain with open veld on the one side and forest on the other, to the west of Ndunu and the Nongqai Camp).

After the uSuthu had formed a semi-circle, they were addressed and exhorted to action by Hemulana kaMbangezeli of the Sibiya clan. He deployed it [the army] as it was getting dusk, and gave it orders to head for Ndunu and to attack at red dawn. Seeing that the Nongqai Camp was on this side of Ndunu, it was ordered to pass to the side of it, and make straight for Ndunu and Zibhebhu.

And the uSuthu acted accordingly. Shortly before daybreak [*kumpondozankomo*, when the horns of cattle became visible] they arrived at Ndunu. The Magagane regiment was stationed in front, this regiment being mounted and mostly armed with guns, with the Prince in person among them, he being in front of his army. As they reached the Mandlakazi, *satsha*! *satsha*!, firing commenced and continued without cessation from the Mandlakazi, and the Magagane were driven back. Then the uSuthu who were on foot closed in, and there were no more questions. Before it was quite light they starting stabbing, and then the 'sparks' [front flankers] on both sides flashed forward, and it was *dudlu dudlu*, thump thump. When the whole of the uSuthu army reached Ndunu, in a very short space of time it got among the Mandlakazi and destroyed them. Well! How long would it take for the uSuthu to finish them off? It overran the whole of Ndunu hill while killing them off singly. And there was the scion of the Ntombela clan, Siqaka kaNgonela, pursuing and spotting and stabbing them for three days, until he met up with his fellows back at Ceza where they had originally encamped.

When the Mandlakazi were defeated and Zibhebhu saw that they were now routed, he ran off into the undergrowth of the Ndunu bush, and abandoned his horse which ran off on its own, whilst he concealed himself. They searched for him but failed to find him. They killed them off almost to a man, very few escaping. They seized the cattle, the uSuthu fellows, even to the scraggiest. The army then marched back to Ceza from where it had launched its attack.

At that time the uSuthu were living under great difficulties in Zululand, as if they were being exterminated, because the Zulu nation was now divided into sections, a majority having deserted to the Government and now killing their own people.

It was at that time that the Prince Ndabuko [Cetshwayo's brother], together with the dignitaries still supporting the Zulu kingship, sent messengers to Ekukhanyeni, to the lady Dlwedlwe [long staff], the daughter [Harriette] of Sobantu [Bishop Colenso],[1] to report to her that as they were being destroyed throughout the whole country, they intended to migrate to a distant country and abandon Zululand. It was then that the lady [*nkosazana*] became alarmed, and she suffered pain to hear this message. After the messengers had returned, she reported this painful matter to the chief representative of the Government in Durban.

While the uSuthu were still at Ceza, Colonel Mansell, Commander of the Nongqai force, took his force to Ceza. Ceza mountain is forested on the one side, but open on the other. He headed for this famous mountain and made for the forest. When Ndabuko saw the force advancing armed, he sent two men, Ndungunya of the Nxumalo clan, and another, to ask what they had done that they should be killed? No sooner had Ndungunya arrived at Colonel Mansell's force, than they stabbed Ndungunya's companion to death on the spot, and they also stabbed Ndungunya himself and wounded him.

When Ndabuko saw the force approaching the forest, he moved his army to the top of the hill to avoid the white people. As soon as the whites reached the forest they opened fire, thinking that the uSuthu were within the forest. When the Falaza regiment was surprised by the sound of the guns, they urged to go down towards it, but Ndabuko took strong steps to beat them back. Then other uSuthu supporters appeared asking the question, 'What is happening there?', hearing the sound of the guns. The others replied, 'They are shooting at the forest'. It was then that the young men broke away on this side of the Prince [Ndabuko], and hastened to where the guns were firing. When they saw the whites down yonder, they turned back and crossed the Black Mfolozi, crossing over towards Mnyamana's residence, Ekushumayeleni. One glance [at the whites] and the young men changed their minds and turned back.[2]

Chapter 58
THE ARREST OF THE PRINCES

After those events the Governor [*Hulumeni*, actually the Government] came to Ekukhanyeni to speak to the daughter of Sobantu [Harriett Colenso, henceforth the Nkosazana], and she informed him that the Zulu people were in a disturbed state, affected by a spirit of hatred and determined to fight the whites, and he asked her to use the influence of her father who had been on good terms with them.[1]

And so there came Manzekofi [Coffee-water] (Harry Escombe, Esq. Q.C.)[2] to speak to the Nkosazana concerning the distressful predicament of the Prince Dinuzulu[3] and the uSuthu people. On Manzekofi's arrival, the Nkosazana sent for Sobantu's headman, Thwayisa Mabaso kaMqambi, and Bubi Mthuli kaNondenisa, who taught children, including me (Magema Fuze kaMagwaza, the compositor). After our entry into the room, Manzekofi started by saying that it was desirable that Ndabuko and Dinuzulu, the son of his brother, remain in Zululand and not go off to some other country. He said it was desirable that the Nkosazana send a message to Ndabuko to tell him not to run away but to remain in his own country and not quarrel with the Government. And he said that if Malimati (Sir Melmoth Osborn, Resident Commissioner for Zululand) arrested them, they were to offer no resistance. He said that if they did as he advised, he would act for them with representations for them to remain in their own country, but if they ran away and deserted their country and fought, he would not act for them. And so Thwayisa Mabaso and Bubi Mthuli were sent with all speed to Zululand to Ndabuko to deliver the message from Manzekofi.

These two arrived and found the country in a bad way, the Zulu people living on the Boer boundary with these Boers constantly inciting them to break away and come over to them, so that they [the Boers] could then fight the English on their behalf for the restoration of the whole of Zululand. But Ndabuko, being clever and knowing the cunning and deception of the Boers, refused. And so when the Nkosazana's messengers arrived, they [the Zulus] accepted all the advice of Manzekofi, even agreeing to submit to arrest.

But their arrest was a procedure that was followed throughout the whole of Zululand. Down yonder at Mpunkunyoni, Somkhele was arrested, and over there at Ndlayangubo the Mangweni headmen, Lugoyoza, Ndabayakhe, Masekwana and Dlemudlemu were arrested being arrested at the instigation of Zibhebhu kaMaphitha, Hamu kaMpande, Sokwetshata kaMlandela, and Mgitshwa kaMvundlana. Shingana, the son of the king [Mpande], was also arrested down at Mahlabathini, who fought and dispersed them who had confined him in the Hlophekhulu stronghold, Nonkwenkweziyezulu. And so the whole of Zululand was now in a state of confusion. Well, listen then! The situation was bad throughout the country, with uSuthu supporters being arrested and killed, including Somopho of the Thembu clan, Bhejana kaNomageje of the Cebekulu clan, and Somhlola kaMvundlana of the Biyela clan.

I do not know how I could go on counting seeing that the country was in constant turmoil. The whole of the Zulu clan [its most prominent members] was arrested, being kept apart, the one separate from the other, at Malimati's place [Eshowe], to be executed or imprisoned. The regiments that had been fighting abducted boys and girls and their mothers. Only one man of rank came out of prison, Somkhele kaMayanda, because the Khwanazis [his people] got very angry and gathered together a large number of cattle, about eighty, and demanded that he be detained outside [on bail]. All the Zulus were imprisoned at Eshowe in separate rooms, the Princes Ndabuko and Shingana and their child Dinuzulu[3] being given their separate room, the Mangweni headmen theirs, and the others theirs. And that is how they were imprisoned.[4]

Chapter 59
THE TRIAL OF THE PRINCES

In due course the day arrived for the hearing of the court cases. The case was heard against Somhlola kaMvundlana, detained at the instigation of his brother Mgitshwa in league with Malimati, in his efforts to destroy the royal house. This was on the 15th July, 1888, as far as I remember. From Ekukhanyeni went the Nkosazana Dlwedlwe, the headman Thwayisa, and Bubi Mthuli and I (Magema M. Fuze). But I followed when they were already ahead. When I went down to Thekwini [Durban] I chanced to meet Mr W.Y. Campbell, one of the lawyers acting for the uSuthu who had come down from Goli [Johannesburg], and we went together to Eshowe. The lawyers acting for the Zulus [uSuthu] were Mr Escombe who was senior to them all, together with Mr Campbell, Mr Dumat, and Mr Samuelson (Bhembhedu) [R.C. Samuelson] who advised them on the Zulu language, and Mr Burgess who recorded the proceedings in shorthand [by writing short words]. The Judge was Sir Walter Wragg, together with Mr Fannin (Makhanda) and Mr Rudolph (Tshela). The Government Attorney was Mr W.B. Morcom, the Registrar was Mr H.C. Campbell, and the interpreter, Mr S.O. Samuelson. Assembled there were Zibhebhu and his followers, Sokwetshata and his followers, the headmen of Hamu and Mgitshwa kaMvundlane, and all the rest who had come to hear their cases; also Tshanibezwe kaMnyamana who had come to lay a charge against Dinuzulu personally, of having murdered his son Madweledwele.

The cases were heard, the trials lasting about four months. In December the Court broke up, it being said that Christmas was to be celebrated in Mgungundlovu [Maritzburg]. And so they dispersed, leaving Magema alone at Eshowe with the task of teaching the three royal princes their letters A.B.C.D.

At the end of December the high officials returned and resumed their sittings as previously. Now approached the day of the trial of the three princes. Ndabuko's case was dealt with first as he was senior. He was sentenced to fifteen years imprisonment. His brother, Shingana, was sentenced to twelve years, and finally their child, Dinuzulu, was sentenced to eight years. The decisions in these cases were preceded by an announcement by the lawyers on the previous day, by which the uSuthu people were refused and told that they were not to attend the following day, the day of judgement, and that only the princes were to do so because only their cases would be decided. For this reason the

AFTER THE TRIAL

people did not attend on that day, but remained in the houses where they were lodged. The next day soldiers arrived, and whilst judgements were being given, remained outside until the conclusion of the proceedings and the princes had been sent to jail. The Government Attorney began to speak on the previous day and continued until mid-day. He was followed by Manzekofi (Mr Escombe), by then a large number of white people being present. On the conclusion of his address, the cases were decided the following day. After that the Court did not remain long in session, but quickly dispersed, leaving Malimati [Melmoth Osborn] and Mmango kaSomtseu [Arthur Shepstone] and Mr Knight [Zululand Magistrates], to deal with the minor cases concerning Nkunzemnyama and Malumbela and others whom I no longer remember.

After the high officials had departed, Mr Dumat and his wife remained behind, and also Dlwedlwe [Harriet Colenso], until every case had been decided. It was Mr Dumat who took possession of all the documents concerning the cases and passed them on to the Secretary of State overseas. I myself remained there teaching the three princes in the Eshowe jail, and after a time the Nkosazana left with Nondela (Master Eric Colenso, the son of her brother, Mnyayiza kaSobantu[1]), and went back to Ekukhanyeni to the Nkosikazi [Mrs Colenso], and then they all went overseas to fight the cases there, and for the Nkosikazi to visit her brother and his children. And so they went overseas, the Nkosikazi, the Nkosazana Dlwedlwe, with the child Sineke and the son Nondela.

Chapter 60
AFTER THE TRIAL

But I continued to remain on with the princes, teaching them, whilst living with Paul Bontsa Mthimkhulu and Lutsha Ngcobo, the son-in-law of Mfunzi of the Xulu clan, an important messenger frequently employed by Cetshwayo along with Nkisimane of the Luhlongwana clan, to be sent to Sobantu at Ekukhanyeni. And so I remained on at Eshowe employed in teaching. The Nkosazana sent me money from time to time to buy food because there was a severe famine in the land, and in Natal the people were usually able to get relief by buying flour and bread which they were able to do by working for the whites in Maritzburg.

On the 15th January, 1890, we received a message that the princes were required to go and be told of the place to which they were to be sent. We all heard that night that they were to be sent to the island of St. Helena where they were to serve their sentences. Wo! There was confusion among us, speaking in low voices about that. And the next morning I was informed that I was required to return home. I then wrote to Manzekofi informing him of where they were to be sent. He replied stating that the Nkosazana and her mother had already passed the island of Madeira by now. He said it was all right, he had heard. After that I made my preparations for departure. I left Paul Bontsa, of whom it was heard that he would also be going with the princes to St. Helena.

But that case consumed a large amount of Sobantu's money, because all the lawyers engaged in defending the Zulu royal family were paid from his purse, and the expense of sending Mr Dumat overseas with all the documents of the proceedings also came out of his purse, causing the manager of the Bank to be tight in advancing the Nkosazana money, wanting to know where the property of Sobantu's children was going. But because the wife was still alive, he agreed to release it on her word. It amounted to about £3 000, if I am not mistaken.

I went down to Durban and slept at the home of Manzekofi. The following morning I went on to Maritzburg. I did not stay long at home because I went to seek work at St. Alban's College, to Hwanqana (Rev. F.J. Green), who was teaching the children at that school. My work was to teach them to set the type. There was a European in charge of the printing press whose name was Mr Braum, from Italy. There were also two other teachers, Sikweleti Nyongwana and another, who taught them A.B.C.D. and other things taught in schools. I remained at St. Alban's College teaching the children my work of setting type.

People from Zululand were constantly coming to me to report on matters from Zululand from the Nkosikazi [Cetshwayo's chief wife], the daughter of Msweli at the Nengwe residence, and from other parts of the country, and also from Sambane kaNhlongaluvale, the chief of the Nyawo clan. But as I had no opportunity to write, I advised them to meet at Ekukhanyeni so that we could write from there when we were all together. The headman who used to bring all the reports to me from Zululand and who was deputed to do so in Zululand, was Mjwaphuna kaMalungwana of the Shandu clan of the Mbatha tribe.

All the money that came from home was brought to me by people who were brought by Mjwaphuna. I would count it and record it, and then hand it over to those who had brought it for them to take it, accompanied by the headman Mjwaphuna, to a high official of the

Government, for transmission to Dinuzulu at St. Helena. Much money was sent to the Prince, at one time £5, or £10, or £15, or £20, or even more than that, according to their efforts.

They quartered themselves in many households at Ekukhanyeni. Their headman, Mjwaphuna, lived at the home of Bubi Mthuli kaNondenisa, a householder who owned a large number of cattle and also money in the Bank, being also a headman for the people of Mahoyiza.

In the year 1893 the wife of Sobantu died, having lived ten years after the death of her husband, he having died in 1883. She passed away shortly after their return from overseas, where she had gone in the year in which the princes had been sent to imprisonment on the island of St. Helena.

After the death of the Nkosikazi, the Nkosazana Dlwedlwe went overseas again to fight for the Prince. She went with Bubi Mthuli kaNondenisa, travelling via St. Helena. She left Nondenisa's son [Bubi] there and went on to London. There she remained working for the cause of the king's family. And Bubi was now engaged in teaching the king's family, as well as the children, Nyawana and Maphumuzana, born to Dinuzulu, and all others wishing to be taught, including Xamandolo of the Zungu clan and others. And Mthuli remained there and taught them.

The Nkosazana continued to contest the case against the king's family. I think it was on this occasion that she met Mr John Joseph Meek when they travelled together to England, with his wife, Jejese kaNongcangca Zulu. It was a matter of great interest for the white people to see Jejese, for they called her 'Princess' Jejese, which is the equivalent of 'Nkosazana' [chief's daughter].

But Bubi was not happy [at St. Helena] because of the interpreter, Anthony Daniels, who constantly offended him because he did not like to see him being favoured by the princes. This led him to ask the Nkosazana in England to allow him to return to his home in Natal. The Nkosazana agreed for Bubi to return as requested.[1]

I was teaching at St. Alban's College, working with the children every day, and on Sundays dealing with the Zulu business. Then word was received through Bubi Mthuli that Dinuzulu wanted me to come and teach his children, even if I stayed only a short time. I had already been to Zululand to see the Nkosikazi, Msweli's daughter [Cetshwayo's chief wife] at her Nengwe residence, where she had slaughtered a large ox in my honour. I then went on to Eshowe where I saw Khwezi (Sir

Marshall Clarke[2]), who held the position of Resident Commissioner. I then returned to our country of Natal. It was the time when I travelled a good deal through Zululand, eventually getting down as far as the home of Bhejana kaNomageje of the Cebekulu clan.

I did not stay long after those days, for word was received from the Prince Dinuzulu in 1896 that he wished me to come and teach his children to read and write at St. Helena: Nyawana, Maphumuzana, Mphaphu (Victoria), Mshiyeni (Arthur) who was then very young, and Bhekelendoda (Samuel), whom I represented [as Godfather] when he was baptised. Ah then! The Prince together with his two uncles remained in detention, being taught to read and write by the Rev. Barraclough, with Miss Burchell of Rupert's Valley teaching him to play the piano. Father Dr Paul was their preacher and provider of medicines if they were sick. Xamandolo of the Zungu clan assisted Paul Bontsa in preaching, and Nyosana Mthembu and his brother Mkolokoto assisted in all the domestic work.

Chapter 61

THE PRINCES AT ST. HELENA

And so the princes lived at St. Helena, being well treated, having plenty to eat and drink, and having as their doctor, Dr Welby, the son of the local Bishop. Even the Governor treated them very well.[1] The Governor was in the habit of holding dinner parties, and he would invite the Prince and Dr Paul to attend at his residence, where white people of high rank were gathered. On occasions a dinner would be given by the Prince, and he would invite Mr Solomon and Mr Yon, wealthy residents, and I may mention the St. Helenian girls. There would be dancing in European fashion, the two royal uncles sitting as onlookers, together with their brides [*abalobokazi*, new wives]. The girls who danced were Miss Cummings and Miss Cressy and her sister, who were brown in colour, their fathers having been captured as children whilst bathing in the Congo river, and Martha Williams.

To the south of Jamestown there is the large building of Maldivia, where all the Zulus lived, completely accommodated in its many rooms, even the three princes, the two uncles and the son, together with their wives and the two brides [*abalobokazi*], and their servants. After a time an old woman, Mbhodiya, was brought there to serve as the children's nurse and as a midwife.

To the east of Jamestown there is a ridge with the place where the great king of the French, Napoleon Bonaparte, lived under detention and eventually died. Towards the west is the large English church where services were conducted by Bishop Welby, the father of our doctor who attended the Prince and his uncles and all the people when they were sick. Below there on the ridge is a military fort. To the west again is the Residency where the Governor lives, which is known as the Plantation. And to the west again, overlooking the sea, is the large building where the Zulus lived when they first arrived from their country, but they were later removed from it on account of its dampness which caused sickness. There are also a number of stores, but the largest is the one owned by Mr Thorpe, at which the Prince usually made his purchases. Mr Thorpe is not white, he is brown in colour.

The arrival of a steamship is the occasion for great celebrations among the 'ladies' [*amaledi*] of St. Helena. Adorned in their finest clothes, they get into small boats which transport them to the ship which they board, to ask for money. The white people who are travellers leave the ship and disperse to visit and view the island, and the sailors usually go about in groups.

On Sundays it is completely quiet, with people only going to church. The Zulus used to attend the English church where services were conducted by Bishop Welby, assisted by the Rev. Barraclough. It was there that the royal children were baptised: David (Nyawana), Solomon (Maphumuzana or Nkayishana), Victoria (Mphaphu, who was born on Queen Victoria's birthday), and Arthur (Mshiyeni, who was born on the day that the Zulus were about to be sent home, and it was said that Mkasilomo, his mother, would be left behind [*shiya*] to follow later), and Samuel (Bhekelendoda, because the people were being killed off completely by Zibhebhu while they [the leaders] delayed saying, 'We are waiting for the word of the man [*sibheke elendoda*, referring to Mnyamana]. It is said that this building is the oldest on the island.

Chapter 62

MAGEMA'S MISHAP

It was here that I received a serious injury, breaking my right ankle, nearly dying at a cliff which had already accounted for four people, on the way to Rupert's Valley from Jamestown. It was dark (9.30 p.m.). The Prince had sent me to Miss Burchell to ascertain whether a letter had arrived from Miss Colenso in London. It was March, Sunday 7th, 1897, when we were expecting a message to come to say that we were to return to Zululand.

The cliff is very high, and I think that by the time I reached the bottom, I was long since unconscious. When I recovered consciousness and tried to get up, I was unable to do so, and wondered what had happened to me. After a long time I made a great effort to get up. Wo! It was not possible because the bone was broken, the foot lying sideways to the ankle! Well! What was I to do seeing that it was so late and also dark? The only thing for me to do was to lie quiet until sunrise, when, if still alive, I would shout for people to come and carry me. I then said the Lord's prayer, in silence, but before I had finished, I heard people talking above me, whereupon I shouted, 'Hullo!' They replied, 'Who are you?' 'I am a dead man.' Then they came to me. They were two soldiers carrying a lantern, because it was very dark. They came and asked me, 'What is the matter? What has happened?' I told them, as I lay there, how I had been sent on an errand by the Prince. They showed great sympathy for me, and went to report to the Governor at the Castle, where he happened to be in person.

Within a very short time as I lay there, Governor Grey-Wilson arrived with Major Peacock and a file of soldiers. They placed me on a stretcher and carried me away. The pain was so terrible that only death could end it, when the broken bones grated against each other, which caused me to faint, and I only recovered when I was having my boots and trousers removed upstairs at the Civil Hospital.

There I found people with sympathy and compassion for me, Miss Williams and Mrs Ellis. Of course it was no longer of consequence to Dr Welby, for he had long since become the victim of liquor ['*sopi*'], the same that destroyed the Hottentots and has now become a world disease. Three days passed without the arrival of the Doctor, but the nurses tended me carefully. The unfortunate thing was that they were afraid to stretch me, leaving the foot to remain as it was. The pain was so intense that the foot could not be touched even with a finger.

The next day the Prince Dinuzulu sent a request that I be allowed to invalid with him, and to be stretched, because he had a doctor who was qualified to do it, Dr Paul. But the white people refused Dinuzulu's request. He sent three requests, pleading, he together with his two uncles, Ndabuko and Shingana, but the whites continued to refuse. When they were refused, they sent Xamandolo to me to tell me not to agree if they [the whites] wanted to amputate my foot. Such was the situation, and I continued to remain in the hospital for two whole months. After that Dinuzulu came down and carried me away in his carriage, and I went to invalid with him.

When I was with him, I asked to be stretched, even if it meant the breaking of the bone. But he refused strongly, saying that I would die if the bone was re-broken where it had re-grown, and that it did not matter if my foot was useless as long as I myself was still alive on earth. When the white people at the hospital asked the Prince for £6 for my stay in hospital, he firmly refused to pay them because they had refused to allow me to go to him.

Chapter 63

THE RETURN OF THE ROYAL FAMILY

The royal family remained on the island for about nine months after that, with me walking on crutches and not on my own like other people. After those months, Dlwedlwe [Harriett Colenso] arrived with the authority for the Prince to return home – the daughter of Sobantu who had inherited her father's heart which never failed to have pity for those in trouble, distress or sorrow, and for those who had no one to help them. About the 24th December, as far as I can remember, we embarked on a ship for our return to Zululand, celebrating Christmas at sea.

Before the return of the Zulu royal family from St. Helena, the son of Nkosibomvu (Mr Saunders) left them and returned to Natal, his place being taken by Mr Madden to share the work of Mr Daniels as interpreter. They eventually returned with all of us, and Daniels went on with Dinuzulu to the Osuthu residence. He remained there a long time after I had left and returned to Natal. But although he had been with the Prince for such a long time, he eventually quarrelled with him,[1] and then I was surprised to receive a messsage from the son of the king summoning me to Zululand to take up my position, it being said that I was again required. It was the year 1904.

And so I went, accompanied by my eldest brother whom I follow in order of birth, Sifile whom they call Bambada, along with my son, Siphongo. When we reached Osuthu and Dinuzulu, he was delighted to hear that I had arrived. We were given a small homestead for our accommodation and we slept well. The following day I was invited to go and see the Prince. He was very pleased to see me, because at the time it seemed that Daniels would be relieved to go elsewhere, and I would take his place. But no! It did not happen like that, and he continued to stay on.

I remained at that small homestead for the use of visitors for some time. In the end we went to live at the home of Nsukumbili kaNtanjana of the Mbatha clan, not far from Osuthu. Nsukumbili treated us very well, and we were very happy there.

After the Prince returned from restoring the Nobamba residence near Mahlabathini, I longed to return home because three or four months had passed without my being given any work to do, Anthony Daniels still being there. My heart began to be sullen and moody, and so I bade farewell to the Prince, telling him that I was yearning for home because I could not simply live without any work to do. Thereupon the Prince gave me £6, and agreed to my returning home. But I asked why I had been summoned then, to be told today that I may simply go again? And where was the money for my many years of service that I had rendered, writing letters for the Zulu people and for the Prince at St. Helena, with me having to go to St. Helena too? Had I not been promised that I would be paid for all this? But the Prince had no answer to that. I then went to his chief councillor, Mankulumana kaSomaphunga of the Ndwandwe clan. He said he knew of such a promise from the Zulus, but he had no authority to give instructions unless Dinuzulu approved. I then went on and reported the matter to the Magistrate at Nongoma. He said that he could do nothing without the approval of the Nkosazana, the daughter of Sobantu. He said I should write to the Nkosazana about the matter. And indeed I wrote to her. In replying she sent me £5, and told me to come back and speak to her so that she could set the matter right.

Accordingly I left Zululand and proceeded to Filidi [Vryheid] where I slept. The next day I boarded the train which took me to Mgungundlovu [Maritzburg]. I saw the Nkosazana and we discussed the matter of the money which I was demanding from the Prince, and she gave me £100, and there the matter ended.[2]

Chapter 64
FALSE REPORTS AND RUMOURS

In the year 1904 people began to speak of many things which they thought the Prince was doing. They began by saying that some white people had visited Osuthu, and he had offered them a beast for slaughter; but when they tried to shoot it, the bullets of their gun stopped at the skin and did not penetrate. In the end he gave one of his own men a gun and said to shoot it, and as soon as he fired he shot it and it died. Secondly it was said that the Prince travelled as far as Maritzburg, travelling without being seen by a single person. On arrival he mounts the Town Hall and there writes letters which he leaves on the table, to be seen by the white people the next day, after he has left. Thirdly, it was said that word was received that all pigs were to be killed, not one remaining. European plates and dishes were to be broken and thrown away, not a single one remaining in an African household. Homes in which these prohibited articles were found would die and perish completely, not a single soul remaining. All European articles were not wanted by the African people.

The year 1905 commenced. On the last day of May a great deluge occurred in the evening, snow fell, large rivers were flooded, and people, cattle and goats perished – it was terrible. Things happened that had never happened before in my memory, for in some places buildings collapsed. That day will always be remembered, even by generations to come. I myself was at Zibomvana (Fitzsimon's Location) when I witnessed this strange rare occurrence. I was sharing a bed with the late Chief Martin Luthuli,[1] his wife being away. We stoked the fire continually because it was intensely cold. One of the houses collapsed during the night, but all escaped who were sleeping in it. Large numbers of Indians in Durban perished owing to the bursting of a dam, and there were many deaths in other places. It was evident that this was the beginning of the many strange things of which we had been told in the rumours reported by people, saying that they were caused by the Prince, the son of Cetshwayo. We saw something which we had never seen before – snow falling in the city of Pietermaritzburg. Deaths from frost and snow were reported from all sides.

Incidents in the life of Dinuzulu, his troubles and unfortunate experiences, began to indicate that he would never grow [into a king], and that the fabrications and lies about him, and the resentment and weariness of him by the people of his own country, would bring his body to the grave. And yet he was a man of peace, this son of the Zulu king, not wanting to quarrel with anyone, no matter what sort or race.

It was at this time that certain chiefs here in Natal began to send messengers to him in Zululand, with persistent questions as to whether it was actually true that he was doing these things about which there was so much talk here in Natal – preventing the white man's bullets from penetrating the flesh of a beast, and mounting the Town Hall for it to be seen in the morning where he had written, and turning himself into a dog. Was it he who had given orders for the killing of pigs throughout the country, and for the discarding of all vessels of European construction, leaving only African clay pots?[2]

When he was questioned about all this, the son of the king expressed astonishment, knowing nothing about all those miracles which they associated with him. But he realised that something serious was going to happen to him.

Chapter 65

BAMBADA'S DISPUTE

In 1906 the Bambada dispute broke out,[1] he being a minor chief of the Zondi clan. He was born of Mancinza kaJangeni kaMagenge kaDlaba, of the junior house of the Ngome family, following after the Nadi and Mphumuza clans, being the last of them. Bambada lived in the Greytown district, in control of his small area. He quarrelled with Dlovunga (Mr J.W. Cross, R.M.), demanding to know why they should have to pay for heads [the poll tax].

It had been previously proclaimed by the Government that all young unmarried men were to pay poll tax; that a young unmarried man [*insizwa*] was to pay a pound, and that all men [*amadoda*] who were unmarried were to pay the same amount. Wo! The whole country was roused to anger to the point of extinction by water on hearing this law. The people were greatly agitated throughout the country, some swearing that they would not pay the tax while they lived [not yet dead – 'over their dead bodies'].[2]

And so many messages were sent to Dinuzulu to ask him what was to be done in the matter. Of course the whole country was hostile, both Zululand and Natal. As for him, he advised all those who questioned him by saying, 'The money demanded by the Government from young men is not that which is payable by the householders who pay tax every year, it is payable by the young men only. Householders should remember and realise that the majority of their sons no longer send money to their fathers, but spend it on themselves. Therefore the Government has done well to tax the young men.' He then took out a pound note and gave it to a servant and directed him to pay it as a tax in his name, so that all the Zulu people should see that it was right that this should be done.

And so all the Natal people who had been sent by their chiefs to the Prince to ask what he thought should be done in the matter, returned with his word to say the tax should be paid; and they delivered the message to their chiefs and their people. Yet at heart the people throughout all the country were opposed to the payment of the tax.

Then one day the taxation date was announced in the district of Greytown. As Bambada kaMancinza was a resident in that district, he went personally to Dlovunga [the magistrate], to question him closely about the matter at the court office in Greytown. They quickly quarrelled at the court office, Bambada saying that he refused to pay the tax. On returning home he summoned the members of his area and told them what had been said between him and Dlovunga. All the people swore and declared that they would not pay the tax. Then came forward among them Magwababa, his father's younger brother, and advised the son of his brother not to take it upon himself to quarrel with the Government, and said that he should comply with what the Government had ordered throughout the country. Bambada got angry and struck him on the knees so that he was unable to go and inform the white people of Bambada's intentions; and he [Magwababa] was incapacitated, no longer being able to walk. Thereafter he [Bambada] rounded up his force and announced the day on which the whites would come to collect the tax down in the thorn country, and the place where it would be collected.

Chapter 66

THE BAMBADA REBELLION

Listen now! The day for the payment of the tax arrived, and Bambada and his force were ready for it. They went beforehand to prepare for the whites who were to accompany the magistrate Dlovunga. On arriving at that place, the incorrigible Bambada prepared his force before the arrival of the magistrate and his Nongqai escort [a force of Zulu sepoys with white officers]. He deployed and stationed his men in places of great difficulty for the whites, overlooking them in this dangerous place in order to trap them unexpectedly against a cliff. He told his men the plan by which they were not to shoot when they saw them passing by, but to let them pass on ahead until they heard the sound of his own gun, and then to rise up and attack. Hau! They drove them headlong against the precipitous places of the cliffs and into the dongas and gullies of the thorn country; but they were not all killed even though besieged by such a force, and some broke away and escaped. It was there that the calabash was broken and its contents spilt [Zulu saying – the fat was in the fire]. As soon as he had committed this despicable act, Bambada proceeded to cross over into Zululand and then make for the Nkandla forest, seeking to establish himself in a stronghold.

The Government now raised the alarm, and started to take action.[1] The whole country raised its eyes, cleaned its ears, and listened intently to what had happened, wondering what was going to be the outcome. The white people followed him [Bambada], keeping him in sight until he entered the Nkandla forest.

It was then that matters became serious with the Fuze clan [Magema's own clan], Mjongo and his Christian followers having revolted and determined to fight the white people over the tax issue. And indeed that happened; the Christians took up arms and fought. But what served to reduce the seriousness was that they fought alone; the clan as a whole remained neutral and did not fight. When they were arrested, they were arrested by Mveli who was in control of the Fuzes, the Christians having taken to a large forest.[2]

Down yonder with the people of Mkhonto kaNtwananhle in the Maphumulo district, it was the same, and they fought. Over there with the people of Khula Majozi, the son of Luntshungu kaNgoza, it was the same, for Mntele kaNgoza, Luntshungu's brother, broke away with a section of the clan. They rebelled and followed Bambada into the Nkandla forest. There was confusion throughout the country, the people being in a state of unrest and division.

Whenever people met on the road they would question each other by the use of passwords they had coined as a form of greeting. The one would say to the other, 'Where do you pay your tax', to which the other would reply, if he was one who had rebelled against the Government, 'The poll tax is a fanciful fairy tale', and so the other one would know that he was on his side. There were large numbers of 'joiners' [*abajoyinayo*] who came from various places to join up with those of different clans, all anxious to fight the white people. The Nkandla forest was filled to the brim with people from many different parts, not to mention those who came with Bambada kaMancinza. I should also mention those who came from various parts of Zululand wanting to fight. But be that as it may, the Prince knew nothing about those people.

After a period of silence, it came to the knowledge of the Prince that the Nkandla forest was full of people. He then sent messengers to tell the people to come out of the forest because he was not connected with that army that was fighting the Government. He sent to the Government requesting that it should allow him to go in person to get Bambada out of the Nkandla forest, but the Government refused.

And now this rogue of a fellow, Bambada, in his cunning, pays a personal visit to the Prince accompanied by one of his wives, and on returning to Nkandla leaves her at Osuthu.[3] But I am not certain whether on leaving her there, he went straight back to Nkandla or some other place. It was this incident that caused the Prince to become implicated, it being alleged that he was in league with Bambada. Well! Even that which is concealed comes to light on close investigation, and so, despite the Prince's assertion [denial] that he did not know Bambada, he was nevertheless convicted by this incident when Bambada actually trod in the courtyards between the houses of the Osuthu residence.

And so it was: the events of that year were very serious indeed, and a great deal of blood was shed because the people were driven to fighting by their hearts, without weapons, and without thought for their bodies.

The Mjongos over there killed one white man, Sgt. Hunt, but as there were many of them involved in the case, they were all shot, having been forced to dig their own graves at Richmond. Those executed at Richmond numbered twelve, the sons of Mncindo kaDangadu kaMnyani of the Ngcobo people, together with others. As they were about to be put to death, they sang songs and clan chants with great gaiety like people on the way to a festivity; and when ordered to dig their own graves, they did so with contentment like people happy to die. Mjongo himself was not among those twelve who were executed at Richmond, as he was sick in jail in Maritzburg with two of his followers. These three were executed later, having been removed from prison after they had recovered from their wounds.[4]

Those people of Mkhonto kaNtwananhle in the Maphumulo district were quickly arrested before they could do anything. Many of them died attempting to fight, without accomplishing anything. Over there in the Nkandla forest, the whole of Bambada's army was persuaded by Sigananda's brother to come to a certain place [Mome gorge], but when it arrived there, the white army had already encircled the place; and they suddenly heard the thunder of artillery, and they were all completely wiped out; but when I say 'all', they did not all completely die even though they were besieged by such a large army.[5]

Chapter 67
THE ARREST OF DINUZULU

After that battle had ended, the white people went to Osuthu to capture the Prince. He offered no resistance, and promptly went with them to the Nongoma Magistracy, where he was arrested.[1] When he was about to be tried, he was sent to Mgungundlovana [Greytown]. Many Zulu people assembled. The Judge that tried the case was Sir William Smith, supported by Mr Justice Boshoff (Stofela) and Mr Henrique Shepstone (Gebhuza kaSomtseu); the Government representative was Mr T.F. Carter, K.C., Attorney-General, and Dinuzulu's advocate, provided by Dlwedlwe kaSobantu, was Mr W.P. Schreiner, K.C., with Mr Eugene Renaud (Mfushane) and Mr R.C. Samuelson (Bhembhedu).

Dlwedlwe attended in person, Bubi kaNondenisa Mthuli accompanying the Nkosazana. I myself was not present. The hearing of this important case lasted many days, and ended with the conviction of the Prince and his sentence to four years imprisonment.[2]

Amongst the witnesses who gave evidence on behalf of the Prince, I recall one who spoke the truth, Ngobozana kaVukuza of the Mphungose clan, a member of the Mboza regiment and a headman appointed by the Government to be in charge of the people at Mahlabathini. He spoke the truth and said, 'All we people were opposed to paying this tax, and it was only Dinuzulu who said we should pay it. We all wished to fight, but he refused . . .', and other such good words which were spoken by this truthful headman.

Dinuzulu was convicted and committed to prison in Pietermaritzburg, together with a number of other Zulus who were convicted of serious crimes. Afterwards he was accused of certain other offences,[3] but the majority of them were lies concocted by the Zulu people who hated him as a person hates a snake, in accordance with the name given him by his father, Dinuzulu [He who wearies the Zulu people, He who is slandered by the Zulu people].[4]

It was at this time that the son of Sobantu passed away. He was an advocate, for whilst the case was being tried here, it was also being tried overseas, the case against the Prince. While he was making his great fight for the truth of the case, he was taken ill with the heart complaint that had also struck his father, Sobantu, when he was engaged in the case of the arrest of Langalibalele.[5] And Sobantu would also have died on that occasion if our eminent and brilliant doctor had not appeared, Dr Gordon, who immediately denied that he was ill, only angry. He treated him, overcame him, and cured him. We know for a fact that Gebhuza (Francis Ernest Colenso) died fighting for the truth on behalf of the Zulu royal family, not wanting to conceal it. It is these whom we know as 'the army of martyrs', when we worship God.

It was not long after his imprisonment in Pietermaritzburg that the Prince Dinuzulu was sent up to the Transvaal to be imprisoned at the Bhalule [Olifant's river], where General Botha bought a place for him,[6] which he named 'Thengisangaye' [Barter with him], meaning that the Zulu people had bartered with him to foreigners. There he remained for a number of years. Dinuzulu suffered from the disorder of the leg that had afflicted his grandfather, Mpande. He was always ill with it, and then it was heard that the doctor attending him resolved to send him to Germany where there were hot springs, for him to be treated there. But the ailment became much worse, despite the efforts of his doctor to help him. Eventually it was heard even here that the child of the king was gravely ill, and in the end the sickness carried him away in great distress [1913].

Then the Magistrate of Middelburg at the Bhalule, with great kindness, sent a message to report to the Nkosazana Dlwedlwe, and she without delay took Bubi Mthuli and set off on the way. The Government showed great consideration by allowing the Zulu people to remove the body and bring it to the royal graves at Nobamba, where are Mageba, Phunga, Ndaba, Jama, and Senzangakhona.[7]

The Nkosazana met the body at Filidi [Vryheid], and when they went on to Nobamba, she went with them, the body being conveyed by wagon, until they finally reached the place of burial.

Chapter 68

THE DEATH OF DINUZULU

After the burial, there was still the business of appointing a Prince to stand in the position of his father. They finally chose Solomon who was Nkayishana whose name was Maphumuzana, the son of his mother, Mkasilomo kaNtuzwa kaNhlaka of the Mdlalose clan, she being the chief wife of Dinuzulu. David Nyawana who was the son of Zihlazile kaQetuka kaMonqondo of the Magwaza clan, became as a younger brother [he was the elder in age], and he was given the area of the Qulusi people.

Thereafter all the mourners dispersed, including the Nkosazana who returned home. And so now the Zulu country resided in the hands of Solomon kaDinuzulu and the Government, Solomon to be in the hands of his uncle, Mnyayiza kaNdabuko, and the chief councillor, Mankulumana Ndwandwe, and all the dignitaries in charge of Dinuzulu's district,[1] in the name of the Government.

But ever since the son of the king left us, people are constantly dreaming and affirming that he is not dead, but in Germany. They say that when the Germans fought the other white nations, they did so on behalf of Dinuzulu. It does not dawn on our people that Germany and all the other white races would not die on account of Dinuzulu concealed by the Germans. But it is not the first time that people have spoken like this of the line of Senzangakhona, for when Mbulazi died in his dispute with Cetshwayo, they immediately declared that he was still alive, concealed by the English in order to install him on the death of his father, as king in succession to Mpande. All the Zulu dignitaries declared emphatically that Mbulazi had been concealed by the white people. All those who spoke thus have now died, many after attaining a great age, but none of them ever saw Mbulazi.

Today Zululand is no longer Zululand, it is Natal, ruled by the English, the original government having passed away and a new one taking its place. The rule of Zulu has disappeared. And why is this? It is because Shaka established it with great force and haste, like a great wind and whirlwind, discarding the old ways of Senzangakhona and his forebears.

When Mpande appeared on the scene to contest against Dingane, he was installed by the Boers who had already discerned that he was a kind person with respect and regard for others, unlike his two brothers,

Shaka and Dingane, who were like wild beasts. We do not know who these two took after, seeing that we know Senzangakhona to have been a kind and considerate person; but from some of his praises [*izibongo*] we learn that he had a violent temper, so perhaps Shaka and Dingane took after him. Only one is known to have been without it: Mpande. This one of today, Solomon, is mild, kind and humble, and one can say that he is indeed a child of Mpande. His father, Dinuzulu, was also humble, but took after his father when angry. But Cetshwayo was very good and kind, and loved all his people.

EPILOGUE

[The first part of the epilogue, which Fuze entitles 'UDinuzulu' but takes five pages to get to that subject (which I have included in the body of the work), is transferred partly to Chapter 20 and partly to Chapter 43. A few paragraphs are omitted as repetitious, and the rest is reproduced here.]

About the Bantu Book: It is with great regret that I have to inform you that as I completed the book which I had been so anxious to publish under the name of *Abantu Abamnyama*, the son of my old friend, the late Nicholas Masuku of Edendale, was taken ill, the son being Mr N.J.N. Masuku of Glencoe Junction.[1] He was taken ill by a sickness which eventually carried him off. For this reason I was shattered with grief, for I was hoping that this work which I had commenced, I would see its successful conclusion by the time I passed away. But the illness of that son of mine set me back. For ever since I made my appeal to you, I have not seen the slightest sign of response from you, except Mr R.M. Siboto of 75 Upper Ashley Street, Cape Town, who, on hearing of my request, sent me £2 to enable me to proceed with the work, and also my son Solomon at Wm. Cuthbert & Co., Bloemfontein, who sent me ten shillings. The majority remained in silent stillness, expecting that the book would publish itself and attain completeness on its own account.

Yet, my friends, there is no work that produces itself. All things are made by humans with their hands and brains. It was so in olden times, and it is so even now. People work with their hands and fingers to produce things which are eventually seen by others; and all those admiring them suggest that they are not the work of human hands.

EPILOGUE

Concerning my own deliberations, gentlemen, I now suggest that we immediately prepare for the benefit of our future generations a record of events to show them where they came from. A grasshopper when it is fertilised at the end of a year and when it feels that it is about to die, digs a hole in the ground and lays its eggs there and covers them with soil, and then settles on a twig to wither and die. After a time the eggs hatch out, and its children emerge as grasshoppers just like it. We should remember that on death we do not come to an end, but by our progeny we renew ourselves to continue indefinitely, and so arise anew as if we were beginning at the beginning. Remember the old proverb, 'A skin cradle is not thrown away because of a death.' I am concerned to preserve. It will be a good thing if even in the future our children gain knowledge about their past, rather than remain ignorant and stupid like the *siphumamangati* eagle.

I will be happy if the One above will allow me to proceed with my work[2] in spite of my present frailty which makes me realise when I walk that, 'Wotshi! The times have advanced! How is it that my knees are so rickety when I walk!' And yet, No! The gifts of our Father are not so. He gives us greater gifts than we think, and offers us more time than we think. It is He who makes us progress and prosper all the days of our existence.

Pietermaritzburg, 1922   Magema M. Fuze

NOTES

AUTHOR'S PROLOGUE
1. *Isisusa*: preliminary wedding dance
2. The Rev. J.L. Dube was the founder of the famous high school, Ohlange, the founder of the isiZulu newspaper, *Ilanga laseNatal* and the first president of the African National Congress.
3. Rather than 'his chief wife bore him four sons', as Lugg has it, for in this context the wife is merely the means of production, as Fuze reflects. In other contexts the mother is important both for herself and for her clan connections.
4. Sir Theophilus Shepstone was firstly 'Diplomatic Agent to the Native Tribes in Natal' and later Secretary for Native Affairs in the Natal Colonial Government. He was the architect of 'native administration' in Natal, and widely regarded as the foremost authority on 'native affairs'.
5. They are both terms referring to relationships through marriage.
6. An Afrikaans word meaning a rascal.
7. Not 'who would thus be enabled to take control', as Lugg has it, for it was not Shepstone's policy to interfere with local customs unless they were 'repugnant to civilised standards'.
8. If Magwaza gives as willingly as Somtseu gives, so should he receive as rightly as a father who gives his child in marriage receives. There is no record that Bishop Colenso took the hint!
9. 'He who nods the head in agreement', or 'He who threatens with a stick'. Zulu names tend to be peculiar to the individual and not selected from a common stock, let alone from a book.

INTRODUCTION
1. *Inkondlo*: grand wedding dance.
2. Or in English, half-breeds, a less generous expression in that it implies that the one half is inferior to the other.
3. The various Bantu languages do not differ greatly in structure, but in speech they are certainly not mutually intelligible – no more so than English, German and Dutch. However, Fuze's knowledge is virtually limited to languages and dialects which are more or less mutually intelligible, but Sotho is not one of them.
4. We have been unable to determine the exact nature of the contribution of Mr N.J.N. Masuku, but it was not co-authorship as the style is consistent throughout, and distinctively so.

EXHORTATIONS
1. *Amangebeza*: bridesmaid's refreshments.

NOTES

2. Literally *madoda* (men): here, as in the opening address to the members of the tribal assembly [*ibandla*], Fuze presumes that his readers will be men only.
3. This sentence is an example of the author's rambling style at its worst, during which he drifts off the point.
4. According to the Zulu legend, at the Creation the chameleon was sent to tell people that they should live for ever, and the salamander was subsequently sent to tell people that they should die. The chameleon dawdled on the way, feeding on red berries, and the salamander arrived first with its message. When the chameleon arrived, the people said, '*sobamba elentulo*' ['We will stick to the word of the salamander'].
5. We cannot clarify the obscurity.

CHAPTER 1

1. The main reference for this section is Bryant's *Olden Times in Zululand and Natal*, but his highly speculative *Bantu Origins* is to be avoided.
2. Recent attempts to account for the origin and spread of the Bantu-speaking peoples are the chapters by M. Guthrie and R. Oliver in *Papers in African Prehistory* (ed. J.D. Fage and R.A. Oliver, Cambridge, 1970); J.H. Greenberg, 'Linguistic Evidence regarding Bantu Origins', *Journal of African History*, XIII, 2 (1972); D. Dalby, 'The Prehistorical Implications of Guthrie's Comparative Bantu', *Journal of African History*, XVI, 4 (1975) and XVII, 1 (1976); D.W. Phillipson, 'The Chronology of the Iron Age in Bantu Africa', *Journal of African History*, XVI, 3 (1975); T.M. Maggs, 'some recent radiocarbon dates from eastern and southern Africa', *Journal of African History*, XVIII, 2 (1977). Recent studies relevant to the Natal Nguni are S. Marks, 'The Traditions of the Natal Nguni: a second look at the work of A.T. Bryant' in L.M. Thompson (ed.), *African Societies in Southern Africa* (Heinemann, 1969), pp. 126–144, and S. Marks and A. Atmore, 'The Problem of the Natal Nguni: An examination of the ethnic and linguistic situation in Southern Africa before the *Mfecane*' in D. Dalby (ed.), *Language and History in Africa* (Frank Cass, London, 1970), pp. 120–132. S.M.
3. He refers to the Ntungwa and the Nguni as though they were the original Bantu stock, whereas they are relatively recent and certainly local, with no relevance to the scale of time and place that he is attempting to describe. He seems to equate Ntungwa with Sotho (see next two paragraphs), whereas Bryant treats the Ntungwa as a substock within the Nguni group. However, it is the people of this Ntungwa-Nguni subgroup who pride themselves on their origin in the Sotho country – *SingabeSuthu*, they say (We are Suthus, i.e. Sothos – see Gatsha Buthelezi, 'The Early History of the Buthelezi Clan' in *Social System and Tradition in Southern Africa*, O.U.P. 1978) – and *Suthu* was the designation of the royalists (Cetshwayo's party) in Zulu politics, and the Zulu war cry. Fuze is stressing a relationship between Ntungwa and Sotho which white investigators have overlooked.
4. Recent archaeological evidence prevents an easy transposition of the term 'Nguni' even into the eighteenth century. On the Babanango plateau, for example, recently excavated building sites resemble Sotho patterns more closely than contemporary Nguni patterns of settlement. Fuze may therefore be nearer the mark than one would have thought even a few years ago. S.M.
5. The term 'Matebele' could indeed indicate a degree of carelessness or indecency in dress.

157

NOTES

6. By which he may mean either 'no longer Nguni but Sotho', or else 'Ntungwa in origin'.

CHAPTER 2
1. He refers to the Bushmen as *abatwa* (*abaThwa*, sing. *umuThwa*) and *izicwe* (*iziChwe* sing. *isiChwe*) with equal frequency.
2. Nhlapo is a typically Zulu name, but this clan is reputed to have intermarried very much with the Bushmen.
3. This is quite incorrect, although some of the Bushmen of Lesotho may have originated in the Drakensberg. Late Stone Age hunter-gatherers once inhabited large tracts of southern Africa, and those in present-day Namibia (SWA) have little relationship to the hunter-gatherers of Natal. For an excellent account of the relations between the Bushmen, the Bantu-speakers and the Natal colonists and authorities, see J. Wright, *Bushman Raiders of the Drakensberg 1840–1870* (Pietermaritzburg, 1971). S.M.
4. Presumably after the defeat of Mbulazi (Mbuyazi) by Cetshwayo at Ndondakusuka in 1856.

CHAPTER 3
1. He refers to the Hottentots as *amalawu*, which also means Coloureds, i.e. people of mixed descent.
2. Fuze's views on the origin of the Hottentot or Khoikhoi herders of the Cape are not correct. For the most recent views, see L. Thompson and M. Wilson, *The Oxford History of South Africa* Vol. 1 (Oxford, 1969). However, in his reasons for their loss of independence there is some truth: their induced addiction to the white man's alcohol and tobacco, which rapidly became the *sine qua non* of the cattle trade in the 17th and 18th centuries, was an important factor in their decline, as well as a symptom of it. By the time Fuze was writing, alcoholism was already a social problem for many of his own people. S.M.
3. This is not strictly correct, as the ancestral spirits do not normally assume a physical form. They may appear as snakes, however, when they want to draw attention to themselves, or they may send snakes as messengers.
4. As is indeed the case!

CHAPTER 4
1. Adam Kok was already of mixed descent when he moved out of the Cape Colony and up to the Orange River, where his followers became known as the Griqua. S.M.
2. Not Adam Kok I but probably Adam Kok III, who had moved with the majority of his followers at the behest of the colonial authorities from Griqualand West (in the northern Cape Colony and western part of present-day O.F.S.) to Griqualand East on the inland borders of the Cape Colony and Natal. S.M.
(A recent 'popular' publication which includes a short account of this move is John Shephard, *In the Shadow of the Drakensberg* (Durban, 1976), Chapters 4, 5, 6. The territory was known as Nomansland until its annexation to the Cape Colony as East Griqualand in 1878, after fifteen years of Griqua independence. A.T.C.)

NOTES

3. He is not at all certain about how to classify the Griqua, as he himself has already admitted. The best short account of the origin of the Griqua is to be found in J.S. Marais, *The Cape Coloured People* (Johannesburg, 1957).
(A recent publication on this subject is R. Ross, *Adam Kok's Griquas* (Cambridge, 1977). S.M.)

CHAPTER 5
1. Here Fuze would seem to be influenced by the fantastic notions of the time on the subject of Bantu origins. S.M. (These 'fantastic notions' are apparently still current in some minds, e.g. Binns, *The Warrior People*, Ch. 1: African Origins (Cape Town 1974) A.T.C.)
2. The monster apparently turned out to be a slave boat.
3. Fuze here reiterates the Zulu belief or pretence as to why folk tales and fairy stories cannot be told during daytime.

CHAPTER 6
1. Fuze had been summoned to St. Helena to serve the Zulu royal family in exile.
2. The ambivalent human animal who plays the trickster in Zulu folklore.
3. He refers undoubtedly to his master, Bishop Colenso.
4. The first traders to visit and settle in Shaka's kingdom.
5. A good question. Fynn's domestic history provides the answer. On Fynn's first visit to Natal (1824 to 1834) he was a subject of the Zulu king and readily lived the life of a Zulu family man, to which his descendents still testify. On his subsequent visit (1852 to his death ten years later) he was a citizen of the British Colony of Natal in which intermarriage was 'beyond the pale', and as a magistrate he could hardly do otherwise than live conventionally with one white wife.

CHAPTER 7
1. This chapter evinces a scepticism and independence of mind that may have contributed towards Bishop Colenso's heresy. Disraeli's famous saying that 'they defeat our generals, they convert our bishops' suggests that Colenso was converted by his converts. Of course Colenso was renowned for his own independence of mind, and controversial subjects such as evolution were discussed in his household, as Fuze reflects.

CHAPTER 8
1. Charles Mackenzie, whose brief, unfortunate and unsuccessful mission as Bishop at the Zambezi is referred to here, not to be confused with the contemporary Douglas McKenzie, Bishop of Zululand (1880–1890).
2. Alice Werner lived and studied and taught in Central and East Africa, as well as with the Colensos in Natal. The climax of her career was her appointment as Professor of Swahili and Bantu Languages at the School of Oriental and African Studies in London, from where she retired in 1930.

CHAPTER 9
1. In the next three chapters Fuze deals with Nguni clan relationships and genealogies. Bryant's *Olden Times* is recommended for reference to the many names of persons

NOTES

and clans mentioned in these chapters; and also for the localities, for Fuze points 'over there' and 'down yonder, but we have no means of knowing in which direction he is pointing! See also *The James Stuart Archive of Recorded Oral Evidence Relating to the History of the Zulu and Neighbouring People*, Vol. I (University of Natal Press and Killie Campbell Africana Library, 1976). Vol. II will appear in 1979 and three further volumes are planned.

2. The Cape Nguni (the Xhosa people – Mnguni and Mxhosa are personal names) are supposed to have moved southward through the Natal uplands, which from Fuze's point of view in the midlands could have seemed like westwards.
3. In this clan praise there is a play on the word *biya*, to fence (to put up a fence), from which the surname is derived.
4. The grandson of Makhasana, who was the grandson of Mabhudu ('Maphutha'), by whose name the people are sometimes known.
5. He is referring to the Tembe-Tonga, a branch of the Tonga in southern Mozambique.
6. The founder of the Swazi nation was Sobhuza, who fled northwards across the Phongolo (Pongola river) after a contest with Zwide kaLanga, where he forged a new kingdom out of his followers and the clans he conquered.
7. From the same stock (Tekela Nguni), not from the Swazi themselves, who were a relatively recent development.
8. Zwide was Shaka's strongest antagonist who fled into obscurity and death after his defeat, and Soshangana was Zwide's army commander who, after the Ndwandwe destruction, settled in Mozambique and founded the Gaza kingdom. His followers became known as the Shangane (Shangaan).
9. Several families are reported to have disputed about castor oil plants on deserted sites, which seems to refer simply to family quarrels.
10. Dingiswayo was the chief under whose protection Shaka emerged to fame.
11. Bryant has none of these names in his version of the Qwabe genealogy, and we have been unable to trace them anywhere. According to Bryant, the name Nozidiya refers not to an ancestor but to the fact that the women wore a distinctive type of apron (Bryant, *Olden Times*, p. 186). It is strange that Fuze makes no mention of the famous Qwabe chief, Phakathwayo kaKhondlo, nor of his famous or infamous brother, Nqetho.

CHAPTER 10

1. In this paragraph, Fuze is giving an account of a non-Nguni chief, Moshesh or Moshoeshoe, founder of the Sotho nation of Lesotho (c. 1786–1870). It was Moshoeshoe who established himself on Thaba Bosiu, rather than his father or grandfather. Neither the 'wandering' or Fuze's 'Swaziland' should be taken literally. For Moshoeshoe, see the two recent biographies, L.M. Thompson, *Survival in Two Worlds, Moshoeshoe of Lesotho, 1786–1870* (Oxford, 1975) and P.B. Sanders, *Moshoeshoe, Chief of the Sotho* (Heineman, 1975). S.M.
2. The Nguni practise clan exogamy, which means that people of the same surname may not intermarry, however distantly related. If they take their surname from a less remote ancestor, however, they may now do so, even although they acknowledge descent from the ultimate progenitor, as is the case with the Ngcobo.

NOTES

3. It was not Shaka who put Matiwane to death, but Dingane several years later. In these circumstances Shaka would not have done so – it would not have been in character.
4. This happened in 1829. In 1812 Matiwane was at the height of his power, whereas Shaka was still living among the Mthethwa, by favour of Dingiswayo.
5. Utrecht was a settlement established by Afrikaners from the South African Republic when they took over a large tract of land from the Zulu in 1884 to form the New Republic, allegedly to reward the services they had rendered Dinuzulu in his struggle against Zibhebhu. S.M.
6. The Lala pronunciation. The Lala dialect is today virtually extinct. It is an extreme form of Tekela Nguni speech, which is also almost extinct in Natal today. SiSwati is 'tekela' whereas isiZulu is 'zunda', or from the Zulu point of view, the standard language.
7. It is apparently deliberately that Shaka addresses Ngcugcwa as Gcugcwa, using the sort of slight that is effective through being so slight.
8. He subsequently fled from Zululand to the Transvaal and later to Zimbabwe (Rhodesia), where he founded the Ndebele (Matabele) kingdom.
9. He seems to suggest that the Zulu may have been known as the Phunga or the Mageba 'at that time', after these two ancestors, but Zulu was the progenitor.
10. Apparently as a youngster, for the ears were pierced about the age of ten.
11. It was considered dangerous for the royal spittle to touch the ground. The king therefore used to spit upon his personal attendant, who thereby absorbed the essence or *insila* of the king – he was in fact known as the king's *insila*.
12. Shenge is still the formal salute [*isithakazelo*] of the Buthelezi chief and people.
13. 'Dust of the deep hole' in the Lala dialect, to which aboriginal group these people belonged.
14. See Note 6 above.
15. Referring to precipitous flight at the time of Shaka's disturbances.
16. We know of no special significance in these eating habits.
17. Of the same stock as the Swazi.
18. The brisket is reserved for the head of the household, but note the similarity of this story to that told in relation to the Qwabe clan in Chapter 9.
19. As Bryant lists about a thousand clans and sub-clans at the back of *Olden Times in Zululand and Natal*, it is hardly surprising that Fuze is reluctant to include them all in his account. S.M.
20. One of the Khabeleni chiefs, whose name means 'sole survivor'.

CHAPTER 11
1. Fuze's Chapter 12.
2. See Chapter 10, Note 1.
3. Faku was the powerful Mpondo (Pondo) chief who ruled from c. 1824–1867.
4. Not so – see Chapter 9, Note 6.
5. See Chapter 9, Note 7.
6. According to tradition, Ndungunya, the father of Sobhuza, was responsible for the introduction of military organisation to the Ngwane people (later the Swazi royal clan). The Embo of Mkhize share the formal salutation of 'Dlamini' with the

161

NOTES

Swazi, but the relationship of the two groups is more recent and more complex than Fuze suggests here. S.M.
7. See Chapter 9, Note 5.
8. Not eating maas is simply a local custom, according to Mr Lugg, and not particularly significant. (See Chapter 10, Note 16.)
9. In fact Mzilikazi's *Bulawayo* was named after Shaka's *Bulawayo* in emulation of its greatness. The nickname *Gibixhegu* is supposed to have been coined by Shaka in commemoration of his destruction of a number of old men who were no longer fit to fight; although some say it was a derogatory reference to his father, and others to Mzilikazi.
10. See Chapter 10, Note 3.
11. See Bryant's genealogy of the Bomvu or Bomvini clan: 'The list is safe as far as Ndlovu (i.e. from Nyoniyezwe backwards to Ndlovu). Beyond Ndlovu, the names are given in any and every order . . . From this fact we would like to believe that the Bomvu first reached the Tugela country during Ndlovu's days (1766–84).' Thus does Bryant sift the evidence of many informants such as Fuze, and present conclusions which should rather be read as hypotheses.
12. In Bryant's account the Mthethwa and the Ndwandwe were at war at the time, and Dingiswayo suffered himself to be captured by Zwide because of a magical spell. Here Dingiswayo went to Zwide *ngobuhle* (in peace and goodness), which he could have done, diplomatically, even though they may have been at war. Such action would accord with Bryant's eulogy of the man (see *Olden Times*, Chapter 11).
13. Phakathwayo's derogatory description of Shaka is obscure, except that the 'stumpy little stick' is supposed to refer to the size of his penis. Bryant translates the phrase as 'he who doesn't know how to use his stick properly' (*ndukwana*, diminutive stick), and his dictionary entry under *igamanxandukwana* is similarly suggestive, though not intentionally.
(Shaka has been likened to Napoleon because of the similarity of their careers, but they were similar in this respect too: Napoleon also suffered from hypogenitalism, he also failed in his relations with women, and he is also supposed to have tended towards homosexuality. Shaka, like Napoleon, has been described as a 'latent homosexual' (see Donald Morris, *The Washing of the Spears*, p. 46, and Max Gluckman, 'The Rise of the Zulu Empire', *Scientific American*, Vol. 202, No. 4, 1960, p. 168, and 'The Rise of King Shaka of Zululand', *Journal of African Studies*, Vol. 1, No. 2, 1974, p. 140). A comparative study of the lives, both public and private, of Shaka and Napoleon, Attila and Hitler, Alexander and other such men, would be interesting if not illuminating).

CHAPTER 12
1. The references for the ethnographical section are Bryant's *The Zulu People* (reprinted 1967) and Krige's *The Social System of the Zulus* (reprinted 1977).
2. Fuze's Chapter 11.
3. One must remember that Fuze was writing at least seventy years after the social revolution brought about by Shaka, which lessens the validity of his observations for social life at the beginning of the nineteenth century, which he regards as a golden age; as does Bryant, one of whose chapters in *The Zulu People* is entitled 'Daily Life in Arcady'.

NOTES

4. Lugg regards this account as erroneous, 'as the Zulu have always been a very warlike people as can be testified by the early settlers'. However, the British settlers arrived at the height of Zulu power, which was certainly not 'always'. He adds, however, that 'the late Ndlovu kaThimuni, a chief involved in the Bambatha Rebellion whose grandfather, Mudli, was Senzangakhona's brother, told a very similar story long ago before Magema wrote his book, and he was probably its originator', i.e. the originator of this story relating to 'some small specific dispute'. However, Bryant describes the self-same method of settling disputes before the days of Shaka, a clash more in the nature of a tournament than a battle. Of course both Bryant and Fuze may have heard the story from the same source; in fact Fuze himself may have been Bryant's source.
5. According to Mr Lugg it is done to release the victim's spirit and to prevent it from haunting the man at his home.
6. The progeny of such *ukungena* marriages (for which no lobolo is paid, as the woman remains within the family which has already paid lobolo for her) are regarded as the children of the deceased.

CHAPTER 13
1. The man's *isicoco* or head-ring (a circlet sewn into the hair) signified a mature man who, in the days of Shaka, had done his service in the army and earned the privilege of marriage and family life. The woman's *inkehli* or top-knot, which is built up by working clay and red ochre into the hair, from a top-knot to a large, high, dignified head-dress, signifies a married woman or a woman engaged to be married. The man's head-ring is no longer in use (a pity, because of its great dignity), but the woman's head-dress is still to be seen among traditionalists, and even, with the growth of Zulu nationalism, among modernists, who have evolved a detachable head-dress for use on occasion.
2. He is not correct, because as Mr Lugg points out, Chief Jobe's quarrel with his son Tana (the brother of Godongwane, later to become known as Dingiswayo) arose over the latter's refusal to wear the head-ring, and the earliest navigators record this form of head-dress. Shaka was responsible for the long delay in the adoption of the head-ring, for a man would be almost middle-aged by the time he had done his service. However, its use throughout the country may have dated only from the time of Zulu dominance through Shaka.

CHAPTER 14
1. *Ukusoka nokuthomba.*
2. According to the authorities, it was already dying out, if not obsolete.
3. Literally to milk straight into the mouth, which is what the boys at the barracks used to do.
4. By 'owner', the author presumably means Shaka.
5. The word used is *soma*, which the dictionaries give as 'illicit sexual intercourse', but the author does not regard it as such. It was important for the girl to retain technical virginity, and we conclude that the author uses *soma* in the sense of *hlobonga* (sexual intercourse without penetration). In fact the distinction is not always recognised, particularly in Natal.

NOTES

6. He is describing the *hlobonga* method of intercourse without penetration, which was allowed premaritally as it did not endanger the girl's virginity.
7. Who need not be one's mother in a polygamous family, although she is always addressed as such.
8. Here Fuze's judgement would seem to be influenced by his Christian background. The object of such songs is not to deter the girls from doing 'these filthy acts', but to teach them how to do them properly! It is sex education expressed in the plainest possible language. The word used to describe these songs and other puberty rites is *thombisa*, the causative form of *thomba* (to attain puberty), indicating that the songs themselves help to bring about puberty, maturity and fertility. One of the causes of barrenness is said to be that these songs and rites were not performed at puberty. (See E.J. Krige, 'Girls' Puberty Songs and their relation to fertility, health, morality and religion among the Zulu', *Africa*, Vol. 38, No. 2, 1968.)
9. It is not clear whether this is a sequence of events or merely a ramble on the part of the writer, from one point to the next.
10. The *ngungu* drum is made by stretching the skin of a freshly killed goat over a pot, and a wetted reed is placed against its centre and the chest of the player, who then slides her hand up and down to cause a droning sound.

CHAPTER 15

1. The isiZulu heading is *ukuganwa nokugana* (getting engaged or married, and marrying). It is the woman who marries [*gana*] just as it is the woman who chooses [*qoma*] and the man has these things done to him. But it is the man who causes the girl to choose [*qomisa*] in courtship.
2. The dress of an engaged girl, bride or wife, or apparently of a girl who wants to be.
3. The author is describing the *ukubaleka* (to run away) form of marriage, when no one of her family is supposed to know where she has gone.
4. It is apparent that the bride's father, like the bridegroom's father, has no option, at this stage, but to consent.
5. The word *isigozolo* is used for the marriage intermediary here, which has the connotation of a parasite or sponger.

CHAPTER 16

1. It often settles by the river or sometimes on a bank or in a donga, but wherever it settles is known as *esihlahleni* (by the bushes); or sometimes as *ezibukweni* (at the ford).
2. Singing and dancing are not separate activities. Thus the word *inkondlo* signifies both a dignified dance and a serious song.
3. These celebrations take place in the arena or open space below the homestead and outside it.
4. Nice, good, fine, right, pleasant. Mr Lugg's 'gay and merry' is not a translation but a description of what he knows the bridegroom's party's wedding dance to be: it is as merry and bright as the bridal dance is slow and solemn.
5. But she does not distribute them until the following day, or even two days later, at a relatively small family ceremony.
6. This beast is alternatively the *umqholiso* beast [*qholisa* means to honour], which elsewhere refers to the beast presented to the bride's mother.

NOTES

7. She may distribute them the day *after* the slaughter of the *umbhubuzo* beast, with its attendant difficulties from the bridemaids, as described here.
8. Not the day of the slaughter of the *umbhubuzo* beast, but one or two days later.
9. *Ngehla nobulembu*, I descend with my fine covering or gossamer veil, literally *spiderweb*, figuratively *hymen*.
10. These observances and many others which he does not mention, and which vary from place to place, especially between Natal and Zululand.
11. She continues to be called *umakoti* or *umlobokazi*, however, for some time, certainly for at least a year.
12. The houses are separate rooms [*zindlu*].
13. Adults, both male and female, normally address one another by their surnames or their correct titles (husband, wife, brother-in-law, son-in-law, bride or young wife).
15. Or *isigcayo*, the front covering sometimes termed a pregnancy apron.

CHAPTER 17

1. Mr Lugg says that it is not the normal rule to do so.

CHAPTER 19

1. There are many references for this section, which comprises the rest of the book. The most concise is Trevor Cope's 'The History of the Zulus' (Chapter 1 of *Izibongo: Zulu Praise Poems*, Oxford, 1968); but other reasonably brief and reliable accounts are to be found in L. Thompson and M. Wilson, *The Oxford History of South Africa*, Vols. 1 and 11 (Oxford, 1969 and 1972); E.H. Brookes and C. de B. Webb, *A History of Natal* (Pietermaritzburg, 1965); and S. Marks, *Reluctant Rebellion* (Oxford, 1970). Of full-scale accounts, the best by far in terms of readability is Donald Morris, *The Washing of the Spears* (London, 1966), 'but it is not always reliable in its interpretations' (S.M.). Bryant's *Olden Times* has a wealth of material on the rise and reign of Shaka; and for a more general appraisal of the rise of the Zulu kingdom, see Omer-Cooper, *Zulu Aftermath: A Revolution in Bantu Africa* (London, 1965). For a major new analysis of the nature of the Zulu kingdom and of the Zulu war and its aftermath, see J.J. Guy, 'The Destruction of the Zulu Kingdom: The Civil War in Zululand, 1879–1884', unpublished doctorate, University of London, 1976 [since published by UKZN Press 2012 under the original title].
2. A section of this chapter has been extracted and inserted into Chapter 14.
3. See Chapter 1, Note 1 for Fuze's use of the terms Ntungwa, Nguni and Sotho.
4. He never does so, for the rest of the book concerns 'the matters that he knows', namely the events of Zulu history. He does not describe Nguni history as he claims, for that would include the Swazi and the Xhosa as well as the Zulu people, on whose history he does no more than shine side-lights, as Mr Lugg says.

CHAPTER 20

1. See Chapter 11, towards the end.
2. In his Epilogue where he repeats this song, Fuze says that 'it is sung neither for joy nor for sorrow, but only at the burial of kings'.
3. Lugg speculates that the origin of the Zulu formal salute [*isithakazelo*] could be a phrase from the Zulu national song, *uNdaba uyinkosi* 'Ndaba is a king', which is

165

NOTES

not quoted by Fuze, namely *uNdaba uyazitha*, 'Ndaba names himself', of which *Ndab'ezitha* could be the participial vocative. On the other hand Bryant recounts the story that Jama son of Ndaba appropriated the Mbatha salute by defeating the Mbatha chief in a duel (*Olden Times*, p. 122). He considers, however, that both the Mbatha and the Zulu clans may have shared the same ancestral origin and hence the same salute.
4. Mbhengi, an earlier chief of the clan, and Nguga, the principal homestead of the Langeni chiefs.

CHAPTER 21

1. It was forbidden for boys in seclusion for circumcision to have communication, even verbal communication, with girls or young women. This act was therefore highly illegal.
2. If Fuze's account seems to suggest some scepticism, it may be not altogether without cause. Recently Professor John Argyle (University of Natal) has pointed out the similarities in the traditions of origin of Shaka and Dingiswayo, and has suggested that they arose to justify the usurpation of power by outsiders. See John Argyle 'Who were Shaka and Dingiswayo?' *Collected Seminar Papers: The Societies of Southern Africa in the Nineteenth and Twentieth Centuries* Vol. 7, Institute of Commonwealth Studies, London, 1977. (S.M.)
(I detect no sense of scepticism in Fuze's account, but it does contribute to Professor Argyle's hypothesis. If this account is correct, Shaka was not only illegitimate but completely illegal, and there was no contact between him and the Zulu clan. A.T.C.)
3. Lugg translates *ayiphelele* as *ayiphilile* (not well), but it actually means 'not intact, complete, perfect', which suggests that the pregnancy was by now plainly apparent.
4. Not '*ishaka*', the intestinal beetle that gives rise to abdominal disorders, which is supposed to be the origin of Shaka's name (see Bryant, *Olden Times* p. 48). Fuze has a different explanation of the meaning of his name (see Chapter 43).
5. Mudli was not his brother but his father in Zulu terminology (actually his paternal uncle), who acted as regent during his minority.
6. Tshaka in the Natal dialect which Fuze uses. He does not relate the name to the word indicating the 'bad body disease'.
7. No mention of legitimisation here, nor of Nandi and Shaka living for a while in the Zulu clan (cf. Bryant, *Olden Times*, p. 49) as recognised wife and son of Senzangakhona.
8. No mention here that Shaka suffered persecution by his fellow herd-boys. (Cf. Bryant, *Olden Times*, p. 62.)
9. No mention that Nandi went too. (Cf. Bryant, *Olden Times*, p. 63.)

CHAPTER 22

1. Presumably because it was the recognition of paternity, brought about by Shaka's fame.
2. Presumably Mbhengi's rather than Senzangakhona's.
3. To signify his right to the chieftainship.

NOTES

4. Not 'returning' as Lugg has it, but 'going' to the Zulu country for the first time in Fuze's account, while his father was still alive. (Cf. Bryant, *Olden Times*, p. 119.)
5. The usual story is that Shaka became Zulu chief with Dingiswayo's assistance in 1816, and that Dingiswayo died at the hands of Zwide two years later.

CHAPTER 23
1. The brother whom Shaka killed for the chieftainship is generally known by the name of Sigujana, but the names Nomkwayimba and Mfokazana are also known to refer to him.
2. The date of Senzangakhona's death and Shaka's succession is officially 1816. Also it is generally believed that Senzangakhona died before the murder of Sigujana some months later, and two years before the death of Dingiswayo.
3. The main branch of the Ndwandwe nation.
4. See Bryant, *Olden Times*, 'The great Hlubi tribe (the people of Mthimkhulu) fights its way to destruction.'
5. Of the Mandlakazi branch of the Zulu royal family, the father of Zibhebhu.
6. Here he breaks into praises of great warriors.

CHAPTER 24
1. Mxamana, Shaka's famous praiser [*imbongi*].
2. Ngqengelele was Shaka's personal attendant [*insila*]. See Chapter 10, Note 11.

CHAPTER 25
1. Dingane was inclined to put to death anyone who had been favoured by his predecessor.
2. The place of execution is generally believed to have been the hill above the donga, now known as Matiwane's Hill.
3. Bryant considers the question of whether the Khambule and the Ncube (both branches of the Mlotsha clan) could have shared the same chiefly line. (See *Olden Times*, p. 115.)
4. 'They who avoid or revere the grass coil used for carrying loads on the head'. (See *Olden Times*, p. 114, for Bryant's suggestion for the origin of the nickname.)

CHAPTER 26
1. Febane kaMjoji was the Zulu name for Francis Farewell, Farewell of King George.
2. Mbuyazwe may mean 'He who returns with nothing'.
3. Fynn has left a vivid account of his experiences: *The Diary of Henry Francis Fynn* (Pietermaritzburg, 1950).
   Another eye-witness account of the experiences of the first settlers is Nathaniel Isaacs: *Travels and Adventures in South East Africa* (London, 1836; Cape Town: 1936).
4. See Bryant's *Olden Times*, pp. 264–271, for further reports of Macingwane's cruelty.

CHAPTER 27
1. The 'stumpy little stick' is supposed to be a reference to Shaka's penis, which is reported to have been underdeveloped, at least in childhood; but the rest of the insult is obscure. See Chapter 11, Note 13.
2. These cairns are known to have existed long before the time of Shaka.

NOTES

3. Or 'spit on it and throw it onto the heap': an obscurity due to a misprint, but both actions are practised.
4. Of the Zelemu clan, which claimed Zulu relationship.

CHAPTER 28
1. This is supposed to have happened before the attack against the Ndwandwe, not against the Khumalo (Mzilikazi's people).
2. Mjokwane was Senzangakhona's praise-name, and Ndaba an ancestor.
3. A visitation from the ancestors.
4. Although it was Shaka who drove Mzilikazi from Zululand, it was during the reign of Dingane that expeditions were sent out against him in the Transvaal, but never as far as Mashonaland.

CHAPTER 29
1. Msikofili was the chief of the Khuze clan during the Bambatha Rebellion, who was severely punished by the Natal authorities for his part in it (see S. Marks, *Reluctant Rebellion*, pp. 193–6 and 321–2). Probably about the time Fuze was finishing his book, Msikofili was accused of ritual murder and sentenced to death. Harriette Colenso was very involved in his defence, but to no avail. S.M.
2. This passage is somewhat irrelevant here, but it reflects Fuze's awareness of the danger of prosperity and the acquisition of private property, in traditional communal life.
3. According to Bryant, the fowl came from the Tembe-Tonga in Mozambique. The ultimate origin may have been the Portuguese. S.M.

CHAPTER 31
1. Cf. Bryant, *Olden Times*, p. 63.
2. Cf. Bryant, *Olden Times*, p. 49.
3. Perhaps he means to say 'even though his father was still alive' – his mother now being *indlovukazi* (Queen Mother). If Fuze's 'even though' were to read 'when', this phrase would make sense.
4. See also Bryant, *Olden Times*, p. 607–608. In his otherwise recommendable book, *Shaka Zulu* (London, 1956), Ritter builds such a rumour (not the Cele girl, but Pampata) into a fictional romance. Ritter presumes that because Shaka's household contained a large collection of girls, he was 'very potent' (p. 375), but Morris (*The Washing of the Spears*) presumes that he was impotent (p. 46, p. 91–92).
5. Lugg unaccountably omits this statement, which is Fuze's firm conclusion on the subject.
6. Thus confirming Ngqumbazi as chief wife to bear the heir.
7. A variation of Mbulazi. It is reported that Mpande (and other members of the Zulu royal family) used to affect the *thefuya* accent, which would render Mbulazi as Mbuyazwe. It would also render *balethe* (bring them forth) as *bayete*, an explanation of the royal salute.
8. Surely a slip; he means Mpande.

CHAPTER 34

1. The truth is the reverse: Mzilikazi named his capital after Shaka's capital. (Chapter 11, Note 9.)
2. *Bhodwe* refers to the whole country and not just to the port. The word 'port' is Zuluized to Bhodwe, which then means 'the place of the pot', because of *ibhodwe*, the iron pot introduced by the settlers at the port. To the Zulu ear there is no distinction between 'pot' and 'port', which are here conveniently confused.

CHAPTER 35

1. The *isizinda* section of a clan was usually located in the original ancestral home, for it was the remnant that was left after the senior sons had moved away.

CHAPTER 37

1. Section 12 of *Izindaba* continues as follows from here. Fuze reproduces Colenso's historical account in full but I have cut it, sometimes drastically, on my own responsibility. Colenso wrote it as material for use in school, and I have retained only the significant or relevant parts, and particularly the parts on which Fuze comments. These comments are, of course, given in full. Colenso's full text can be found in *Izindatyana zaBantu kanye nezindaba zase'eNatal* (Pietermaritzburg, 1859). This is a very rare volume but a few copies are available in libraries.
2. Fuze's footnote: He lived with his mother's people in the Langeni clan. (He also lived with his grandmother's people in the Mthethwa clan. A.T.C.)
3. Given by Fuze at the end of Chapter 27.
4. Given by Fuze at the end of Chapter 26.
5. Usually known as Mbuyazwe.
6. Fynn estimates that about seven thousand people perished.

CHAPTER 38

1. Lugg omits this phrase, but it is important because the reason usually supplied is that Mpande was weak in the mind, not that he was deformed or diseased in the leg. This phrase could refer to his mother, Songiya, as the construction is ambiguous, but it is not likely.
2. Fuze's footnote: 'The blind wanderers, Nhlanganiso and Mphezulu' – this was the song that was composed at that time and sung about these two unfortunates, who were condemned by this wicked man who had no pity whatever.
3. A.F. Gardiner: *Narrative of a Journey to the Zulu Country* (London, 1836; Cape Town, 1966).
4. Cory (ed.): *The Diary of the Rev. Francis Owen* (Cape Town, 1926.)
5. Fuze's footnote: Our people state that when the Boers arrived, they were provided with quarters from which they paid visits to the king at Mgungundlovu. During the evening they were in the habit of leaving their quarters to encircle Mgungundlovu at night; but they were seen by the night watchmen (*ogqayinyanga*) who were not asleep. It was for this reason [*isizondo*, animosity on the part of the Boers] that Dingane killed them, realising that although they said they had come with goodwill, they had evil in their hearts; for why did they want to surround his residence during the night?

NOTES

CHAPTER 39
1. There were a few survivors, of which Dick King was one.
2. The Battle of the Tugela in historical records.
3. Fuze's footnote: It was on account of that battle that there died Dabeka kaDube, the Qadi chief, and Nobanda, the Mphumuza chief. I think I am correct in saying that both of them remained at that battle [as casualties].
4. It is interesting that the word *ichwebe* is used instead of the word *itheku* from which *eThekwini* is derived. It is highly likely that the Zulu name for Durban refers to an animal with only one testicle (the Bluff being the penis and the Bay being the testicle), and that the meaning of 'lagoon' is derived from the place name as a euphemism, perhaps to save embarrassment to the whites.
5. Senzangakhona's praise-name.
6. Although most historians have followed tradition in judging Mpande as a simpleton, Colenso's version accords better with Mpande's shrewdness and later strategies. See S. Marks: 'Mpande has, to my mind, been much underestimated in almost all the secondary sources on Zulu history: after all, it must have required a shrewdness akin to genius for a brother to have survived both the Shaka and Dingane regimes. Mpande learned 'the politics of survival' at an early age and in a very rough school. It would not be surprising if he continued their practice in the changed circumstances wrought by the arrival of the Trekkers and the British on the scene'. ('The Nguni, the Natalians and their history', *Journal of African History*, VIII, (1967), p. 537.) S.M.
7. Dingane did not disclose to his people what was going on.

CHAPTER 40
1. The name of two hills near Magudu near the Swazi border.
2. Fuze's footnote: 'There was also another, Nzobo kaSobadli of the Ntombela clan.'
3. Such a sentence defies the rules of syntax!
4. Lugg's account of Dingane's death, as set out in *A Natal Family Looks Back* (Durban, 1970), may be summarised as follows: Dingane sought the protection of Silevana, the regent for Sambane, the heir to the Nyawo chieftainship; but Dingane was too dangerous to be allowed to live. Silevana and his brother and the heir, Sambane, with the help of a local headman, Nondawana Mdluli, killed and buried Dingane. The three royal persons each placed a stone on the grave, but the commoner was not allowed to do so, and he was later killed for having taken part in the murder of a king. See also Lugg's account of his discovery of Dingane's grave.
5. Those entrusted with property often filch a little for themselves.

CHAPTER 42
1. Fuze interrupts the flow of Bishop Colenso's narrative to comment on a point unimportant to the story but important to him, so much so that he makes a separate chapter of it; whereas it is simply a continuation of 'The Establishment of British Rule in Natal'.
2. This section does not concern the Zulus, but I decided to include it to show not only the style but the relative neutrality of Bishop Colenso's historical account, in matters of imperial policy, British-Boer relations and English-Zulu relations.

NOTES

3. For more up-to-date views on the Bushmen or Late Stone Age hunter-gatherers, see M. Wilson, 'The hunters and herders', in M. Wilson and L. Thompson, *The Oxford History of South Africa*. In this paragraph, even Bishop Colenso seems to have accepted the conventional settler attitude towards the Bushmen – an unusual position for him. S.M.

CHAPTER 43
1. He omits the name of Zulu from the genealogy!
2. *Umhlola:* an event which is unusual at least, at most portentous.
3. A euphemism for sexual congress; literally to come together.
4. The usual explanation is that Nandi's pregnancy was at first attributed to intestinal trouble [*ishaka*].
5. Literally 'to call them', which is what one does to one's ancestral spirits. Life in the world of the spirits depends upon the existence of children.

CHAPTER 44
1. Most accounts report that the bull was killed without an instrument, but by force, strangulation and suffocation.
2. And which, according to Mr Lugg, is to be found particularly in the plants growing in the vicinity of the graves.

CHAPTER 45
1. Songiya was also Mpande's mother; they were therefore full brothers.
2. The house of Hamu kaNzibe, although he is usually known as Hamu kaMpande, in spite of the arrangement Fuze describes here, whereby Mpande 'raised seed' to his deceased brother to preserve his house, according to the Zulu custom of *ukuvusa*.
3. Zulu kings do not normally die, they either bow down [*khothama*] or go home [*goduka*, the word used here]; they die only abnormally by assassination.

CHAPTER 46
1. This chapter is composed partly of Chapter 43 and partly of Chapter 44. Fuze's Chapter 46, 'Offences for which the penalty was death', is mostly transferred to Chapter 14, and the somewhat confused and disjointed remainder omitted.
2. The codification of Zulu law by white authority has rendered it inflexible and incapable of adapting itself to time and circumstance.

CHAPTER 47
1. 1818–1828.
2. Dingane ruled for 12 years: 1828–1840.
3. Thus there is no incompatibility between belief in ancestral spirits and God.
4. An expression used of people so old that they have to be fed on liquid foods.
5. 1840–1872.
6. This dispute had arisen twenty years earlier, and had been decisively settled at Ndondakusuka by the death of Mbulazi.
7. Fuze here refers to Mbulazi as Mbuyazwe, the form of his name used by the royal family who affected the *thefuya* accent. See Chapter 31, note 7.

NOTES

8. Lugg omits this phrase referring to the effect of the charm, but it is important because of the word *bhungula*, to desert, which implies loss of loyalty to the family and loss of control by the family.
9. Cetshwayo's rivals who were devastated at Ndondakusuka.
10. He reigned for seven years, 1872–1879, and it was in the seventh year that he was destroyed.
11. It is difficult to translate the sarcasm of *abelungu bansondo*.
12. Hamu was physically Mpande's son, but by Zulu law he was Nzibe's son, and as such far removed by all the sons of Mpande from a claim to the throne. He turned traitor during the course of the War of 1879, in the furtherance of his claim for greater recognition.

CHAPTER 48

1. Or the consummation song of his wife [*isimekezo somkayo*], which is more likely seeing that the man was travelling either on his own or on his own account [*izihambela*], although the expression may mean 'just travelling along'.
2. It was because of Cetshwayo's suspicions that his brothers Mkhungo and Sikhotha were rivals for his position, that they had fled in fear to Natal. Their mothers (Mpande's wives) had joined them later. Shepstone was now trying to persuade Mpande to release the princesses also. Cetshwayo naturally resented his brothers' safety and freedom under European protection.
3. The literal translation is, 'Now Mpande was heard', for the praises are the man, and the praises of the king are the spirit of the nation.
4. Langalibalele was not actually killed. He was captured, brought to trial, sentenced, imprisoned, and finally exiled.
5. In 1873 Langalibalele had difficulty in getting his people to comply with a government order that they register their firearms, which they thought would mean confiscation. He was twice summoned to appear before Shepstone, but failed to appear and finally fled into Basutoland, seeking refuge with Molapo, as Fuze states. Colonial troops sent in pursuit were fired on by a section of the Hlubi, whereupon the affray was regarded as a 'rebellion'. Langalibalele was arrested and handed over to the Cape Mounted Rifles, and later deposed and exiled. The Hlubi lands were confiscated. In the trial, Langalibalele was defended by Bishop Colenso and his daughter, Harriette, who regarded it as a total travesty of 'British justice'. See Brookes and Webb, *A History of Natal*, pp. 113–21. S.M.

CHAPTER 49

1. The Zulu first fruits ceremonies were far more than magico-religious ceremonies to strengthen the king and the nation and to bring about fertility throughout the country. Under the Zulu kings they developed additionally into national, political and military rallies.
2. This statement is also puzzling, except that unpredictability and indiscriminate execution seem to have been features of Zulu kingship. It has been suggested that the Zulu kings consciously used them as a means of control and government. See E.V. Walter, *Terror and Resistance* (New York, 1969), Chapters VI to X.

3. The relationship of Hamu within the royal family is explained at the end of Chapter 47.
4. Fuze's footnote: 'Hamu was begot by Mpande, who begot him for the family [*umuzi*] of his own brother Nzibe, who died in the campaign against Soshangana during the reign of Shaka. When Nzibe remained behind [on the battlefield], Mpande used the cattle of Nzibe's Mfemfe homestead [*umuzi*] to lobola a girl of the Nxumalo clan [to become Nzibe's wife, according to the custom of *ukuvusa*, to raise seed], and begot Hamu in it [the homestead and household].' The point I am not clear about is which was the senior of the two sons of Songiya, Mpande and Nzibe, because even Cetshwayo, together with all the members of the royal family, when roused to take a serious oath swore by 'Mpande' or by 'Nzibe who lies at Soshangana's'. An interesting point. Nzibe's seniority would have given Hamu a claim over the sons of Mpande, although seniority of birth is not the only or even the main consideration in the matter of succession.
5. Gebhuza (paw the ground and toss the head, as a bull) was also the Zulu name for H.C. Shepstone, son of Somtseu.

CHAPTER 50
1. Some of Langalibalele's followers who had taken refuge with the Bishop in 1873, at the time of the 'rebellion'. S.M.
2. Matshana kaMondisa was a Natal chief who had fled into Zululand after a skirmish in court with John Shepstone, who succeeded his brother as Secretary for Native Affairs in Natal in 1875, and who, before that, had headed the Native High Court, where his arbitary conduct was notorious. S.M.
3. The contact between Cetshwayo and Sobantu (Bishop Colenso) seems to date from the Langalibalele affair. Cetshwayo realised fairly early in his reign the advantage of having a spokesman like the Bishop of Natal. S.M.

CHAPTER 51
1. Very neatly and nicely expressed: the question was whether retribution had come in Zululand, or murder in Natal.
2. The word *vinjezelwa* means to be besieged rather than attacked.
3. He was nevertheless responsible for the deaths of several at Ndondakusuka, and for the attempts on the lives of several others, and for the murder of the son of Nomantshali in front of his father, Mpande.
4. Fuze is quite correct in seeing the Sihayo episode as merely the pretext for a war which had already been decided upon. S.M.
5. The invasion took place in January 1879.
6. The rally cry is reported to have been, 'The little branch that beats out the fire (Cetshwayo) did not order this'.
7. The number was about a hundred and thirty, but there were about thirty invalids in the building that had been converted into a hospital.

CHAPTER 52
1. Fuze gives a very sketchy account of the Anglo-Zulu War, but I suggest that he sees it in its proper perspective. The Zulus were defeated but not destroyed by the

NOTES

War of 1879. They were destroyed by the post-war 'settlement' and by the civil war, for which the British persistent recognition and support for Zibhebhu as an independent chief was largely responsible. Fuze pays far more attention to this period (1879–1888) than to the 1879 War.
2. Lord Chelmsford was in command at the battle of Ulundi (Ondini), the king's capital.
3. In 1883, when the decision had already been taken to restore him to Zululand, which was now in the throes of civil war.
4. Fuze omits mention of Sir Garnet Wolseley's 'settlement' after the Zulu War, whereby Zululand was divided under thirteen chiefs, referred to in Natal as 'Kilkenny cats'. He quite rightly regards this period (1879–1883) as an interregnum rather than a settlement.
5. In fact Cetshwayo was met at the Cape by the British Governor, Sir Hercules Robinson, who explained the conditions of the return to him. He was met by Shepstone at Port Durnford on the coast of Zululand. S.M.
6. The land was not exactly to be retained by Natal: it was to be constituted as a 'Zulu Native Reserve' under a British Resident Commissioner, in which people unwilling to come under Cetshwayo's rule could take refuge. In fact, however, John Shepstone, who was appointed the first Resident Commissioner, appears to have given the impression that the Reserve had come *de facto* under Natal rule. (See JJ. Guy, 'The Destruction of the Zulu Kingdom: The Civil War in Zululand, 1879–1884', unpublished doctorate, University of London, 1976, p. 275) (S.M.)
(Fuze does not mention the Zibhebhu Reserve to the north in which Zibhebhu was recognised as an independent chief, and does not associate this condition with the civil war which followed. A.T.C.)
7. Fuze is not entirely accurate: even in London, Cetshwayo was warned that he would be allowed to return to Zululand only under certain conditions, including the forfeiture of a certain portion of his land. The precise limits of this land and the purposes for which it was to be used, were not spelt out to the king, whose objections were nevertheless clear. S.M.

CHAPTER 53

1. Zibhebhu's great-grandfather had been adopted as an orphan boy by Cetshwayo's great-grandfather. He had married on attaining manhood, but had died before producing an heir. A member of the Zulu royal family was nominated to 'raise seed' for him (the *ukuvusa* custom), so that the line became Zulu by blood as well as in name, the Mandlakazi Zulu line. The Mandlakazi's antagonists maintained that the wife had already been pregnant at the time of her husband's death, thus denying royal blood to the line. This is the background to the friction between the Mandlakazi and the uSuthu section of the Zulu royal family, which eventually erupted into the conflict which destroyed Cetshwayo and, during the reign of his son, the Zulu nation. Of course there were other factors contributary towards this friction and conflict, not least the interference of the whites.
2. This expedition, which oral accounts confirm left without Cetshwayo's permission, came at the end of a long series of provocations by Zibhebhu which went back to the period during which he had been put in charge of Cetshwayo's family and

close followers after the war. The immediate cause of the invasion of Zibhebhu's territory was the report that he was continuing to harass and oppress the Suthu loyalists in his territory. The crucial battle of Msebe took place on 30th March, 1883. Confident in its superior numbers, the expedition fell into an ambush laid by Zibhebhu. In this battle, as in the struggles which followed, Zibhebhu relied on a small group of armed horsemen. This defeat at the hands of Zibhebhu was followed by further attacks from Hamu, who joined up with Zibhebhu's forces, burning homesteads and raiding cattle in their wake. As a result of the battle of Msebe, Zibhebhu emerged as the most formidable rival to the king's power. (See Guy, 'The Destruction of the Zulu Kingdom', pp. 284–9). S.M.
3. According to Guy, the real tragedy 'lay not so much in the magnitude of the slaughter – though that was terrible enough – but in the number of uSuthu leaders who were killed. For at the time of the attack the king had gathered round him the most important and loyal of his supporters'. Most accounts agree that more than fifty of the most influential men of the nation were wiped out on this occasion. (See Guy, 'The Destruction of the Zulu Kingdom', pp. 303–4, and others) S.M.
4. By this time Colenso had in fact died (20th June, 1883), although it is perfectly correct that William Grant was sent by the Bishop to Zululand in response to Cetshwayo's pleas for a literate white to communicate on his behalf with the Government. In fact, Grant was a totally unsatisfactory choice, being more concerned to curry favour with the authorities than to advance the uSuthu cause. S.M.

CHAPTER 54
1. Lugg omits this phrase, but it is most significant in view of the events which followed.
2. Cetshwayo was widely believed to have died from poison, 'a fact which is not now disputed by those who are in the best position to know the truth' (Sir Rider Haggard, *Cetshwayo and his White Neighbours*, 1888). The doctor's verdict was 'fatty degeneration of the heart', but there was no post-mortem examination. Poison is a common cause of death, in Zulu belief, in situations of strained personal relations.
3. Seawater, as he was conceived at sea, on board ship.
4. Dingane is omitted from this list, perhaps by oversight on the part of either Cetshwayo or Fuze, but probably deliberately.
5. The king moved to Eshowe on 17th October, 1883, and died there on 8th February, 1884. S.M.

CHAPTER 55
1. The previous interpretation (Chapter 43) was 'he wearies the Zulus' (*udin' uZulu*). Here the isiZulu version is given as *udinwa nguZulu* ('he is wearied by the Zulus'). The first interpretation seems more likely.
2. Under the post-war settlement of Sir Garnet Wolsley, the king was replaced by thirteen independent chieftains, some of whom (including Mnyamana of the Buthelezi clan) were successors to these chieftainships which had been independent before the unification under the Zulu kings.
3. There have been a number of interpretations both of Mnyamana's refusal to accept Sir Garnet Wolseley's offer of a chieftaincy and of his withdrawal of support from Dinuzulu. According to his own evidence before the 1879 Boundary Commission,

175

NOTES

he refused the chieftaincy because the proposed territory excluded two-thirds of the land of his followers, which was to come under Hamu. (See Guy, 'The Destruction of the Zulu Kingdom', p. 99). As to Mnyamana's relationship with Dinuzulu, Mnyamana was always against Dinuzulu's decision to seek assistance from the Boers in his struggle against Zibhebhu, and appears to have favoured some sort of rapprochement with the British. (See Guy, 'The Destruction of the Zulu Kingdom', p. 316 and p. 320). His son, Tshanibezwe, did indeed give evidence against Dinuzulu in the treason trial following the latter's arrest. S.M.

CHAPTER 56
1. Dingane is deliberately omitted (see Chapter 54, Note 4).
2. The Boers may have thought so, but it was hardly an accurate perception of reality. S.M.
3. The battle took place on 5th June, 1884. S.M.
4. The decision to allow Zibhebhu to return to the lands from which he had been expelled in 1884, came at the beginning of 1888, although Zululand was still suffering from unrest and disturbance. Osborn, now British Resident Commissioner over the whole of Zululand which had been annexed as a Crown Colony in May, 1887, convinced the British Colonial Office that only a very few uSuthu supporters would be affected. In fact the removal of some 5 000 people was involved, and major violence erupted again in the north of the country. For an account of the events of these years and of the miscarriage of justice which Fuze cites, see H.E. Colenso, *The Zulu Impeachment of British Officials in 1887–8 confirmed by the official records in 1892* (London, 1892). S.M.
5. An example of the white man's justice: it was the Mandlakazi who were originally at fault!

CHAPTER 57
1. She was so named because she was the 'staff' on which her father leaned in preparing his defence of Langalibalele and of Cetshwayo. S.M.
   (The term also described her appearance, in accordance with the Zulu flair for noting and naming simultaneously the inner and outer nature, for she was tall and thin and very erect. A.T.C.)
2. It was on the basis of this evidence that Harriette and Dinuzulu's defence counsel argued that the royal princes had no intention of committing treason, and that their sole quarrel was with Zibhebhu. S.M.

CHAPTER 58
1. Bishop Colenso himself had died in 1883.
2. Escombe was one of the principal architects of Natal's Responsible Government of 1893, and a prominent member of the first cabinet. S.M.
   (He was called Coffee-water because the first thing he did when he woke up in the morning was to shout for hot water to make coffee. A.T.C.)
3. Fuze never recognises Dinuzulu as the king, presumably because he was never officially installed, having never regained control of his father's kingdom. (A further reason is that it was still dangerous to recognise Dinuzulu as the king in Natal: as

NOTES

late as 1916, three years after his death, a drunken Zulu who reported that Dinuzulu was still alive and ready again to lead the Zulu people, was given a jail sentence of three months with hard labour. S.M.)
4. As Cetshwayo's brothers, they would be his fathers and he their child.

CHAPTER 59
1. Dr Robert Colenso, by this time living in London. S.M.

CHAPTER 60
1. Anthony Daniels was an 'exempted native' from Natal, who served as Dinuzulu's secretary both on this occasion, on St. Helena, and later in Natal, having been chosen for the purpose by the Native Affairs Department in Natal in 1890. He had been educated at Lovedale, and had passed the Cape university entrance examinations – high qualifications for an African in those days. On both occasions he was employed by Dinuzulu, the relationship ended in recriminations, and he was dismissed on allegations of fraud. In 1906 the bad blood between them came to a head when Daniels reported on Dinuzulu's alleged treasonable activities during the 'Bambatha rebellion' in terms calculated to do the chief the maximum damage. See S. Marks, *Reluctant Rebellion*, p. 254. S.M.
2. Lieut. Col. Sir Marshall Clarke had served in Natal, the Transvaal and the Cape Colony, before becoming Resident Commissioner in Zululand. Unlike his predecessor, Sir Melmoth Osborn, Clarke soon became disenchanted with the activities of Dinuzulu's opponents, and by the end of his first year of service in Zululand (1893), he was advocating the return of Dinuzulu and his uncles from exile. This was delayed by the Natal Government for another four years. S.M.

CHAPTER 61
1. The good treatment the royal princes received on St. Helena was bitterly resented by the Natal colonists. Most of them were convinced that the familiarity with which Dinuzulu had been treated by the Governor of St. Helena and the tastes he had acquired in exile, could not fail to be deleterious. See S. Marks, *Reluctant Rebellion*, pp. 110–111. S.M.

CHAPTER 63
1. See Chapter 60, Note 1.
2. Fuze's footnote: 'Here I reimbursed Magema from the money of the Prince Dinuzulu which he had placed in my care. So say I. Dlwedlwe kaSobantu. 24 Feb. 1923.' (Which strengthens the view that it was Harriette who was responsible for getting Fuze's manuscript into print. S.M.)

CHAPTER 64
1. Chief Martin Luthuli was the elected chief of the Christian community at Groutville, an American Zulu mission settlement. He was the uncle of Chief Albert Luthuli, who later also headed the Groutville community before his deposition by the South African Government for his activities on behalf of the African National Congress, of which he became the President in 1953. In 1957 he won the Nobel

NOTES

Prize for Peace. Fuze's link with Martin Luthuli again shows the nature of the African Christian community in the early twentieth century. Like John Dube, Martin Luthuli was one of the founding members of the Natal Native Congress (later to become the provincial branch of the African National Congress), and was closely in touch with Harriette Colenso over its establishment. S.M.
2. For a full account and interpretation of the rumours which filled Natal and Zululand at this time, the messengers sent to Dinuzulu and the government's reaction, see S. Marks, *Reluctant Rebellion*, Chapter 6. S.M.

CHAPTER 65
1. Bambada, alternatively Bambatha. (The correct isiZulu spelling is probably Bhambatha.) The most recent account of the Rebellion is to be found in Shula Marks, *Reluctant Rebellion*.
2. Even before Bambada's actions, martial law had been declared and several chiefs punished for failure to pay the Poll Tax. S.M.

CHAPTER 66
1. The Government's action began with the declaration of martial law on 9 February 1906, after a small group of Christian separatists in the Richmond area resisted paying the Poll Tax. Bambatha's resistance came nearly two weeks later, when some of the younger men of the Zondi clan refused to pay the tax. After refusing several summonses from the magistrate, Bambatha disappeared and made his way to Zululand and ultimately to Dinuzulu. His overt resistance to white forces came nearly a month later, in April, after his return from Zululand and his capture of his uncle Magwababa, who had been appointed Zondi chief in his stead. On the 3 April he attacked the magistrate and police escort sent to investigate Magwababa's capture, and on the 5 April successfully ambushed a party of police in the Mpanza valley, which would appear to be the engagement Fuze describes here. After this, accompanied by between 150 and 200 of his followers, Bambatha made his way to the dense Nkandla forest. See S. Marks, *Reluctant Rebellion*, Chapter 8. S.M.
2. Mjongo was the leader of a group called the Presbyterian Church of Africa. For an account of the incident and Mveli's reaction, see S. Marks, *Reluctant Rebellion*, pp. 174–180 and 189–192. S.M.
3. From the evidence led at Dinuzulu's trial, it would seem that Bambatha's wife was left at Osuthu on the occasion of his first visit there. There is little evidence, however, to support the conclusion which was later drawn by the Natal Government, that Dinuzulu therefore knew of Bambatha's plans and indeed encouraged him to rebel. Dinuzulu's actions at this time were extremely ambiguous, for his position was practically intolerable. See S. Marks, *Reluctant Rebellion*, Part V, Zulu Hamlet. S.M.
4. These three were tried and sentenced by the Natal Supreme Court in Maritzburg. The previous twelve had been tried and sentenced by court martial at Richmond. S.M.
5. Bambatha's army was annihilated at Mome Gorge on 10th June. The devasting 'sweeping movements' of the white troops continued in the Maphumulo district until martial law was lifted at the beginning of September. S.M.

NOTES

CHAPTER 67

1. Fuze has somewhat telescoped the events. Dinuzulu was only arrested more than a year later, on 7th December, 1907, after martial law had once again been declared and three thousand troops sent to Zululand from Natal. His trial took place between 19th November, 1908, and 3rd March, 1909, after an extremely lengthy preparatory examination. S.M.
2. Dinuzulu was found guilty on three of the twenty-three counts of high treason brought against him. That the outcome was relatively favourable to the chief is to be attributed to the constant vigilance exercised on his behalf by Harriette Colenso, to the concern of the Colonial Office which she aroused, and to the services of W.P. Schreiner which she acquired, one of the most brilliant advocates of his day. For the trial, see S. Marks, *Reluctant Rebellion*, Chapter XI. S.M.
3. He was accused of implication in various murders which had occurred in Zululand in the wake of the disturbances. The evidence was flimsy, being largely brought by people who had reason to incriminate Dinuzulu in order to lessen their own guilt, and none of these allegations led to further prosecutions. S.M.
4. See Chapter 55, Note 1, for the meaning of the name.
5. Fuze refers here to the valiant activities of the Colenso family to rouse British humanitarian opinion and the Colonial Office on Dinuzulu's behalf. There was no actual 'trial' of Dinuzulu in Britain. There were, however, four libel suits connected with the Dinuzulu trial, led by Alfred Mangena supported by F.E. Colenso, which arose out of Mangena's public denunciations of the Natal Government's actions. Fuze's view of F.E. Colenso as a martyr to the Zulu cause was certainly shared by his family. S.M.
6. One of the first actions of the first Union Prime Minister, General Botha, was to release Dinuzulu from jail, though he was to be exiled to the Middelburg district of the Transvaal, with a handful of wives and followers, for the rest of his life. S.M.
7. The Union Government did not share the paranoia of the Natal authorities about the Zulu royal family, and was in general far readier to recognise its position amongst the Zulu people, and to use it. S.M.

CHAPTER 68

1. After the return from St. Helena, Dinuzulu was not recognised as the Zulu king by the Government, but only as the chief of the uSuthu section of the Zulu people, with jurisdiction over an area round Nongoma. His son, Solomon Nkayishana, sought in vain for recognition, but it was not until 1952 (almost 60 years later) that Solomon's son, Cyprian Bhekuzulu, was recognised as Paramount Chief of all the Zulus. His son, Goodwill Zwelithini, was subsequently recognised as the Zulu king.
2. Zululand was annexed in 1887 and incorporated into Natal in 1897.

EPILOGUE

1. See the author's Introduction, first and last paragraphs.
2. He did, and Fuze proceeded to give his account of Dinuzulu, which appears here in the body of the work as Chapters 55 to 68.

Printed and bound by CPI Group (UK) Ltd, Croydon, CR0 4YY
06/04/2026

14854580-0004